YUMMY Discoveries

Worry-Free Weaning

Felicity Bertin and Dr Anna Walton

ROBERT HALE • LONDON

© Yummy Discoveries 2014
First published in Great Britain 2014

ISBN 978-0-7198-1307-8

Robert Hale Limited
Clerkenwell House
Clerkenwell Green
London EC1R 0HT

www.halebooks.com

The right of Felicity Bertin and Anna Walton to be identified as
authors of this work has been asserted by them
in accordance with the Copyright, Designs and
Patents Act 1988

Yummy Discoveries is a registered trademark. All rights reserved.

A catalogue record for this book is available from the British Library

2 4 6 8 10 9 7 5 3 1

Design by Eurodesign
Printed in China

YUMMY Discoveries®

Worry-Free Weaning

Other Yummy Discoveries titles

Yummy Discoveries:
The Baby-Led Weaning Recipe Book

Contents

Acknowledgements

We would like to thank all our patients, their families and our fellow health professionals for trusting us with their problems, allowing us into their lives and giving us the opportunity to work with them and learn from them.

We give special thanks to all at Robert Hale, especially Gill Jackson, Nikki Edwards and Ruby Bamber.

Our thanks go to Luci Lishman, registered nurse, midwife, international board certified lactation consultant (IBCLC) and tongue-tie practitioner. Her contribution to this book has been invaluable.

We would like to thank our husbands, Dave and Adrian, for their endless support, infinite cups of tea, love and absolute faith in us through the writing and re-writing of this book.

Finally, to our children, the ones we have lost, the ones we have and the ones yet to be born. We thank them for reminding us of what's truly important in life.

Introduction

'Nature does not hurry, yet everything is accomplished.'
Lao Tzu

Purées, finger-foods, 'They eat what you eat', 'Food is for fun in under ones', 'Wake early, wean early' ... There is so much conflicting advice around introducing solid food to your child (in this book, solids are all foods aside from infant milk) that it can be difficult to know as a parent whom to believe and where to start.

Research has shown that eating habits are established by the age of two and how a child is weaned and introduced to food in the early years has an enormous effect on their relationship with food in later life. Yet parents often become confused and befuddled under the weight of all sorts of advice from well-meaning friends and families, as well as out-of-date recommendations from books and health professionals[1][2]. Is it any wonder that it's become difficult, as a parent, to feel like you're making the right decisions? Weaning can feel like a minefield where one bad move might make it all go wrong. Given the endless opportunities we have to subject our children to the limited, hyper-calorific and energy-dense (but nutrient-sparse) diet prevalent today in Western culture, is it any wonder that the strategies our parents used aren't working in the same way for us? Why are we surprised that research shows a rise in childhood obesity and type II diabetes?

It doesn't have to be like this.

Every child is different and every parent is different, so why should one rule apply to all families when it comes to weaning? As a parent, you have an instinct for what is best for you and your family and our aim is to help ensure that your child establishes a healthy relationship with food. By presenting you with the facts and dispelling the myths about the weaning process our aim is to empower you to make an informed decision about the best way to introduce solids to your child. Many parents who formulate their own unique approach to weaning rather than following a prescriptive method find mealtimes less stressful and have less anxiety about their child conforming to a rigid standard of 'normal' behaviour.

As a team comprising a psychological therapist (Anna) and an osteopath (Felicity) – more about us below – we work together running workshops and family consultations for people with children under five years of age who are fussy eaters, educating families on how to wean their children using a variety of complementary methods. Our holistic and relational approach means that our advice considers your child's physical and psychological development and the relationship between you as being key for successful weaning. It is not our intention to promote any brands or products in this book and we do not recommend any brand as being superior or inferior to another; our mission is to empower you by presenting you with the information so that you can make informed choices.

This book is an outpouring of many years of experience and research and we hope you enjoy reading it as much as we have enjoyed writing it for you.

About the authors

Dr Anna Walton is a counselling psychologist with a longstanding specialist interest in child development. She has a doctorate from the University of East London (DCounsPsych) and a Master's degree in Child Development (MSc with Distinction) from the Institute of Education (University of London). She works in private practice with Felicity Bertin, supporting families of children with weaning and fussy eating issues. Anna also helps adults, teenagers and families with a wide variety of problems, giving counselling/psychotherapy and coaching sessions. She lives in Buckinghamshire with her husband, two cats and two horses and she and her husband are currently trying for a baby.

Felicity Bertin has studied infant feeding and child development for a number of years. She is a registered osteopath, specializing in paediatric and cranial osteopathy, and a voluntary breastfeeding support worker. She lectures in embryology, developmental biology and neuro-musculo-skeletal medicine and works in private practice with Anna Walton, supporting families of children with feeding issues and fussy eating difficulties. She also uses her osteopathic skills and helps babies and mums-to-be with a range of issues. After following the principles of baby-led weaning with her son, she co-authored *Yummy Discoveries: The Baby-Led Weaning Recipe Book* in 2012. Felicity lives in Hertfordshire with her husband and young son Lucas, and is eagerly awaiting the arrival of her second child.

Chapter One

What is Weaning?

Weaning is creating opportunities for your child to explore food; it is *not* the stopping of milk feeds

Traditionally, many parents and health professionals have viewed weaning as a baby's transition from milk to solid food, which involved stopping milk feeds. Over the years, though, much research has shown that breast milk has enormous benefits for babies, so nowadays, weaning is understood as the introduction of solid food alongside milk rather than stopping milk and 'converting' babies to solid food. When you start weaning, the introduction of solid foods is not for nutritional purposes but to offer your child opportunities to discover new tastes and experience food while they are still gaining all the nutrition they need from milk feeds.

Offer your baby the chance to try food, rather than feeding them

It's as simple as that. Weaning is about facilitating your child's journey of discovery in the world of food. You are offering your child the opportunity to explore food; you are not feeding them. If they're not interested, don't worry and try again at the next mealtime. You may start to panic at this point that your child is not eating enough but until around nine months, they will be getting everything they need nutritionally from milk feeds and possibly a vitamin supplement (see p.143).

Throughout weaning, continue to offer regular milk feeds and gradually your baby will reduce their milk intake as their ability to manage food grows. Breastfeeding whilst introducing solid foods can be a huge advantage since you won't be hung up on the volume of milk consumed as you aren't able to measure the fluid ounces or millilitres after each feed.

Learning how to eat

The idea of 'learning how to eat' might sound relatively easy, because it sounds like your baby is just learning to do one thing – eat. In reality, in order to make the transition to solid food, your baby will have to learn lots of things in many different ways, using all of their senses. Don't forget that, as adults, we learned everything we could possibly need to know about eating so long ago that it's become second nature. Thus, all of the actions, comprehension and sensory cues (e.g. texture, smell, taste, temperature) that we need in order to make sure that we eat nutritious and not poisonous foods have been firmly reinforced in our brains by so many years of eating. Our brains are expert navigators through the world of food and we don't realize how many unconscious cognitive processes are happening when we eat.

In contrast, your baby's brain needs to learn absolutely *everything* about eating, from the biomechanical aspects (e.g. hand-eye and hand-mouth co-ordination) to the sensory experiences (e.g. becoming familiar with tastes and textures) to the cognitive understandings (e.g. recognizing an apple) and even the emotional aspects (e.g. experiencing frustration). Your baby's brain has a *lot* of work to do in a relatively short time! When you understand just how much your baby's brain needs to absorb in order to learn to eat, you can see why it makes sense to have a good few months to learn new things and practise them over and over again, before they depend on receiving nutrition from solid food. If weaning *were* about your baby needing to get all their nutrition from solid foods from day one, they'd be likely to be undernourished by the time they learned *how* to eat, and if it really *is* all about 'energy', then surely parents should be discouraged from weaning with low-energy foods (e.g. puréed carrot) … but more about that later.

With weaning, your aim needs to be that by nine to twelve months of age – which is when the nutritional content of solid food becomes more important and your baby begins to rely less on milk for nutrition – your baby has learned and practised enough new eating skills to move themselves seamlessly from milk feeds to more solid food. Notice that we said move *themselves*? Yes, your baby can and should be making their own choices and taking control over their eating … more about *that* later, too.

Combining spoon-feeding purées with finger-foods

Many parents report that they do a 'combination' of spoon-feeding their child shop-bought purées and offering them finger-food to play with alongside these. Their reason is often that it helps them feel satisfied that their child is getting the nutrients they need from the purées. If you are considering

taking this approach for that reason let's draw your attention to some research conducted on the UK baby food market. The research analysed the nutritional content of shop-bought baby foods between October 2010 and February 2011. It found that the majority of products on sale had an energy content similar to breast milk and would not serve the intended purpose of enhancing the nutrient density and diversity of taste and texture in infants' diets[3]. So, knowing this, if you are considering spoon-feeding your child shop-bought purées to ensure they have more nutrients and energy then you are better off offering another milk feed instead. From this research, it is evident that the nutritional value from breast milk far outweighs that of the shop-bought purée; breast milk also contains a similar number of calories. Formula milk contains more calories and high nutrients so it will also nourish your baby more efficiently than shop-bought purées (although see p.130 for the potential

Shutterstock

Many parents report that they do a 'combination' of spoon-feeding their child purées and offering them finger-food to play with alongside these.

problems with its high calorie count). It's worth mentioning that the same research has shown, unsurprisingly, that home-made purées are more nutritious than those that are shop-bought.

This reinforces what we know: that weaning isn't about nutrition – if it were, then these baby foods certainly wouldn't be up to the job. Weaning is about giving your child the opportunity to explore a wide range of tastes, textures and flavours – another element these jars, pouches and tubes of baby food often seem to be missing. This same piece of research found that 'The UK infant food market mainly supplies sweet, soft, spoonable foods targeted from age 4 months'[4].

So, we know that these commercial products are aimed at children from four months of age, an age when most children are not developmentally ready to try solid foods (the current World Health Organization (WHO) guidelines recommend breastfeeding exclusively for six months)[5]. We also know that consistently serving these isn't going to do much to expand the palate of your child and that they don't supply any more energy or nutrition than breast milk, so ask yourself again 'why am I serving these to my little one?'

The final thing to consider here is the process of spoon-feeding itself. Research conducted by the Department of Health (DH) showed that the majority of parents spoon-feeding solids to their children are over-feeding them. They examined the food and nutrition intake of 2,683 children aged between four and eighteen months and found that 75% of boys and 76% of girls are consuming around 100 more calories a day than they need[6]. Commercial baby food and formula milk were found to be the main contributors to this.

What is driving this excess supply of calories? It's unlikely to be a regulation issue in the children, but rather an external influence from our own needs to reduce waste, finish a bottle/jar or ensure they have had enough so they sleep through. By removing the spoon-feeding and allowing your child to self-feed, you are removing your own external influence and allowing your child to eat for their own personal needs. If you want to offer purées then preload the spoon and allow your child to self-feed (more on this on p.43).

Does the doctor always know best?

An approach of strict parent-led weaning and forcing food on a child, in line with a man-made date, regardless of whether the child is ready or whether the parent feels it is appropriate, fits in with the twentieth-century approach when 'men of science' were assumed to know better than mothers, grandmothers and families about how to raise a child. In those days, it was assumed that the adults should be 'in charge' of the relationship, which can bring about certain problems. There are two people in any relationship, and each person must have their own sense of agency. This includes taking responsibility and making decisions – although these things happen in different ways for you than they do for your baby, your baby will flourish if they're given the space to make their own decisions, even though those decisions won't be as sophisticated as yours. You do things at your level, while facilitating them to do things at their level.

Adopting the attitude that you and your child are in a relationship together and that you are both equals in terms of both being human beings can yield huge rewards. Of course, you as the parent have more power in the relationship in that you make decisions about what's good for your child and they are dependent on you. But if you remember that it's your job to go on their developmental journey *with* them, rather than being in control of them, it is easier to allow them to make decisions and learn from them. You need to think of the weaning journey as just that, a journey you take together, so that any mistakes also belong to both of you.

So often, problems are being located in the child when parents say: 'My child is so stubborn, he won't eat X.' In fact, mistakes are created by both of you and any behaviour you see your child showing is a result of your parenting + your child's reaction. If you can think of weaning as a process that shapes your relationship in the way that other activities – like playing together – do, then it becomes easier to remember that weaning is about finding the best way forward for *both* of you, as you go. All humans have different temperaments, stressors and beliefs – one size doesn't fit all, and so even if you've weaned a child before, it will be different with your next child because the combination of you and your baby is a unique one. By listening to your instincts and your baby, you will be able to find the way that works for you and your family, and that's empowering.

Parenting + child's reaction = behaviour

Weaning around the world

Interestingly, at the time of writing this book, the New Zealand Ministry of Health does not recommend baby-led weaning for New Zealand babies[7]. It states that there isn't enough evidence on the benefits to support it, yet this doesn't stop some New Zealand mothers participating in what they feel is right for their child. A quick Google search shows plenty of social media groups interacting and discussing baby-led weaning. So why do these mothers go against the Ministry of Health's suggestions?

Perhaps they've educated themselves enough about baby-led weaning and its use in other Western cultures to feel safe that it is a sound approach. Equally, perhaps it's all about having the confidence to trust their instincts as parents, and believing that they know best about weaning (and other) decisions. Of course, this isn't easy (particularly if you're a first-time parent) when you have no way to evaluate what the impact of your decisions will be. Every parent wants to do the best for their child, as they're the most important thing in the world to them, so every decision can feel like it's loaded. Decisions also aren't easy when there's so much out there that claims to 'know' what's best or frightens you by saying that if you don't do a certain thing then there will be consequences that will either make your life harder or negatively impact on your child's health and well-being. But remember, official healthcare recommendations can change and, even now, recommendations in some countries are different to others. Is that because New Zealand babies are different to British babies? Of course not. So trust yourself regarding what's right for you and your baby – you're the one who is there observing your child at ground level.

For innovation in approaches to weaning, perhaps parents around the world could learn something from the French. In France in 1987 'taste lessons' were established in a select number of schools[8]. The results of this programme are difficult to come by since no systematic research has been conducted, but it is worth mentioning that this programme aimed to teach young children to become aware of the quality and differentiation of foods through their smells, textures and tastes. Behind this study was the consideration that children's awareness is developed by awakening their interest and curiosity towards foods by exercising their senses – does this sound a lot like how a child interacts with a toy to you?

So what sorts or activities did they do in these 'taste lessons'? They explored all the senses such as hearing a carrot being grated and smelling onions being fried – things your child will experience whilst you're cooking dinner. Children saw bananas ripening in the fruit bowl and tasted the different flavour and texture at different stages – these are all things that you can do naturally if you expose your child to 'real' food. Each time you sit down with your child at the table and give them the opportunity to interact with different foods, you are helping them engage with their palate. So if you're enjoying breakfast, lunch and dinner together, that's three taste lessons each day that can stimulate their curiosity for food. Each time you cook a meal and the smell wafts through the house or you pierce a tomato with a fork and it squidges and squelches, your child is learning about food and is less likely to be fearful of it (for more on the importance of this see p.116).

The 2004 National Guidelines on Infant and Young Child Feeding in India recognize how the introduction of solid food to your child can mean much more than just eating. They mention how the way in which food is introduced can 'provide significant learning opportunities through responsive caregiver interaction, enhancing brain development in the most crucial first three years'[9]. They recommend the staple cereal of the family be used to make a porridge as a first meal – thickening with fat and sugar to provide more calories. Once the child is eating the porridge, the traditional foods of the family can be introduced. Many years of research have passed since these guidelines were introduced and so we wonder whether an updated guideline will be issued soon? Only time will tell.

Two interesting studies[10] are taking place at the time of writing, which could have a profound effect on guidelines across the world. In Guatemala, Pakistan, Zambia, the Democratic Republic of Congo and China research is taking place to evaluate meat as a first complementary food for breastfed infants. Fear about depletion in the body's iron stores at six months (see p.144) is a common reason for parents to introduce iron-fortified goods such as infant formula or baby cereals, which (as discussed on p.70) are not necessarily optimal first foods. In developing countries this has the added problem of iron-fortified foods being expensive and not accessible to all since they are commercially manufactured products. If the evidence shows that introducing these children instead to local, affordable, non-iron-fortified foods that can be sourced at home will offer the high intakes of iron, zinc and vitamin B12 that their parents seek, then this can only be a positive thing for these poorer communities.

Pre-mastication

Pre-mastication is where a parent or caregiver feeds pre-chewed food to an infant. It is sometimes called 'kiss-feeding' and as the human species evolved it was likely to have been used by our early ancestors as a way of supporting an infant's growing nutritional needs when breast milk alone was not enough[11].

As a behaviour, it is suggested that pre-mastication developed from the regurgitation of food behaviour that is still demonstrated by other animals (e.g. wolves), who also nuzzle

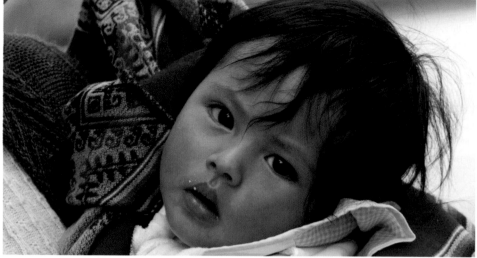

Shutterstock

Pre-mastication is still practised in some non-Westernized cultures.

their young with their mouths in order to bond and communicate socially. Interestingly, pre-mastication is also observable in our closest animal relatives – apes – alongside ritualized mouth-to-mouth contact for bonding and social reasons. This supports the idea that both pre-mastication and kissing evolved from similar roots. That's probably quite an odd idea to us nowadays – that kissing (and particularly French kissing, which is considered to be just like pre-mastication but with the absence of food) evolved from socially rooted feeding behaviours! As strange as that may sound, it is currently thought to be the most likely evolutionary explanation.

Written records of pre-mastication have been found dating as far back as Ancient Egyptian society and it is believed to have been a common practice in Roman times. Pre-mastication has largely disappeared as a usual practice in Westernized societies, but is still practised in some more traditional cultures. It may not be a coincidence that populations that have abandoned this practice generally have access to modern food-processing techniques. Alongside this, modern definitions of hygiene have framed pre-mastication as an unhygienic, and even unhealthy, practice.

For many parents, the thought of chewing food and then passing it to their child (often with their tongue) to eat fills them with horror and it's not for them – they see it as unsavoury and unsanitary. However, not everyone feels that way – the mother standing next to you in the supermarket queue might find the prospect fits in well with her beliefs. Neither of you is wrong, you are both merely finding your own unique way to feed your child. So whether you feel disgusted by the idea or you're considering it, bear with us; we're not trying to persuade you of anything. This book is about giving you the facts, and with that in mind, if you *are* considering it, the argument that 'we used to do it' isn't enough to justify doing it now. Let's look at the facts, then, so that you can make your own decision about whether pre-mastication is something that you feel would suit you and your child.

For all mammals, breast milk has historically provided a secure nutritional source for infant survival. However, as a child grows older, breast milk alone isn't enough to support their needs. Many people look to the animal kingdom for ways to do things and we have heard many parents support their decision to pre-masticate food by making statements such as 'animals do it'. It's really important to consider the difference between humans and these other species, though, as there are key developmental differences that should inform our decisions when it comes to pre-mastication. Humans develop more slowly, both *in utero* and postnatally, achieving the characteristics to survive independently later than other mammals[12]. This is particularly true of tooth development, which develops later, with molars erupting at around eighteen to twenty-four months. Our ancestors must therefore have found a way to support this period of transition. Some people therefore see pre-mastication as a little like puréeing foods – it was simply what we did before the blender existed. This could be considered true, because pre-masticated food has historically been introduced to children at one month (sometimes even as early as ten days) old. Most parents who have chosen this practice have introduced it at between three to four months and stopped at five months[13]. During this period, a child is less likely to be anatomically or physiologically ready to accommodate solid food, which is a common reason why purées are introduced early in society today.

It's also worth considering how cooking techniques have changed over time. It has been reported that the most frequently premasticated foods are 'tough foods' such as meat and nuts[14]. Over the years, our knowledge of cooking skills has increased, which means that even the toughest of meats can now be tenderized using techniques such as marinading or slow-cooking.

One benefit that can't be ignored is the transference of saliva that comes with premastication. It is current scientific opinion that saliva 'may not only have immediate digestive, immunological and other protective benefits but also long-term immunocompetence and immunotolerance benefits'[15]. Babies can find it difficult to digest complex carbohydrates (such as rice and potato) because they do not produce adult levels of pancreatic amylase[16] until the age of nine months. Similarly, they do not produce adult levels of salivary amylase[17] until the age of six months and both of these enzymes are necessary for digestion, to break complex carbohydrates down into glucose. It could be thought, therefore, that pre-masticating these foods means that the parent's saliva will start their break-down so they can be used by the baby. However, if the baby isn't introduced to complex carbohydrates until the age of around six months – when they will have plenty of salivary amylase for themselves to do the job – then there isn't really a biological need for the parent to do it for them. Given that, historically, pre-masticated food was introduced to children under six months, it's clear why, under those circumstances, exposure to saliva would be beneficial, and even necessary.

One study in Thailand found an increase in bacterial contamination of foods being pre-masticated and given to children[18]. The authors of this study speculated that certain types of bacteria might be passed from mother to child through the act of pre-mastication. For example, the bacteria associated with dental caries (*streptococcus mutans* and *streptococcus sobrinus*) are likely to be transferred through saliva[19] so a thorough assessment and evaluation of the risks and benefits of pre-mastication really needs to be conducted before any healthcare organization considers recommending this approach as part of their guidelines.

It is impossible for researchers (or us) to say at this stage whether pre-mastication is a 'good or bad' thing since very little research exists. More questions need to be asked and answered in this area, but we hope that the information here helps you along the way a little, and that more studies will be conducted to better inform us as parents of the facts we need in order to make these decisions for our children.

Your baby, your decision

Everyone will probably have an opinion on which method of weaning you should be doing – health visitors, family, friends, etc. Your mum may tell you that she weaned you at four months by putting baby rice in a bottle and giving you a rusk to nibble. Your friend may have started at six months to the day by spoon-feeding her child a purée pouch. It's enough to make anyone worry about whether they'll get it 'wrong' – after all, weaning is such an important time.

The good news is that there's no absolute 'right' or 'wrong' about weaning. Societal approaches, just like healthcare recommendations, change over time and trends come and go. Societal and medical opinions about food for adults aren't much different: one minute butter is terrible and we shouldn't eat it and the next it's healthy[20].

Nobody knows your child better than you

What is the one constant that you can rely on? The fact that nobody knows your baby better than you. No one has the connection you

have with them and no one can sense their needs like you can. The most important thing is to remember that and *trust your instincts*. Your baby relies on you to sense what they need and you do this many times a day, so why should mealtimes be any different? Arm yourself with the facts, then tune in to yourself and your baby and have confidence in your choices.

Guilt!

Guilt is an emotion that we encounter a lot when we talk to parents, particularly when it comes to weaning their babies and dealing with their young children's eating. Guilt is something that we all feel at different points in our lives, as we may worry about whether we've got it 'right' or 'done the right thing' in lots of areas. Some of us experience this more than others, and that all comes down to what our relationship with ourselves is like – if it's built more on compassion and acceptance than criticism, then we're likely to feel less guilt. However, if it's underpinned by anxiety and insecurity, then we're likely to experience guilt more regularly. An example of this might be the person who never tells someone close to them when they're angry or upset about something the other person did, because they feel so guilty about 'upsetting' other people that they'd prefer to subjugate their own needs and dismiss their feelings about things.

At least, though, in most areas of life, we're not thrown in at the deep end when the stakes feel like they're the highest they've ever been. When you're a parent, however, that is the situation you have to deal with – a feeling of complete responsibility for ensuring that your child, who is completely dependent on you, develops physically and psychologically. The stakes couldn't be higher – it's a pretty unique situation, compared to all the others we will encounter. No other human being we meet in life is completely dependent on us and our decisions, every single day, for their healthy development. The hugeness of the responsibility of being a parent, then, is perfect for evoking feelings of insecurity and anxiety about getting it 'right' in even the most secure people. Anyone who was prone to feeling guilty/anxious/insecure before they had a baby is therefore likely to feel it in a much more intense way when they become responsible for another human being. It's really important to pause and notice how you relate to yourself, because guilt is not a helpful emotion – it keeps us stuck and blaming ourselves and that's no good for anyone – it makes it much harder to parent effectively too.

What's my relationship with myself?

It's really important to be aware of what your internal dialogue is. We all have an internal critical voice but for some of us It's much, much louder than for others and we may more strongly believe what it says. Although we all tend to believe the things we tell ourselves, these voices aren't speaking 'the truth'. They are regurgitating ideas that we've taken in and taken on as true as a result of our experiences as a child. For example, if you had a critical parent who always made you feel like nothing was good enough, that's the voice you'll have loudly in your head as an adult, bugging you no matter what you do – putting you down and making you feel like you're never quite getting anything right and giving you hell for making any mistakes. This, plus a hard-wired evolutionary parental need to keep your children well-nourished, can create anxiety and guilt that can underpin pressurizing strategies when it comes to eating, like the 'clear your plate' tactic. That

doesn't work for anyone (see more on this later on p.80 and p.170).

What should I do?

The first absolute 'do' is to try your best to park that judgmental voice in your head. It's often not that easy to do but if you feel like it's getting in the way of your life then a psychotherapist can help you to deal with it. Otherwise, simply become aware of it and remind yourself that it's not 'the truth' and that you would like to speak to yourself in a kinder way – we often speak to ourselves in such a harsh voice, one that we would *never* be rude or cruel enough to use when speaking to another person!

If you notice that your internal dialogue is always telling you off for doing things 'wrong' or it's telling you that you never get things 'right', stop and consider this. If it's telling you that things never work out well or that they always go wrong when you're involved, stop and notice it. Decide that you're going to treat yourself with kindness and compassion during this process, without judgment. It's not a smooth process and you're dealing with two of the most important things in your life – you and your baby – so you're bound to have a myriad of positive and negative emotions and it may feel like a bit of a rollercoaster. Be prepared for that, and decide that when things don't go well you won't judge yourself and that if you get frustrated or feel anxious you'll take a moment out to calm down. Ignore that judgmental voice in your head as much as you can – there is no room for it in the wonderful journey that is parenting your baby. Believe us when we say we know that it's easier said than done, but don't be afraid to get help if you need it. Awareness is the first step towards deciding not to buy into that voice – only you have the power to be kind to yourself.

Once you've got yourself into a positive emotional state, you're ready to start thinking about the practical elements of weaning (see p.92).

What's my relationship with feeding my baby?

Now you've thought about where you are, it's time to consider your feeding relationship with your baby so far.

- Have you enjoyed feeding your baby?
- Was breastfeeding easy and a painless process for *you*?
- Many mothers find establishing breast-feeding can be challenging. If that was your experience, how did you feel about that?
- Could you breastfeed for as long as you wanted to?
- Could you breastfeed at all? How did that make you feel?
- Do you feel you were let down by health professionals who should have been there to support you?
- Were you able to access the help and support you needed to help you breast-feed?
- Did you feel judged for the choices you made?
- Did you judge yourself for the choices you made?

If you have or have had difficulty breast-feeding, it can set you up to have a complex and difficult relationship with feeding your baby – it's a minefield for many mums. You have undoubtedly come across innumer-able posts, tweets, articles and remarks about why 'breast is best'. Breastfeeding is apparently 'the most natural thing in the world', so it's assumed that it should be easy. But what about the cracked, bleeding nipples, the bouts of mastitis, the toes curled in pain and the tears of exhaustion that so many mums experience? Despite the numerous visits to the lactation consultants and breastfeeding cafés, for some mothers breastfeeding just doesn't work out the way they hoped.

Harsh and prescriptive attitudes and remarks are responsible for a lot of unneces-sary guilt and anxiety among mothers, which can roll over into the weaning process if you don't become aware of how you've been feeling up until now and make a conscious decision to put that aside and start weaning as a new journey. Many mothers have strong feelings of failure around breastfeeding and feel it impacts on their value as a mother. Have you felt these things? How might they impact on your feelings around weaning now?

Negative feelings eat up your attention and emotional energy. Being caught up in a mire of negative feelings about yourself can take your attention away from relating to your baby and cherishing the developing relationship between you. If you have lived in fear of the next feed, then become aware of how this may affect you as you embark on the weaning journey with your little one. Guilt, in particular, can be a singularly unhelpful emotion, as it is usually associated with anxiety and can lead you to become stuck. The presence of ongoing guilt and anxiety will not help you to positively develop your relationship with your baby via weaning. On the contrary, these negative emotions will hinder your capacity to connect with your baby over food. Don't forget that your baby has no idea about the internal dialogue you've been having with yourself, so try to put those feelings aside and think of this as a new chapter.

Chapter Two

Weaning Through History to the Present Day

Why is there so much confusion and division of opinion out there over something as simple as introducing solid food to your child? Over the years, ideas about breastfeeding and weaning have changed significantly. For example, the age when babies have been introduced to solid foods has varied greatly as the evidence and guidelines have changed and no doubt they will change again (another reason you should have faith in your ability as a parent and do what's right for you and your family).

1900s (recommended weaning age: one year old)

In the 1900s parents were encouraged to introduce solid foods when a child turned one year old. To prevent scurvy, cod liver oil and orange juice were also recommended. During this time, formula milk was highly expensive and was considered a luxury for the rich and wealthy so 85% of babies were breastfed exclusively[21]. By comparison, in 2010 only 17% of women were breastfeeding at three months[22].

1920s (recommended weaning age: two to six months)

In the 1920s, evaporated milk was used in infant formula, which rapidly lowered the price and made it a more affordable option. With formula feeding previously having been seen as an exclusive act for the rich, it held a certain glamour, so mothers quickly hopped on the formula bandwagon to show their wealth. Babies were introduced to solids

earlier and earlier as fears of iron and vitamin deficiencies enveloped the minds of mothers.

1950s (recommended weaning age: three to six weeks)

In the 1950s, things went one step further and the recommendations for introducing solid food changed again to when a child was

SIX-HOUR FEEDING SCHEDULE
Given Mothers at Time of Leaving Hospital

Feedings at 6:00 a.m., 12:00 noon, 6:00 p.m. and 12:00 midnight.
Water between feedings.

At 2–5 days of age:
Cereal at 6:00 a.m. and 6:00 p.m.
(Oatmeal and barley suggested as starters.)

At 10 days of age:
Strained vegetables at 12:00 noon.
(Peas, beans, carrots suggested as starters.)

At 14 days of age:
Concentrated cod liver oil, 2 drops a day to start.
Increase one drop a month up to 5 drops daily.

At 17 days of age:
Strained fruits at 6:00 p.m.
(Applesauce, peaches, pears suggested as starters. May decrease cereal.)
Midnight feeding may be dropped at any time.

At weekly intervals add:
3 weeks – Orange juice and sterile water, equal parts of each, up to 2 ounces of each at 6:00 a.m.
4 weeks – Strained meats
5 weeks – Mustards
6 weeks – Soups
7 weeks – Mashed banana
8 weeks – Egg
Formula as indicated.

Suggested meal planner for 3-month-olds from 1953.

between three and six weeks old[23]. Introducing solids at this stage was seen as an achievement and a milestone many parents strived for. Parents would see it as an accomplishment if their 'clever' child was eating solid foods at a young age. Medical journals even printed research by doctors claiming success in feeding 2-day-old babies solids and printed suggested meal planners for 3-month-olds (see previous page)[24].

This feeding schedule for very young babies[25] gives an idea of this very different approach.

Early 1970s (recommended weaning age: before three months)

In the 1970s parents were encouraged to add rusk or baby cereal to bottles for babies between three to four weeks of age[26], with the majority of babies experiencing solids by the age of three months.

Mid 1970s (recommended weaning age: four months)

In 1974 the Department of Health guidelines recommended delaying solids until after four months of age[27].

Late 1970s (recommended weaning age: four to six months)

In 1979 the World Health Organization recommended that normal full-term infants should be exclusively breastfed for 'four to six months'. (See Chapter 9 for information about premature babies.)

1980s (recommended weaning age: three months)

In the 1980s the European and American paediatric committees and the National Health Service recommended solids be introduced no earlier than three months, but suggested waiting until four months[28].

1990s (recommended weaning age: four to six months)

In 1994, the Department of Health issued guidelines that recommended that the age range of four to six months was the ideal time to introduce solids to full-term babies. In 1995, the World Health Organization recommended that infants be exclusively breastfed for four to six months with the introduction of complementary foods (any fluid or food other than breast milk) thereafter[29]. This was misinterpreted by many health professionals, parents and others to mean that all babies should begin weaning at sixteen weeks.

It's easy to see how the era of puréeing foods evolved, because a baby who is introduced to solid food at four months is unlikely to be developmentally ready to manage 'real' food. However, a child who is developmentally ready for solids (see p.94) won't need purées and will benefit from experiencing a variety of textures.

2003 (recommended weaning age: six months)

In 2003 the World Health Organization updated their recommendation to 'exclusive breastfeeding for 6 months', a recommendation that was then echoed by the NHS.

Current recommendations

At the time of writing, the American Academy of Pediatrics[30], the World Health Organization[31] and the European Academy of Allergology and Clinical Immunology[32] recommend avoiding solid food for at least the first four months of life. (Many of these guidelines have been in place since 2004.) There is evidence to show an increased risk of eczema associated with earlier introduction of solids[33].

Following the WHO decree in 2003, the Department of Health issued a statement declaring: 'Exclusive breastfeeding is recommended for the first six months (26 weeks) of an infant's life as it provides all the nutrients a baby needs.'

However, many products exist on the market today stating 'suitable from four months', and some of these products are from new brands which started *after* the guidelines were announced back in 2003 recommending exclusive breastfeeding for six months.

WHO recommended that exclusive breastfeeding should continue until six months of age to protect infants from morbidity and mortality associated with gastroenteritis. Following this statement, much research and debate has taken place over whether this applies to *all* children. WHO make recommendations based on worldwide populations rather than local populations so their statements and guidelines encompass not only you but also mothers living in a mud-hut with a five-mile walk to the nearest well.

It is thought that the justification by WHO for this statement that breastfeeding should continue exclusively until six months is due to there being numerous cases of gastroenteritis in developing countries associated with formula and complementary foods. It only takes a quick Google search of 'Nestlé and formula milk' to understand why this decree by WHO has become necessary. But the question remains, should this apply to developed countries, like the UK, where the risks of gastroenteritis are thought to be less?[34][35][36] It is interesting to note that one UK study estimated that 53% of hospital admissions for diarrhoea could have been prevented by exclusive breastfeeding, 25% by partial breastfeeding[37].

In 2001 The UK Scientific Advisory Committee on Nutrition (SACN) reviewed the evidence from the 2001 World Health Organization's global strategy for infant and young child feeding and advised that: 'there is sufficient scientific evidence that exclusive breastfeeding for 6 months is nutritionally adequate'.

However, they also noted that 'early introduction of complementary foods is normal practice in the UK and that mothers do this for many valid personal, social and economic reasons'. They 'therefore recommend that there should be some flexibility in the advice, but that any complementary feeding should not be introduced before the end of 4 months (17 weeks)'.

Your child is unique

So, each child is an individual – no surprises there, then. With this in mind, it makes sense that a standardized approach to weaning where one size fits all and you 'have' to wean by a certain age or date just isn't going to cut it for your child. That simply focuses on the crowd and not the individual (by which we mean either you or your baby). It makes a lot more sense to start with the individuals involved and wean according to their needs. Your child isn't like anybody else's child. Each child reaches developmental milestones at different times – rolling over in their own time, babbling and sitting upright when they are ready, and speaking, crawling or walking at their own pace. As their parent, you may encourage them and facilitate their development as much as you can but, when it comes down to it, they develop at their own pace. Why should being ready for solid food be any different?

Both WHO and the Department of Health recommend one thing that is so often ignored: 'that each infant must be managed individually'[38]. That statement is so important that we're going to say it again in even bolder text and give it its own page …

'Each infant
must be managed
individually'

The politics of weaning

Over the years, the power and influence of the food industry giants has increased dramatically[39]. They have convinced many parents and even health professionals that parents are incapable of preparing their own children's food. Many animals choose the food that their offspring to eat and teach them how to eat by example. Mothers have been feeding children for generations without needing to check with a health professional, so why the shift towards purée pouches and jars and the need for reassurance from a health professional who knows more about current government guidelines than about who you and your child truly are?

Food is for fun when under ~~one~~ nine months

Despite extensive searching, it's difficult to know where the phrase 'Food before one is just for fun' came from. However, one thing is for sure – it didn't come from any reputable body such as the WHO, the AAP or the DH. It's our guess that whoever coined this phrase had good intentions to try to encourage parents to relax around feeding their child solid foods and to ensure they continue to offer milk feeds as the main source of nutrition. This popular phrase has reassured many mothers that milk feeds contain all the essential nutrients a child could possibly want. However, is milk *really* the complete nutritional offering for babies up to twelve months old?

This is what the WHO has to say in its 2004 Guiding Principles for Complementary Feeding of the Breastfed Child document:

Breast milk can make a substantial contribution to the total nutrient intake of children between 6 and 24 months of age, particularly for protein and many of the vitamins. However, breast milk is relatively low in several minerals such as iron and zinc, even after accounting for bioavailability. At 9–11 months of age, for example, the proportion of the Recommended Nutrient Intake that needs to be supplied by complementary foods is 97% for iron, 86% for zinc, 81% for phosphorus, 76% for magnesium, 73% for sodium and 72% for calcium[40].

It is interesting that a Cochrane review has shown that formula milk may contain more nutrients than maternal breast milk but it lacks the antibodies and other substances present in breast milk that protect and develop the gut of the maturing baby[41]. There are also questions around the bioavailability of nutrients in formula milk (it contains a synthetic nutrient but there is some debate about how easily a baby's body is able to convert this for use, another reason perhaps why a formula-fed baby may consume more than a breastfed baby). More research is needed in this area to help parents make informed choices.

With this in mind, we advise that it is at around nine months of age rather than twelve months that nutrition from solid food becomes important for all babies:

The Expert Consultation concluded that the potential health benefits of waiting until six months to introduce other foods outweighs any potential risks. After six months of age, however, it becomes increasingly difficult for breastfed infants to meet their nutrient needs from human milk alone[42].

If we presume the average child will be developmentally ready to start exploring food at around six months of age then it is unlikely that they are going to, at that point, quickly grasp the skills needed to eat successfully to gain nutrition. Some children will grasp it quite quickly but other children will take a bit longer, so it makes no sense for nutrition to be of paramount importance from the moment a child starts solids.

We like to see it as something roughly like this:

- Six to nine months is a time to learn how to eat
- Nine to twelve months is a time when the solids increase and milk feeds start to reduce
- Twelve months onwards is a time when eating is established and solid foods are the main source of nutrition

Remember, all children are unique so this is a rough guide and does not mean that there are exact ages at which certain milestones should be reached.

Night feeding

Children who are between eight and nine months old may still need a milk feed at night, whereas milk feeds become less relevant by the age of twelve to eighteen months as much of the child's nutrition is then coming from solid food. (This does not mean you must stop breastfeeding at this point, as long as you consider the issue of overall calorie intake – see p.131.) Sadly, there is no way to *know* for sure in younger children whether they are hungry, which is why it's not always ideal to stop middle-of-the-night feeds until a child is at least twelve to eighteen months and, even then, it should be on your terms. If you are happy to continue offering feeds in the night then go right ahead – just adjust your expectations of solid food consumption the next day.

+ + + **Tip** + + +

The general rule of thumb for older children (roughly twelve to eighteen months) is one milk feed = one meal so if you offer a milk feed at night then reduce your expectations for food consumed the next day.

+ + + + + + + + +

NIGHT-WAKING AND FOOD VOLUMES

As your self-feeding child learns about volumes of food, they will often get it wrong – but getting it wrong is a natural part of the learning process. If you look at your child's development in other areas, you will see that they made thousands of mistakes before getting something right – whether it was learning how to roll over or batting a toy under the baby gym. The way we learn is through trying and getting it wrong, over and over again, until at last we succeed.

So, be prepared for some turbulence: sometimes your child will under-eat (and may wake up in the night feeling hungry) and sometimes they will overeat (and may vomit). It's common for parents to respond automatically to night-waking in babies with a milk feed, because it's the quickest way to get the household back to sleep. That isn't going to do much harm as a one-off event, but if you repeatedly adopt this strategy over extended periods of time, it may encourage your little one to refuse their dinner. It doesn't take a child long to learn the link between actions and consequences – a child will soon recognize that crying brings milk or that a bath means it's bedtime.

Please be aware, this does not apply to young babies who certainly will need milk feeds through the night. This refers to children who are between twelve and eighteen months and, again, this is just an average. You know your child best.

It's far better for your baby to form an association of crying = comfort, rather than crying = food. It is also a better association for you to be making as the parent, rather than becoming accustomed to reaching for food whenever your child is upset in order to help calm them down. It's easy to slip into it as a habit because it often works, but soon you may find yourself held to ransom by a toddler who won't stop screaming unless you give them a biscuit, and you can see where that one might end up! In terms of your child's associations, the problem with this strategy as a general rule is that you're teaching your child that food (and probably sugary food or a carbohydrate) is what helps them to feel better when they're upset – these are the roots of teaching your child to be an emotional eater. We already all have a complex emotional relationship with food (and we all eat for emotional reasons at times, which is fine if it's not that often). However, don't set your child up to cope with negative emotions by eating as that can increase their chances of obesity, as well as it not being an emotionally healthy way to cope with emotions as a go-to strategy.

If you offer your toddler a milk feed each time they wake in the night, they will also soon learn that they don't need to eat dinner because milk will arrive in the night. This contradicts what you're trying to do in terms of teaching your child to regulate their food intake, to learn action and consequence, to understand mealtime structures and to plan ahead. Having milk in the night means they don't need to plan ahead for how to get through until the morning. It may also then lead to a refusal of breakfast, as they may still be full and may not even be hungry by breakfast time. This does not mean that your child is being manipulative or vindictive; they are merely responding to the knowledge that they will receive food during the night, and then to the feeling of fullness in the morning. They are learning how to regulate these feelings, but their efforts are focused around their night milk feeds, instead of around mealtimes. Eating a meal for a child is initially hard work – as humans we are programmed to always take the easy route, so why would your child be any different? It's a lot easier to fill their tummy with milk than to eat a meal. As a parent, it is therefore your responsibility to facilitate your child to learn to eat.

This is not a recommendation to stop breastfeeding. If you are happy to respond to your child in the night with a breastfeed then go right ahead, but you will need to adjust your expectations of your child's eating of solid food in the day. For example, if they have

---

+ + + **Tip** + + +

As a general rule, when your older child cries because they're upset about something, respond with a cuddle and reassurance rather than automatically turning to milk.

+ + + + + + + + +

+ + + **Tip** + + +

Do not ignore your child's cry. They need to know you are there and that you will respond to them. Cuddle, comfort, love and soothe for as long as they need you.

+ + + + + + + + +

a milk feed at 6 a.m. and you offer breakfast at 7 a.m., don't expect them to be particularly interested in the solid food. Read more about breastfeeding and meals on p.98.

If your child (who is over twelve months) is waking at night and you choose not to feed them then what else can you do?

+ + + **Tip** + + +

Offer a drink of water to a child who is calling out for milk in the middle of the night in an open-top cup. Drinking from a bottle or sippy-cup is much easier than from an open-top cup so this reduces the chance of your baby using one of those items as a comforter rather than because they genuinely need water. You need your child to tune in to their thirst and drink because they are thirsty.

+ + + + + + + + +

Remember, every child is different and every parent is different. If you choose to continue to offer feeds in the night then that is your decision – we are giving you options and choices and you should select those that best suit you and your unique family.

First foods through to nine months

As we have discussed, weaning and eating until nine months of age is not really about nutrition. It's about introducing your child to eating and enabling them to become familiar with foods that you hope they will eat throughout their life. Most parents know what their child *should* be eating, but getting them to eat it can be a problem. Despite the ubiquitous five-a-day messages, the level of fruit and vegetable consumption among children is not increasing[43]. You have the power to lay the foundations for your child to have a healthy relationship with food for life from the moment that they are introduced to food, before they need to eat it for nutritional reasons.

Under six months
During the first six months, breast milk is all a baby needs. If you are breastfeeding and didn't take a vitamin D supplement during pregnancy then you may be advised by your health visitor or GP to give your child a vitamin supplement from the age of one month. Formula milk is fortified with vitamins and so a supplement is not necessary.

Six to nine months
This three-month period is all about allowing your baby to learn how to feed themselves. They are developing their familiarity with and understanding of food, figuring out how to swallow, how much to put in their mouth, what hunger and fullness feel like – all things we take for granted as adults when it comes to eating.

Around 75% of your baby's diet will be made up of milk feeds. This will vary between children as some will learn quicker how to manage solids than others, but take your time and follow your baby's pace, allowing them to reduce their milk feeds gradually as they increase their solids.

At this stage, don't rush your baby. You may hear all your parent-led weaning friends telling you about how many jars of purée they polished off and taking a purée pouch being squeezed empty as a sign that their baby has had the exact right amount, but by offering your child the chance to learn for themselves how to eat and, from this young age, to recognize hunger and fullness, you are setting them up for a healthy relationship with food.

Continue to offer foods during this time regardless of the uptake. If your child is not interested, or only picks – that's their choice, not yours. Your responsibility is to decide what foods to offer and when to offer them to your baby. Remember, *you* make the big decisions and your baby makes the small ones – that way everyone feels they have some say in the matter. Tricking, bribery and spoon-feeding are not necessary. Instead, continue to offer milk feeds and allow your little one time to figure it out.

At this age, expose your child to a variety of foods to allow them to learn to use their tongue to move solid food around the mouth in preparation for swallowing. Spoon-feeding a single texture, such as purées, will have little effect on tongue manipulation and so texture variety is key. Your child is also learning to recognize food by sight and so hiding foods in sauces is going to do nothing to help your child gain familiarity with foods. Hiding vegetables in a cheese sauce is a classic method for getting a child to eat their veggies. This solves a problem short-term but long-term your child is missing the opportunity to become visually familiar with a food and build their database (see p.57).

Although it's impossible to really know whether hiding vegetables in a sauce at this point is going to cause any trust issues later, the point is that it's not a helpful tactic because sooner or later it *will* lead to your strategy being one of deception, which *will*, at some point, cause trust issues if your child ever finds out. If you're hiding vegetables in sauces, even at this age, it suggests that you're feeling anxious enough about your child eating those vegetables to resort to deception tactics, even when the eating of those vegetables is not particularly relevant for nutritional purposes. Ask yourself why you're doing this and what it means about how you're feeling. What effects could this have on your overall approach, if you don't nip it in the bud? Sensing raised anxiety from you is more likely to make your child feel distressed and it's more likely to lead you towards pressuring tactics, for example. So there is never, ever a reason to hide one food with another.

The tactile stimulation that your child receives from the food they engage with also adds to the database – messy food and messy play build familiarity with textures. Research shows that the muscles of mastication (chewing muscles) develop most markedly between six and ten months. However, they can only develop if your baby has experience of having food in their mouth[44]. Serving purées exclusively therefore does little for your child's oral development. Milk feeds are important during this phase since your child's motor skills will probably not be good enough initially to allow them to swallow food, but as the muscles are used and become stronger and your child practises with different textures, they will soon master this skill.

Nine to twelve months

At around nine to twelve months, you may notice your baby getting to grips with feeding. Their interest in the milk feeds will start to reduce as their stomachs become increasingly full on solid foods. Continue to offer the milk feeds but bear in mind that, at this stage, nutrition from solid foods is becoming increasingly relevant. Regularly offering solid food three times a day is a good idea, because it gives your child more opportunities to engage with solid food and it also embeds the pattern that we sit down at the table three times per day in your baby's neural pathways. This begins to establish a structure around eating, where your baby will understand that they have three 'mealtime' opportunities to eat per day and two smaller snack opportunities (or however you structure your meals/snacks – see p.164 for a discussion on this).

Twelve months to two years

From twelve months, your little one's previously rapid growth will start to slow as the focus moves away from gaining weight and gross motor skills towards cerebral development. This is the time when the nervous system begins to develop rapidly, as talking, walking and co-ordinating all begin, and so nutrition becomes more important – food contains the raw materials that will allow your little one's body to develop.

Having had roughly six months of practice, your little one will be well on the way to mastering solids at this stage and, by the time your baby is around eighteen months old, milk and solids will probably be at around a fifty-fifty split. By two years old, around 80% of your baby's nutrition will come from solids, until you feel ready to stop offering milk feeds altogether. (Remember, if your ratios are different to the average mentioned above then that's fine. Similarly, some parents stop breastfeeding earlier, others later – your child is unique so it's your decision.)

Food parenting beyond the toddler years

Once you've safely navigated the minefield that is weaning your baby and you feel like you've triumphed (in that you've made decisions that you're happy with and they seem

to be working for the most part) you're home free, right … ? Wrong, unfortunately. Like everything else about parenting, children's eating behaviours need to be continually shaped within a flexible (yet not too flexible) framework led by their parents, which facilitates choice-making while accommodating the child's abilities and capacities from a developmental perspective.

We frequently speak with parents at our fussy eating workshops and consultations who are pulling their hair out because their child used to eat well as a baby or toddler and yet somehow they've ended up with a fussy eater of three-and-a-half. They don't understand how it happened and it's very tempting to locate the problem in the child, but this is not always the case.

It's all about the relationship between you and your child

Our approach to feeding your child past toddlerhood is similar to how we think about weaning, in many ways. The relationship with your child is central and so, as such, successful parenting around food centres on awareness and management of your relationship. If you provide clear boundaries in life, while allowing your child to take some control and to learn to make decisions (and make mistakes with those decisions), then you'll find that this will easily extend into the food arena. If, as you're reading, you realize that you aren't practising this, then start today. When it comes to food parenting, you don't want your relationship with your child to be dominated by struggles that are nothing to do with food but that manifest themselves at the table. Your job is to model healthy food habits and attitudes, and in doing this to help your child to develop a balanced relationship with food. If you're battling for control at every mealtime, then you can't do your job.

Eating is a sociable and enjoyable occasion. Avoid leaving your child alone at the table to eat.

What's fussy eating about, then?

Fussy eating is therefore typically, in our experience, a manifestation of other things if there are no complicating factors (like recognized developmental issues). Maybe your child is struggling for control. Maybe your anxiety about whether they're eating enough has led you to hover over them as they eat, making them feel pressured. Perhaps you've been telling them that they need to finish their food when they feel like they've had enough. Maybe you aren't letting them make decisions at the table or throughout the day. Maybe you're giving them their dinner, leaving them to eat it alone because you're busy and they are trying to get your attention. Perhaps you're feeding them something different than what you're eating. Maybe every time they pull a face you whip away the food and suggest you make them their favourite thing.

The possibilities are endless as to why fussy eating might develop, but what's for certain is that it'll be a combination of your behaviour around X combined with their behaviour around X. In other words, you're *co-creating* whatever eating behaviour you see in your child – you play a large part in shaping it and in enabling it to continue. A lot of fussy eating behaviour is underpinned by parental anxiety about whether your child is eating enough (which is complicated by all sorts of unhelpful other issues, like guilt, competitiveness or insecurity, for example). This anxiety is so strong that it can lead you to behave in a way that is intended to alleviate that anxiety in the short term, but a) that doesn't work long term and b) it means you're attending to your own emotional needs instead of to your child's emotional needs when it comes to eating. If you don't notice what's happening, things can easily descend into exhausting patterns – cooking a different meal for each family member, never leaving the house without a bag full of snacks or giving them food just after mealtimes just to reassure yourself that they have eaten something.

Shutterstock

Fussy eating issues can be incredibly frustrating and lead many parents to dread mealtimes.

Whose problem is fussy eating?

If you do find yourself doing the above things, it can encourage you to start thinking about it as if your child 'has' the problem, your child is being difficult, being manipulative or deliberately resisting your efforts to get them to eat. If you view it that way, it can only breed more frustration, more guilt and more intense feelings of powerlessness as things continue (and often get worse as time passes).

As we hope you've gathered by now, it's not about blame. It's nobody's problem; no one *owns* it, as such. It's something that's developed *between* you, in your relationship, as a result of your interactions with your child around food, and you need to take responsibility for your part in creating that. For example, if your child will only eat sausage rolls and pizza, how did they get to that point? How did they develop that habit? Did they go to the supermarket, buy them, make them and eat them themselves? Or did this develop over time because you enabled it? The chances are that it is the latter, so (without beating yourself up unhelpfully) consider: how did that happen? For example, do you offer such foods a lot? Does the child-minder/Grandma offer them a lot? Do you automatically use them as a 'go to' option the minute your child pulls a face or refuses something else? Do you give them as snacks in between meals so that your child knows they don't need to eat as they'll get a sausage roll if they're hungry? Permit yourself to have made a mistake, or talk to Granny, and decide to do something different moving forward.

Does everyone have these problems?

Fussy eating seems to be a problem that rears its ugly head a lot more in certain cultures than in others. It's a huge problem in the UK and in the USA, for example, whereas in some other cultures it's just not something that often crops up. We can speculate as to why that may be, but it's likely to be a result of a combination of lifestyle factors, cultural food choices, attitudes to food, cultural approaches to eating and parenting around food.

Irena and Zarya

Irena is Croatian. She grew up there and moved to England during her teens. When she had a baby and got to the weaning stage, she began to worry about how she would introduce food to Zarya and whether she was eating a wide enough range of foods. She began to find it stressful, and she had to stop herself cajoling her daughter to eat healthy foods. She tried very hard to avoid giving Zarya processed and sugary foods like cakes when she was a baby/toddler, but she soon discovered it's nearly impossible to keep a child away from these treats forever. Once Zarya tried them, she loved them and always made a beeline for cakes whenever they were around, losing interest in any other foods.

This made Irena want to start bargaining with Zarya — 'finish X and then you can have Y' — a common sentence among parents eager for their child to eat their dinner.

We met Irena when we were speaking at a baby show and were chatting with her about her concerns. During the course of our conversation, Irena remarked that she didn't remember there being a big fuss around food, or vegetables, when she was young. She said that things were much simpler — eating was practical and social. The family always ate together at the table, with no exceptions. She was one of seven children, and they were told what was being served for dinner. They were all presented with their meal on a plate and were expected to eat it (but she didn't recall having to 'clear the plate' — they naturally stopped when they'd had enough). There were no alternatives, no persuasion. There was no bargaining or deal-making around food, and vegetables weren't more or less interesting than other foods.

This lack of 'strategies' around eating probably reflects the fact that Irena's mother didn't worry about whether they were getting enough fruit and vegetables, for example. Their family ate different fruit and vegetables according to what was in season and all of it came from local markets. Vegetables weren't positioned as being more or less healthy than other foods, such as meat, either — it was all just part of getting a good solid meal. All foods that were encountered day to day were equal and were regarded as just foods, rather than being loaded with desirable/undesirable, good/bad or healthy/unhealthy characteristics. As a result, the family's non-emotionally-loaded attitude towards food was transferred to Irena and her six siblings, who simply accepted the culture — eating wasn't an issue. Another very interesting memory that Irena told us was that, as a child, she spent a lot of time outdoors and she was therefore usually starving hungry by the time mealtimes came around. When it came to sweets and chocolates, Irena recalled that her mother gave them sweets only very occasionally and that, for them, there was no question of demanding or expecting chocolate, biscuits or dessert every day. There certainly wasn't a sweet cupboard in the house.

Irena's food upbringing isn't an unusual picture in a lot of cultures. In many countries, the culture is rooted in cooking fresh and varied foods from scratch (meaning very little exposure to foods containing a lot of added salt/sugar) and eating together. Many cultures have embraced processed foods much less than we have in the UK and their supermarkets are overwhelmingly full of locally sourced foods. Families consistently eat together and their habit of eating seasonal local produce as a matter of course ensures that there is always a variety and wide range of healthy food that children consume, as part of that family eating culture. Parents therefore don't need to worry about whether their children are consuming enough healthy food – most of the food that's available is healthy so the nutritional balance is naturally there, and the range of processed foods that become a part of everyday life is relatively small. In those cultures, parents' main concern is whether their children are getting *enough* food, rather than being concerned with what they're eating.

THE DAMAGING SIDE-EFFECTS OF THE PROCESSED FOOD REVOLUTION

The ratio of natural versus processed foods has become completely inverted in cultures like the UK (and the USA). The development of various processing techniques has enabled the food industry to make cheaper and cheaper food, but the real cost of processing is that the food has less and less nutritional value, yet seems more and more palatable. Children are surrounded by readily available processed foods in a way that they never were in the past, and it's very easy for their palates to become accustomed to very high levels of sweetness and saltiness in their food, which often leads to them 'liking' and demanding these foods more and more and 'disliking' and (therefore refusing) natural foods more and more, because their palates are no longer sensitive to the flavours in natural foods, which consequently seem 'bland'. This is undoubtedly one factor in the rise in prevalence of fussy eating, with daily battles at mealtimes and supermarket tantrums being exhaustingly common obstacles to feeding children healthily. It's tiring just thinking about it!

HOW EVOLUTIONARY HARD-WIRING ISN'T HELPING

What the change in the natural to processed ratio means in the real world for parents is that, given the opportunity to navigate the world of food they encounter completely freely (without any input from parents), children will follow their palates and make a beeline for the strongly (and artificially) flavoured foods. Children are hard-wired to consume as many nutrient-dense foods as possible, as their evolutionary task is to reach adulthood and to be as well-nourished as possible. They are therefore designed to choose food with the most flavour and most calories in it. Unfortunately, the disproportionate addition of fat, salt and sugar to foods nowadays means that those foods are likely to be the processed ones, like chicken nuggets, fizzy drinks and chocolate. This hard-wiring is very difficult to overcome – even those children who may eat well with you at mealtimes, when you have some control over what's available, can't easily eat well when left to their own devices.

There's no doubt about it, you're up against their evolutionary hard-wiring, because it doesn't happen to work in our present culture. So it's your job to create a strong enough 'nurture' attitude to balance out the 'nature' one. When it comes to eating, your goal has got to be nurture over nature.

UNHELPFUL FOOD CHARACTERIZATION

We have become inclined to categorize foods and give them labels – e.g. 'good' or 'bad'. This tendency we have developed can create particular emotional associations with food that it simply shouldn't have, which easily transfer onto us, becoming personal associations. For example, if a food is 'naughty', before you know it, you're naughty for eating it – how many times have you heard someone say: 'It's so naughty and I shouldn't, but I can't resist that chocolate cake – I've been good all week'? That one statement promotes many unhelpful ideas. It's labelling food and oneself as naughty (i.e. bad), it's framing 'naughty' foods as irresistible (i.e. they have a particularly strong appeal and it's impossible to control your desire to eat them), suggesting they 'should' be resisted (so you've failed); the list could go on. That kind of statement – which is so commonly heard that we don't even notice the judgmental undertones, undermining who we are and our self-worth, dictating who we should be and berating us for our failure to be that – is a sign of how far we've gone, culturally, in creating unhelpful attitudes to food and shows just how dysfunctional a relationship many of us have with food, and ourselves in that domain.

By not noticing the undertones of those kinds of statements, by allowing them to be a normal part of how you talk to yourself about food in front of your child, as well as making them a part of how you talk to your child about food on a day to day basis, you're setting your child up to develop food habits that are increasingly defined and controlled by their emotions, rather than their physical feelings of hunger and satiety. Labelling certain foods as 'healthier' than others, which is where the 'eat your vegetables' argument comes in, may increase a child's emotional resistance to vegetables, for example, because they don't want to do what they 'should'; perhaps because they're bullling with their parent for control in other areas. These kinds of labels can therefore be really powerful, in terms of how their regular use can shape unhelpful associations and behaviours that will become more and more entrenched, eventually defining your child's relationship with food, and with themselves around food, in adult life.

But how do you avoid teaching your child that cakes and sweets aren't to be enjoyed as frequently as fruit and vegetables, we hear you cry? Well, it's a question of expectation. Think back to Irena on p.30. Her mother didn't tell her that cakes were 'naughty', she just supplied them only very rarely, and thus Irena learned that this was the normal way of things, without unhelpful emotional labels being attached to sugary foods. And while it may be true that Irena's mother had less of an uphill battle on her hands, as sugary and other processed foods were less common in her surroundings, the impact you as a parent have on shaping your child's view of the world cannot be underestimated.

What did our parents teach us?

Many of us were brought up being taught to 'finish what's on your plate'. That's partly a leftover from times that previous generations lived through when food was either rationed or otherwise scarce (e.g. during the Second World War) when parents were anxious about their children getting enough to eat. The effects of it were less harmful, in many ways, than a similar attitude is today, partly because there were fewer processed foods consumed in daily life (so most food was actually nutritious, and in general was less calorie-dense) but also because children played outside more and for longer than they do today, with less television viewing or computer gadgets available to occupy a child's time. There are certainly too many calorie-dense, nutrient-scarce foods available for that to be a helpful approach nowadays. It also overrides your child's connection with their own body and their decision-making skills about when it's time to stop eating, and that's what we all need in an environment as food-plentiful as ours is.

It's important to remember that the strategies you choose to employ around food are establishing lifelong feeding 'rules' that your child will internalize. Don't forget, the time period when you are controlling everything your child eats is a limited one. When they are left to their own devices, you don't want them assuming that everything in front of them needs to be finished, as those 'rules' will apply no matter which food they might be faced with and may give rise to incredibly strongly rooted habitual eating behaviour. An older child (or an adult) who has internalized a rule that says: 'always finish what's on your plate – it's rude/wasteful not to' will find it incredibly hard to decide they've had enough and leave half a piece of chocolate cake. It will just feel wrong to them, so they are much less likely to listen to themselves and much more likely to behave on autopilot, because it 'feels' more familiar (and is thus interpreted by the brain as feeling 'right').

What can I do?

Make conscious decisions about how you're going to parent around food so that you can actively create your own approach to food parenting, according to what kind of 'food culture' you wish to create in your family. As for techniques, many of the methods we talk about throughout this book will work well for children who are pre-schoolers as well as for babies and toddlers, for example, encouraging choice-making and experiencing the consequences, or creating a culture where everyone eats at the table together and they don't leave until everyone has finished.

The most important thing is to shape your own foundational principles for food parenting, based on an awareness of what type of eating behaviour and relationship with food you would like your child to develop.

Here are some tips to help you:

- Purposefully create your family's own food culture. Awareness is really important. Stay mindful of the fact that the food culture we live in may not guide your child in the direction you would like when it comes to food. This means that you need to notice what's happening and purposefully create something different for your family, rather than getting swept along in what everyone else does.

- All foods should be created equal, from an emotional perspective. Some attitudes towards food in other cultures lead children to develop less 'loaded' emotional associations with particular foods, e.g. vegetables or cakes. Follow their lead. All food is equal. Avoid using unhelpful labels like good, bad or healthy – carrots are yummy, as is chocolate. It's just food.

- No bargaining, no persuading and no alternatives. Encourage independent choice-making with consequences – the same techniques we mention on p.182 work beyond the toddler years and for young children.

- Let go of anxiety about how much your child is eating. This isn't an easy one, but this outdated mentality leads to bargaining and unhelpful associations. Unless your child is ill or losing weight, they're fine.

- Keep your goal in mind. Your aim is to empower your child with balanced long-term eating habits/behaviours and an emotionally healthy relationship with food.

- Don't sacrifice creating a long-term healthy psychological approach to food in your child by using short-term strategies that prioritize your need for quick compliance or your anxieties about their intake.

- Don't automatically copy how your parents parented you around food. Reflect on what your own relationship with food is, and your habitual eating behaviours. Do they serve you? Do they feel like the healthiest attitude for you or do they cause you problems? Make choices based on what you think actually works, rather than just automatically doing something that feels familiar.

- Take control of the food environment in your house. Serve as many non-processed foods as you can, with a wide range across all food groups. However, equally, relax a little. If your child goes to a party and has a tummy full of sweets and cakes during a two-hour period, it's okay as long as this isn't the norm.
- Have conversations with your child about creating a balance. This means that you might explain that we eat certain foods often (e.g. fruit, meat, vegetables), while we eat other foods sometimes (like cakes) because we eat foods that give us a good balance for our bodies and that *that* (i.e. the balance of foods that we create along with our balanced attitude towards what we choose to eat) is what keeps us healthy, *not* individual foods.
- Create a reliable meal framework that suits your family. For example, three meals and two snacks a day is a standard common approach. You need to decide when these will be, according to when meals and snacks fit in with your family's daily routine. Creating this structure as a first step eradicates grazing in between meals and also teaches your child that food is predictably supplied at known intervals throughout the day (although this doesn't mean it has to be forced down regardless of feelings of hunger!).
- Take only half the responsibility for your child's eating and let them have the other half (see p.169 for further details).

Flexibility and compassion for yourself when things go wrong are very important, as not every strategy will work with every child (of course). We can't address everything about parenting your children through the toddler years here (that's a whole new book!) but we hope that this will help you to think about the relevant issues and factors so that you can shape your parenting strategies in a thoughtful and considered way. Most importantly, remember that whatever you choose to do has to work for *you* and *your family*.

Chapter Three

Building Your Own Approach to Weaning

How do you build an appropriate food culture in your home? Well, it starts at the weaning stage, so let's begin by having a look at the introduction of solid foods from the ground up.

The principles of weaning

Weaning can be empowering for you, as a parent, and it can help you to be creative and feel confident in your own judgment. There is no 'weaning by numbers' approach since each child and each parent are different. There's no absolute guide to what you need to do. Instead, you will learn the skills to understand what *your* baby needs at that particular time. You will learn to interpret what they are trying to tell you so that you can *meet your baby where they are* and judge what to do next for yourself. This communication isn't through baby signing or baby whispering, but through tuning in to your baby and understanding your child's needs.

There are certain principles that tell you how your baby is developing cognitively, emotionally and physically. By using your bond with your baby you can positively influence your baby's development in all of these areas. Armed with that knowledge and tips to keep in mind, you can work with your baby at a pace and in a way that suits you both. Understanding your own emotions around food and infant development will enable you to make those judgments and wean successfully, in the best way for you and your

baby as individuals. All you need to do, then, is to keep these simple principles and ideas in mind. These principles are grouped into sections so that you can think about the different dimensions of weaning your child.

Weaning approaches

There are currently two main approaches to weaning, although, as we have said, trends come and go, like everything else. These can be generally described as:

Parent-led weaning: this is where the parent decides when and how to introduce solid food and when to stop milk feeds. The parent also controls the feeding process. Food is often puréed and the child is spoon-fed by a parent or caregiver.

With baby-led weaning, the child decides what food to eat – there is no spoon-feeding and no purées.

Shutterstock

With parent-led weaning, the parent decides what food the child eats.

Baby-led weaning: this is a way of introducing solid foods that allows babies to feed themselves and control the feeding process – there's no spoon-feeding and no purées[45].

We recommend an approach to weaning that is based on one of the most prominent psychological child development theories in recent history, which we wholeheartedly support. It's called attachment theory[46]. We take elements from baby-led weaning (such as self-feeding) and elements from parent-led weaning (for example, the idea that your feelings count too) but we believe that successful weaning depends more on how you parent your child around food than on the food itself. It's not about following a rigid set of rules but about feeling your way to success – it's a journey for you and your baby.

Attachment theory

Attachment theory suggests that the relationship (or the bond, the attachment) between child and parent is the most important thing for every aspect of a child's overall development. If the parent (or main caregiver) consistently provides the child with warm, timely and appropriate attention and care, then the child thrives and forms a view of the world where they are wanted, valued, supported and where they feel worthy of being loved and nurtured. They develop what is known as a secure attachment (rather than an insecure attachment) relationship with their parent, which means that the bond feels secure to the child. They then begin to feel secure in themselves because they know their parent is always there to attend to their needs. This allows children to gain confidence and to explore the world. Much research has shown that secure attachment leads to better physical, psychological, emotional and cognitive development because secure children are more curious, more independent, and more inquisitive. They also become better able to engage with difficult tasks and learn how to problem-solve, for example. This process of attachment begins in infancy and continues throughout childhood – actually, your attachment patterns and key childhood relationships are acknowledged to influence and shape your adult relationships, too. So it's pretty important!

Attachment parenting

Attachment parenting[47] is an approach to parenting that is based on attachment theory. It prioritizes the relationship between child and parent and involves techniques such as birth bonding, babywearing, co-sleeping and breastfeeding. You may have heard parents calling themselves 'AP Parents' and there are plenty of social media sites and forums discussing the subject.

Bearing what we know about attachment theory in mind when we think about weaning brings the relationship between parent and child into the spotlight. Weaning naturally, in a way that focuses on your relationship with your baby and sees weaning as something that happens between you instead of something you do to your child, is one of the most important things. By adopting this approach to weaning, you can enhance your baby's psychological and physical development and develop a stronger bond with them as you introduce solid food. The approach also focuses on you as much as on your baby, giving you the tools to tune in to your-self and your little one, so that you can feel confident about how you go about helping your baby develop a healthy relationship with food for life.

Your capacity to create a healthy attachment relationship with your child is an extremely important factor in their development. Links have been found between children who fail to thrive and mothers manifesting an attachment disorder[48]. 'Failure to thrive' may be defined as: 'a significant interruption in the expected rate of growth compared with other children of similar age and sex during early childhood[49].' It can have a negative impact on long-term social, intellectual and psychological functioning and is associated with neglect. If parents aren't able to provide affection or behave in a socially appropriate way, this may underpin the child's failure to thrive. Research suggests that many social factors might mean that a child becomes neglected. These may include having no help or support from friends or family, social isolation, substance abuse or violence, as well as parental absence or having inadequate emotional resources to nurture a child[50][51]. These are thought to contribute to a child not receiving adequate nutrition, in various ways.

Of course, it's important to remember that these associations have been found in scientific studies and that all studies have limitations. It's the take-home message that's important, which, in plain English, is that how you interact emotionally with your child can have a real effect on their feeding as babies and their eating later on, as they grow up. Your ability to tune in and create a strong emotional connection with your baby is therefore of paramount importance for their feeding, nutrition and physical development.

No labels

As humans, we are multi-dimensional beings, so labelling ourselves as one thing or another doesn't always fit well. You may recognize yourself as a parent who breast-feeds and babywears but you may choose not to co-sleep … what category do you fall into? Are you an attachment parent or not? Does it even matter which label we would give you or which label you give yourself? No. What matters is what works for you and your baby and if that means using theories from different camps then go right ahead.

That's why there is no label for this approach to weaning. It is not a prescriptive approach, there is no telling you how you should do things, and there's no schedule or routine to follow. How you wean your baby shouldn't be about following a particular method and a set of rules, it should support the fact that your baby is an individual and so are you, just as it should be in all areas of parenting. You decide which bits work for you and which bits don't. We simply hope that you will use the ideas and the evidence we give you to find an approach that is label-free and uniquely yours.

The bond between you and your baby is a priority, as is introducing your baby to food and to the vast array of textures, tastes and temperatures that accompany food whilst supporting your own beliefs and happiness. How you are with your baby, and how you introduce foods, via self-feeding, instead of focusing on which foods you offer, are key to this approach.

'Mothers and babies form an inseparable biological and social unit: the health and nutrition of one group cannot be divorced from the health and nutrition of the other'[52].

Your welfare and happiness is just as important as your child's

Your baby is certainly unique, but you are too. One thing that's noticeable about weaning approaches throughout history is that they are entirely focused on which foods to give your child and when. No one seems to focus on the other side of the equation, when it's actually *you* who has the responsibility for your child. As well as considering what may be right for your child, isn't it also important to value what might be right for you? After all, you're the one guiding the process.

With official health guidelines and weaning recommendations seeming ever-changing, is it any wonder that parents are confused? Much of the advice you may receive will be based on other people's experience and, if you're a first-time parent, it's hard to know who to listen to because you are in a completely unknown situation. Like so many other parents, you might have found yourself wondering: should they be sleeping through the night by now? Should their poo be that colour? Are they following the right weight centile? Many parents feel insecure in their parenting, relying on advice from friends, family and health professionals and finding it difficult to trust themselves or follow their instincts for fear of doing something 'wrong'.

Just as your child has the need to feel part of a group and be accepted by their peers, you as a parent also have the same need to fit in with other parents. If the fellow parents in your antenatal group or circle of friends are following one method, you may find it hard to go against the pack mentality and take your own approach. This doesn't apply just to introducing solids but also to sleep-training methods, babywearing, television viewing – the list is endless. So it can be helpful to remember that your peers are experiencing something different – their own baby, their own pressures and their own relationships, and their needs may not match yours.

With weaning, like in so many other areas of your child's life, there are certain facts that can inform you as a parent; the ideal situation is for you to use these facts but trust your instincts to make them work for you. All the statistical evidence in the world isn't going to help you if something doesn't feel right to you and you're going against your internal voice. There is a lot to be said for 'gut instinct' when you become a parent. We are passionate about helping parents to feel empowered in their parenting around food, so we will present you with relevant scientific evidence and weaning information but encourage you to consider yourself in the process too and to follow what you feel is right. It's all about empowering you to make what you believe to be the right decisions for your family. Then, when your mother reports 'I weaned you at three months and you turned out okay' or your neighbour says 'I bottle fed both my babies and they are fine' you will have more knowledge and evidence to base your decisions on and the confidence to go with what feels right for you, rather than doing something based on simply knowing that it was okay for someone else. You see, what might be right for them might not actually be right for you and your child. It might not fit in with your beliefs or emotions, and your welfare and happiness is just as important as your child's in the weaning journey that you embark on together.

You decide which foods are available, your baby decides which (if any) to eat

You decide on a range of foods that you're happy offering and your baby chooses to self-feed from a variety of foods of different textures. It's all about focusing on being together and having fun while you wean. This approach takes both you and your baby into consideration – it's not just about your baby's capability, personality and approach; it is also about *yours*!

This approach creates a hierarchy of responsibility and accountability so that both of you have an element of control over the situation.

Your goal with weaning is to form eating habits, not to fill your little one's tummy

Research suggests that the two important factors in the formation and changing of children's eating habits are:

- The characteristics of the child (temperament)
- The characteristics of the parent/caregiver (parenting style)[53]

Weaning styles are commonly either solely on the characteristics of the child (as in baby-led weaning) or the characteristics of the parent (parent-led weaning). *Both* sets of characteristics should be taken into account for a successful experience and interaction with food.

What about baby-led weaning?

Baby-led weaning has become a much-used method in recent years, and it was an extremely positive development in terms of weaning approaches, because it debunked some very entrenched ideas and allowed parents to think about things differently. For example, it suggested that babies can handle non-puréed solid food, and that eating the same foods as a family (being included) is a positive thing for a baby to experience. It also proposed that babies can feed themselves. Indeed the first Yummy Discoveries book, *Yummy Discoveries: The Baby-Led Weaning Recipe Book*, was born out of Felicity's need to find easy recipes to make for Lucas when she was weaning, that were appropriate for him but which also minimized waste as they could easily be converted into adult-friendly meals. However, as with anything, research moves on, and there are some aspects of traditional baby-led weaning that are not supported by current thinking, for example, the 'no purées'[54] rule (see p.43 for why they need not necessarily be forbidden).

Another concern with traditional baby-led weaning is that it is very much centred around following your baby's direction with no focus on what's happening between you and how your relationship with your baby can strengthen as you help them to discover food. It doesn't really address you as the parent, in terms of helping you to become aware of and manage your own needs and emotions. It also doesn't consider how the way you parent your child around food might affect your existing family structure.

Both you and your baby are present so you should both be considered here. There's nothing more important than the relationship between you both and, when it comes to weaning, this is simply contextualized within food and eating. The ideal approach considers what works best for both of you, parent and baby, allowing you both to make decisions about food – after all, you need to feel good to guide the process. Your baby's personality is developing and you want to encourage them to feel confident and proud of themselves. Give yourself permission to do whatever makes you feel most comfortable

Weaning is about offering your child the opportunity to explore food (and cutlery).

as a parent. For example, if you choose to offer your little one purées and cutlery from the moment you introduce solids, then that is your decision. If your baby is happy to pick up purée and pop it into their mouth with a spoon or their hands then that is their decision, as is them choosing to chomp on a chunk of steak or tuck into the family cottage pie.

Just as our *Baby-Led Weaning Recipe Book* aimed to advise in a non-prescriptive, non-judgmental way how to facilitate your child's self-feeding according to the latest research, so this book hopes to expand on this by drawing in the compelling theory of attachment in the hopes that this will help you find a way to wean that suits your whole family. Our aim is not to prescribe any set-in-stone approach, but rather to facilitate parents to digest the current evidence and have the confidence to create their own way of weaning.

So what is baby-led weaning?

It is suggested that what separates baby-led weaning from conventional feeding is that babies are exclusively offered finger-foods, which makes purées and spoon-feeding obsolete[55].

Baby-led weaning isn't new[56]. Many parents have allowed their infant to self-feed for reasons of convenience, or because their infant refused to be spoon-fed, for generations. The practice of baby-led weaning has probably always existed[57] but by explaining and outlining the benefits of waiting until your child is ready and allowing them to self-feed we hope it has become more accessible to the later generation of parents who were most likely spoon-fed purées and so know little else.

Baby-led weaning involves no purées, yet puréed food is a valid new taste dimension for a baby and weaning from a perspective that involves exposing your child to the whole variety of food textures supports its inclusion as a way for food to be offered. Consider the elaborate meals you see cooked in top restaurants – a purée is often smeared across the plate to allow the diner a different texture.

Offering up foods that can be eaten with a spoon and other cutlery can help with a child's motor development (see p.211) so sticking solely to finger-foods is not necessarily going to suit all children (or you for that matter) all the time. Recall also that your child wants to copy you so seeing you eating that lamb chop with cutlery is something they are likely to want to mimic and experience also.

In 2008, Rapley and Murkett suggested that when a baby makes the transition from a milk-only diet to one including solid (and ideally family) food, food should be offered as graspable pieces so that the baby learns to feed themselves[58].

The baby-led weaning ethos focuses on your baby being offered foods that the rest of the family are eating (i.e. the family has 'chosen' the meal, which is offered to the baby). We recommend a weaning approach that ensures your child has a choice over what they eat, thereby including them in family choices about food from the beginning. Yes, your child will eat what your family is eating, but that's because everyone has chosen a part of the meal.

Some schools of thought consider babies to be natural grazers and recommend that you offer them food six or more times a day for several years. It is also sometimes suggested that there is no need to make a distinction between meals and snacks (also in terms of where they happen) before the age of eighteen months. However, we believe that weaning with a focus on eating together within a structure (i.e. there are meal- and snack-times) helps your child to understand how the social aspect of eating works, as well as to experience its benefits. It also teaches them that food isn't simply sitting around the house at all times and that decisions need to be made around food within a framework. It's hugely important that your child is included in your family's eating experiences as much as possible – they are wired to want to be included and there's no reason to feed them separately, or to encourage them to graze rather than to take part in the normal structure of your family's eating patterns. This means sitting down with your child at as many mealtimes as possible and eating together, even if you're having a cup of tea or a small portion of dinner while saving the rest for later on. You can always create a family structure around eating and you should maximize your baby's opportunities to eat with the whole family as much as you can.

If your child is at nursery or with a childminder then of course you won't be able to sit with them to enjoy every meal. But fortunately it is common practice in these settings that children eat together with their peers so they will experience the same sense of inclusion as they would at home. Remember that the important thing is for your child to explore food and experience eating as the social activity that it should be for us all, as humans.

But shouldn't I listen to my baby's cues?

Listening and responding to your baby's cues and being truly 'led' by them are two different ideas. As parents, it's our job to 'lead' our babies in the world, in terms of showing them how the world works – we are literally teaching them how to survive. But that means knowing the difference between imposing our ideas on them in areas where they should be given the freedom to explore (i.e. self-feeding vs. spoon-feeding) and times when we need to impose our ideas on them for their well-being (i.e. not allowing them to run out into the road). It's all about guiding them by providing a framework that facilitates discovery. By being attentive to their cues (e.g. their ability to sit up unaided as a cue for being ready for weaning), you'll know more about what they're ready for or what they can cope with. That can then shape the way you parent them around food. So we prefer to think of this approach as guiding your baby while staying attuned to what they're trying to tell you.

Is it okay for me to offer my baby purées?

Yes! If that's what you feel comfortable with doing, then do it. Now, there are going to be baby-led weaning purists out there gasping in horror at this, but hopefully if you've read up to this point, you already understand why purées are okay. It is imperative that you, as a parent, are relaxed at mealtimes and are not transmitting anxiety and stress to your child. If you're hovering with your hand over their back or leaping up at every screwed-up face or gag, then you might be happier with offering purées, at least at first, and this may well be more productive. Parents pummelling their child on the back at every cough and croak does not create a harmonious, calm eating environment. Your baby is attuned to you and feeds off your signals. Only *you* know what sits comfortably with you – don't be led by copying your friends or listening to your in-laws. Your baby, your decision.

Parents often ask us whether their baby can eat mushy foods with their hands or whether they should spoon-feed these. The answer is that babies who are developmentally ready to wean can manage sloppy foods – if they have a purée in front of them, then they may stick their hands in it and smear it all over their faces, putting their fingers in their mouths – that's absolutely fine! Babies can also pick up foods like steamed broccoli florets and bring them to their mouth to explore, if they are developmentally ready. Self-feeding is the key here – if it makes you feel happier when using purées to include a spoon, then pre-load it and let your child use it; however, let them make the choice about whether to use it or not. Just don't be put off purées by the worry that your baby won't be able to use their hands to eat them.

Unfortunately, the decision about whether to serve purées or not isn't always as easy as it should be, because they are pushed by the baby food industry to such a huge degree. We promised you the facts, and this includes the facts on the baby food industry and how they are potentially marketing to you and making you feel that your baby needs 'baby-grade' ingredients, or that a purée pouch of apple and pear is somehow better than something you might make at home for a fraction of the cost. That assertion is absolutely false.

Brands emerged in the nineteenth century to protect the public from contaminated or falsely described foods but food-cheating has been going on for years, such as padding bread out with sand in ancient times[59]. Brands indicated trust as the provider could be traced. This book, however, is being written at a time when a horsemeat scandal has recently hit Great Britain, and branded products advertised as containing beef have been found to contain as much as 100% horsemeat. It is clear now that the 'brand' is not there to improve nutrition but to manipulate the psychology of the buyer to maximize profits. Brands with bright logos, cheerful packaging and soothing nutritional claims are popping up everywhere, trying to convince you to buy their baby porridge as it's suitable for babies … but what's wrong with serving regular porridge oats to babies? Absolutely nothing.

The puréed baby food industry is now worth more than £450 million – compared with £191 million in 1989. According to the *Daily Mail*, 'Four out of five British babies now rely on tinned and jarred products' for their food[60].

'It's on-the-go snacking, on-the-go nourishment. It moves with kids and puts the control in their hands.' This is the opinion of the chief executive of a popular baby-food company in an interview with the *New York Times*. He is talking here about the food pouch, a product toddlers slurp while roaming around. The question to ask yourself in response to these kinds of comments is: why would I *want* to encourage on-the-go

snacking and nourishment for my child? By 'on the go', we mean 'eating while moving around' – although snacks may be eaten in different places, we strongly recommend that you do not allow your child to eat while running/walking around.

This is because the body isn't set up to eat and run around at the same time. When blood and energy goes to the legs, the digestive system shuts down and is much less effective, and your child is wired not to *want* to eat. They are also distracted from the experience of food if they're 'on-the-go' when they are eating, not to mention that they're nearly missing out on the eating experience altogether if the 'meal' they have is nothing more than mush in a pouch which they cannot even see. If you look at the contents of one of those pouches their colour and texture has no resemblance to real foods. Where are the different foods, with their different appearances, textures and tastes? They're all blended together into one mush of a flavour that's not actually teaching your child anything about any of those foods. So the next time they encounter a piece of lamb or a parsnip, they will have made absolutely no association between that lamb and parsnip purée pouch and the food in front of them.

This is not to say that these products do not have a place, but the problem comes when the ratio of offering these to your baby outweighs their experience of real food. There is, after all, no such thing as a bad food (see p.161) but the volume it is offered in makes all the difference. If your child is experiencing only these purées and is missing out on making food choices, self-feeding and seeing food in its real form then you probably needn't have even bothered with the purée pouch, especially since research has shown that these purées contain no more nutrients than a milk feed[61].

That's without even *thinking* about what you're not teaching your child about how eating works in the family, at nursery or in society – that is, we all sit down together and eat – when you give them a meal in a pouch. If you're giving your child food 'on-the-go' then why would they be able to sit down with the family and have a meal? How are they learning to regulate their eating or make decisions about when they've finished, in line with the rest of the family? Children learn by repetition and familiarity, so the patterns of sometimes giving them pouches as and when, while sometimes expecting them to sit and eat with the family, can be a way to create confusion and even eating issues.

These purée pouches, when used continuously as a meal replacement, can therefore be a perfect recipe for producing a fussy eater, who doesn't know how to fit in with the eating patterns that society requires, and who is also potentially obese.

A focus on bonding with your baby over food

The relationship between you and your baby is the foundation for everything you teach your child. Weaning is an opportunity for you to facilitate your baby's discovery of the exciting and delicious world of food and to make that journey together. With an understanding of how you influence your baby's moods and reactions, food becomes an opportunity for discovery and having fun together, instead of a source of stress and anxiety as it is for many parents.

Weaning includes you

As a parent, you have a huge impact on your baby's relationship with food. That's because you and your baby are programmed to tune in to each other. Why? For the answer to that one, we go back to attachment theory. It suggests that when your baby is born, their only 'job' is to survive to adulthood. A baby succeeds in becoming a self-sufficient adult if they can get the right emotional and physical care from their parent until they can provide it for themselves – that's why you're programmed to tune in to them. But food and cuddles aren't enough – they also need to 'fit in' with other people so that they can survive in society. They need to make sure that they get your attention, so that you give them everything they need. That's why they're programmed to tune in to you.

How does my baby tune in to me?

Humans tune in to each other in lots of ways – through body language, expressions and behaviour, for example – but we can also just 'sense' other people's feelings. Scientists have actually measured waves emanating from our hearts that 'transmit' our emotional state to other people who are near or touching us[62]. So we are always 'transmitting' how we're feeling. Think about how you can sense someone else – do you know when someone you love has had a bad day without them having to say a word? Have you ever met someone you just don't like, who you don't like being around, even though you can't put your finger on why? If you're with someone who isn't feeling happy but is trying to cover it up, you can tell, can't you? That's because you're tuning in, even though you may not know it.

Your baby tunes in to you in lots of different ways. Let's see what can happen when a baby tunes in to their parent's negative emotions, when food is involved.

Jane and Jack

Jane had read all the research around baby-led weaning and decided it was best for Jack. She decided to wait until he was six months old and, on that day, her husband came home early from work and they sat down with the dinner of home-made lasagne, broccoli and peas that she had lovingly prepared using specially-bought salt-free stock cubes. They weren't sure how to start, so they simply waited anxiously for Jack to eat. Jane was also petrified that Jack was going to gag or choke on the solid food. Had she got the broccoli soft enough? Were there any clumps of beef in the lasagne that might get stuck in his throat?

Jane was so worried that she couldn't relax. Jack started to pick up pieces of food and put them in his mouth, but Jane couldn't bear to let Jack just stick pieces of food in his mouth and explore at his own pace in case he choked, so she ended up interfering with what Jack was doing. She hovered over him and jumped up at any hint of a gag, patting Jack on the back. Jack started to get frustrated and stopped eating. Jane became more flustered and Jack started to cry, which upset her even more. The more she tried to persuade Jack, the more he refused to eat and his crying escalated into screaming, which made Jane feel even worse. She tried everything she could think of, but Jack didn't eat any of the food on offer, and Jane gave up after twenty minutes, feeling like the whole thing had been a huge failure. She started questioning everything: maybe he wasn't ready? Maybe he doesn't like broccoli? Maybe there's something wrong with his mouth? Maybe he's tongue-tied? Maybe it's because she didn't offer a milk feed before offering solids? Maybe he was teething? She felt sure that he wasn't going to get the right nutrition if things continued like this. She had no idea what to make, either, and hated that the food ended up in the bin. All of this anxiety set Jane up to worry at the next mealtime too and, needless to say, a similar course of events took place. Jane became more and more confused, less and less sure of herself and, soon, she began to feel like a failure.

What happened?

Emotionally:
- Jane didn't begin by tuning in to Jack. Instead of looking for the signs that he might be ready for food, Jane chose a date, which may not have actually been related to Jack's readiness to eat
- Jane unwittingly set the tone, as she made the event a big deal and was anxious about it before they started
- Jack was automatically 'tuning in' to Jane, because all babies and young children do that. He sensed her anxiety, and through a mixture of this and her behaviour, he became frustrated and distressed
- Jane wasn't aware of how she was feeling or how it impacted on Jack, so she persevered
- Jack resisted Jane even further as he became more frustrated. He became increasingly upset the more she persevered with trying to feed him
- Jack was unable to 'self-soothe', and so he needed Jane to help him calm down (more on small children's inability to self-soothe on p.82), but

Jane was too preoccupied with the 'task' of getting Jack to eat to take time out and tune in to his needs

- Jane was unknowingly setting both Jack and herself up to associate mealtimes with stress, which made eating the last thing that was likely to happen

Physically:

- When Jack became stressed, his body released adrenaline and his fear-fight-flight response was initiated. We look to our ancestors for why this happens. Imagine you are a caveman encountering a sabre-toothed tiger. Your body will divert all its resources to your brain so you can think clearly and your legs so that you can run away — now is not the time to be hungry or to expend precious energy digesting food
- As part of his stress response, Jack's digestive tract was put into a kind of hibernation. The last thing his body wanted him to do was eat. Think about how you have felt if you have had a shock or been very upset in the past — you probably lost your appetite, or you might even have vomited. For the body, an extremely stressful experience is understood by the body to require a 'fight, flight or freeze' response and it is handled in the same way every time, even if the cause wasn't a 'danger' as such.

Why did this happen?
It's developmental — babies and children need to survive in society too and childhood is partly about working out how the world works. Children are constantly trying to make sense of the world, within the confines of their cognitive capabilities, which are changing as they develop. They don't know what's dangerous or what's safe, so picking up on how you feel teaches them how they should feel about any situation. You're transmitting how you feel to your baby, and they're programmed to tune in to, and be affected by, your emotions.

If mealtimes had continued as described above, Jane might well have ended up with a fussy eater. But adjusting her approach to weaning helped her to manage her feelings and relax, so that mealtimes soon became enjoyable for both of them.

Why food can become a problem

Why is eating such an issue for some families? Well, eating is often tied in with a lot of emotion and it may well be because nourishing your child is a basic, visceral human action. It might even be that you're programmed to become upset if you don't perceive that you're adequately nourishing your child because nature needs you to have a really strong desire to persevere, no matter how difficult things are, in order to keep your child alive. Many parents we have met often wish they weren't so anxious about weaning and feeding their children but they also don't understand why they feel that way. It can help to think that you're designed to care. A LOT. In fact, it would be a concern if you didn't. The fact that you are taking the time to read this book shows how much you care about feeding your child, and that is a positive thing for their development, so try not to beat yourself up about any anxiety you may feel around mealtimes.

Shutterstock

The weight of your baby is often unhelpfully used to judge how 'well' you are feeding your child and how 'well' you are doing as a parent.

The current attitude to parenting in Western society can actually be very unhelpful, and may increase your anxiety around food and feeding. For example, from the moment your baby is born, there is a focus on their weight. After announcing whether it's a boy or a girl, the next question is often: 'How much did they weigh?' Then there's the worry on day five about whether your baby has lost 10% of their birth weight and whether a health professional is going to recommend that you offer 'top-ups' of formula milk. From then on, each visit to the health visitor involves a weigh-in, and discussions with fellow parents often include comments like 'He's on the fiftieth centile', and so on. In the Western world of science, we seem to be obsessed with measuring, defining, labelling and categorizing.

Weight gain as the measure of how well you're doing as a mother

In Western society, it's not surprising that parents become pretty obsessed with weight, which of course is directly related to your own ideas about how 'well' you are feeding your child. This can leave you open to judging yourself, if your child isn't eating 'well'. In this environment, where both perceived and real judgments come from inside and outside, it's easy to see how your baby's eating can become some kind of imagined 'measure' of how you are doing as a parent. Then, just as you might think you've got milk feeding sorted, solid food comes into play. Of course you may find yourself getting anxious!

If you are aware of how you feel about

things, then you can take responsibility for your emotions and handle them in a healthy way so that they don't intrude at mealtimes. Your emotions and how you parent your baby around food can then become more positive, which will make you feel good and in control, instead of stressed.

What about me?

Let's think about you:
- What is your history with your baby since birth?
- Was it a difficult birth?
- Did you need IVF to conceive?
- Has this influenced your emotional space – i.e. are you feeling worried about your baby or about something happening to them?
- Did you have difficulty bonding or did you experience post-natal depression? If so, how has this affected your feelings now?
- Do you feel guilty or worried about getting everything right?
- Are you still feeling low and more likely to feel irritable?
- Are you constantly comparing your parenting or your child with other children?

You may not have realized it, but all of these factors will influence how you approach introducing solid food, which is another huge milestone in your baby's life. If you have been through (or are going through) a difficult time emotionally, then you will be more vulnerable to feeling overwhelmed, low, guilty or anxious when things don't go 'right' as you see them. However, if you can go into the process with self-awareness and compassion for yourself, then you can prevent yourself from becoming overwhelmed or

feeling emotionally out of control without knowing why. It's *really* important to treat yourself with kindness at all times and not to beat yourself up, which can be remarkably difficult!

The benefits of a relaxed approach to weaning and self-feeding

- You bond with your child as you wean
- You become more attuned to yourself and your baby
- The structure you introduce around food is likely to have a positive effect on your parenting (and your relationship with your child) in other areas
- Babies gain independence by exploring food for themselves, at their own pace
- Babies develop healthy eating habits as they learn to self-regulate their feeding
- Children decide the pace and the amount they eat, based on their own individual requirements
- Babies are exposed to many different tastes and textures of food from the start, making them more open to trying them as they grow
- Finger-foods encourage babies to chew, bite and suck, which helps develop the muscles used for speech
- Self-feeding can improve hand-eye co-ordination
- Babies are less likely to become bored and frustrated at mealtimes as they are feeding themselves

Do babies develop good and bad habits?

Working with new mothers, it saddens us to hear mothers say they aren't picking their child up to cuddle them as much as they would like because they don't want them to develop a 'habit' of only falling asleep on them or falling asleep on the breast. As mentioned, being held stimulates a calming response for babies, so it's no wonder that they feel most soothed and safe when they're held and doing the most natural thing in the world – feeding. From an evolutionary perspective, it's also safest for a defenceless infant to sleep in their mother's arms – away from predators.

So it's entirely natural, but whether you're happy with that can only be your decision. Either way, it can be unhelpful to think of things in terms of habits, as that can lead quickly to the idea of babies developing 'bad habits', which adds a negativity to managing your child's behaviour, rooted in judgments of 'good' and 'bad' that isn't necessary and probably won't help you to manage things calmly.

Instead, it's probably more helpful to think of it as familiarity – babies and children can become familiar with a certain food, a certain response or a certain routine very quickly. No familiarity is 'good' or 'bad'; it just is what it is – it's up to you to decide how you want to parent around that familiarity. For example, a child will quickly become 'familiar' with chocolate if you offer it to them but that doesn't mean you want to offer it often. Equally, your child could become 'familiar'

with apples, but you might want to offer this more often.

The idea of 'good' and 'bad' habits is based on your judgments of how things 'should' or 'should not' be. If you can, reframe this a little and remember that, if your baby becomes familiar with something you'd rather they didn't, you can always implement parenting strategies that give them less of that experience, while creating a new type of familiarity that you'd prefer, which undermines the old one. For example, toddlers who graze during the day while playing can quickly learn that meal- and snack-times have structure and that everyone sits at the table. Our brains (but particularly developing brains) have great plasticity, meaning that they can be moulded and shaped by experience – this gets more difficult as we reach adulthood but remains surprisingly possible. Think of people who lose a limb and learn to perform tasks with other limbs, or stroke victims who may lose the power of speech and then regain it over time – that's related to brain plasticity and its capacity to adapt to the demands of the environment.

Your baby is therefore designed to become familiar with the world around them and with what happens in their relationship with you. You can shape and reshape those familiarities according to what feels right for you (for more on this see p.125).

Chapter Four

The Biology of Weaning – Physical and Brain Development

The biomechanics of eating

You are probably so well-practised in eating that you don't need to even stop and think about it; but it hasn't always been like that. You have years of practice behind you, rehearsing the co-ordination of managing food without even thinking about it. There are more than forty muscles involved in controlling the complex process of 'eating'. Sucking, chewing and tongue action prepare the food for swallowing. Then, in the pharynx, the foods are swallowed and guided into the oesophagus. This complicated neuromuscular process requires co-ordination and relies on your baby being anatomically and neurologically ready before tackling it. This is why watching for signs that your own baby is ready for solids is more important than going by a calendar – some babies will be ready sooner and others later. Each child is different.

The British Dietetic Association offer the following recommendations for full-term infants:

The introduction of solid food should commence 'at around six months of age' in line with DH guidance. The DH guidelines acknowledge that babies' individual development varies widely and that some babies may be ready for solid food before, or after, this time. The introduction of solid food should commence no later than six months (26 weeks) of age, but not before four months (17 weeks)[63].

Reflexes

When a baby is born they have several oral reflexes in place for good reason – they are there as survival mechanisms so that nothing other than milk is swallowed, especially because the digestive system isn't yet ready for solid food. During the first year, each of these will be either suppressed or integrated as your child develops. Weaning is about introducing your child to solid foods that will engage these reflexes, enabling lifelong oral motor function, which will help your child establish the foundation skills needed for eating and speaking. It's *not* about focusing on getting food and nutrients into your child from the moment they wean.

The suck reflex

The sucking reflex emerges at around eighteen to twenty weeks of gestation and disappears by around three months after birth, fading out to be replaced by voluntary suckling. You may have stroked your sleepy newborn's cheeks, lips or palms to encourage them to breastfeed, to stimulate the sucking reflex. Anything put inside the mouth will also stimulate the reflex, such as a

Many toys are sensibly labelled as unsuitable for young children. However, the gag reflex is there as a natural mechanism to help prevent your child from swallowing things they shouldn't. But children should never be left unsupervised with items that could be dangerous if put in the mouth.

finger or nipple since the inner wall of the mouth, such as the gums and palate, are stimulants of the sucking reflex.

FROM REFLEX SUCKLING TO VOLUNTARY SUCKING

Newborns are able to suckle at the breast in order to gain breast milk. The wave-like movement from the front of the tongue to the back helps draw breast milk from the nipple and this movement is established *in utero* by the end of the first trimester, which is how babies manage to taste the variety of flavours in your amniotic fluid. At around six to nine months of age the sucking action is said to mature to a more up and down movement under voluntary control. It is now that the ability to swallow without a preceding suck also comes about[64].

I FEEL LIKE A CHEW-TOY – MY BABY SEEMS TO ALWAYS BE SUCKING!

Sucking for reasons other than wanting food has been shown to help with the maturation and development of a baby's gut. Most parents know how important it is for their baby to have sensory stimulation to help with their development. The abundance of baby sensory, baby massage, baby yoga and baby signing classes available today, which many parents are encouraged to fill their day with, demonstrate a growing awareness of this. The action of non-nutritive sucking (sucking but not for food reasons) stimulates the release of digestive hormones and helps with the growth and development of your baby's digestive system. It can also calm a baby's heart rate and relax their stomach.

Sucking in a newborn may also be a way for a baby to relieve pressure from the birth. A baby's skull is designed to pass through the birth canal and many parents comment on their baby's unusual head shape in the hours and days after delivery. This 'natural moulding' of the skull often lessens as your baby suckles, cries and yawns so sucking is all part of this natural unravelling – a little bit like an adult sucking sweets to try and clear the ears when travelling in an aeroplane.

The effects of tactile stimulation (touching and holding your baby) have been shown to stimulate your baby's sympathetic nervous system,[65] which may stimulate gut maturation. So when someone comes along and tells you that your baby will be spoiled because you cuddle and feed them often, you can now tell them … well, we'll leave it to you to decide how to phrase it!

The gag reflex

At around twenty-five weeks of gestation, the gag reflex emerges. When the posterior two-thirds of the tongue or back of the mouth (pharyngeal wall) is touched it will stimulate the gag reflex to eject the object that has stimulated it. This reflex is a protective mechanism in place to prevent objects being swallowed. Over time it reduces, and at around six months of age it is less intense and only around a quarter of the posterior part of the tongue is sensitive, triggering the gag reflex response.

The swallowing muscles

Have you ever thought about how many muscles in co-ordination are needed to achieve the simple act of swallowing? It takes practice to work out how to move food to the back of the throat with the tongue and co-ordinate all those tiny muscles to enable the swallowing action. Your child will therefore undoubtedly make mistakes, but that's how they learn. To swallow food the tongue needs to be able to perform a side-to-side movement, which again takes practice and repetition so there should be no expectation on your baby to actually swallow food when they are initially exposed to solids. The gag reflex comes in there, too. Eventually they will work out how to get the right-sized food to

the correct part of their mouth and it will get easier to co-ordinate all those muscles. That gag reflex will no longer be as necessary and it will start to recede, as you watch your little one become an efficient eater.

Liquids and solids

Swallowing liquids and solids requires different skills – imagine how you feel swallowing a tablet versus liquid medicine. Whilst learning how to eat, your child may treat the food as a liquid and try a 'liquid swallow' technique since this is, of course, what they have been used to. The food may then come into contact with the sensitive back of the tongue, causing coughing and gagging as they attempt to move the food forward to try again. Occasionally a vomit may be triggered to clear the back of the mouth and, although this can be alarming, it is normal and part of learning.

The snorkel

When your baby is taking their milk feeds, you probably notice that they can drink and swallow whilst also breathing at the same time. They don't need to stop every few seconds and have a breather – they can maintain an effective latch for hours. This is down to them having an anatomical snorkel: the larynx. In babies, the larynx sits high in the nasal cavity enabling your baby to swallow and breathe at the same time. This doesn't last for long as, at around three months of age, the larynx drops slightly lower in the throat, so now when drinking milk it can go 'down the wrong way' and into the lungs. At this time many parents discover their baby coughing and spluttering during milk feeds or coming off the breast regularly to have a look around. Because this 'larynx-

Claire Curran

Children use their mouths to explore the different dimensions of toys, objects and food.

Anatomy changes to explore solids

So with the gag reflex receded to the back of the tongue and the mouth shape ready to explore non-liquids you can see how your baby might be ready to experience and explore solid foods. With most of these changes not taking place until around six months, you can probably also see why many children are not ready to explore food until that age. These anatomical and physiological changes don't mean your child is suddenly ready to switch from milk to solids – they mean they might be ready to manoeuvre a substance other than milk around their mouth and tongue and start exploring a new dimension in food.

Goodbye, chubby cheeks!

Your newborn probably has lovely chubby cheeks, which you love to snuggle into and kiss. These chubby cheeks are due to fat pads that have been sitting there inside the cheeks creating a funnel shape in the mouth and directing the milk to the back of the mouth to be swallowed. Over time, these fat pads will lessen to make more space in your baby's mouth for the tongue to start to move side to side – an important movement for your baby to learn in order to manipulate solid foods. The tongue also previously had a groove running along the midline – again, another way of channelling the liquid milk to the back of the mouth to be swallowed. This groove will start to diminish and, as your baby's head grows, the lower jaw (mandible) moves downwards so the mouth is more spacious. It is now geared up and anatomically ready to explore foods other than milk.

drop' makes choking whilst drinking milk much easier, it seems like a design flaw, but it's this movement that now gives your child the capacity for speech. You'll know it's happening as your baby starts to 'coo'. If you have a little boy, then the larynx will drop even further during puberty to give the lower voice we associate with men.

Exploring toys with the mouth

You will spot your little one putting different objects in their mouth to explore them further. This 'generalized mouthing' helps your baby explore a different dimension to objects and this is the groundwork for exploring solid foods. As time goes on the mouth becomes even more important as the neurological and muscular control over the lips, teeth and tongue become more developed. As your child uses their mouth to discover different textures and weights with both toys and food they are building their database of how to manage and manipulate different foods: what feels slimy and sloppy won't need as much chewing, for example.

Your baby's anatomy changes to accommodate solid food. The fat pads in the cheeks reduce and the grooved midline of the tongue will alter in due course.

The Asymmetric Tonic Neck Reflex (ATNR)

The Asymmetric Tonic Neck Reflex (ATNR) Is often called the 'fencing reflex' as the baby adopts a fencing pose when the reflex is activated. When a baby turns their head to look one way, the arm on the side they are facing extends and the arm on the opposite side flexes. It is a key precursor to hand-eye co-ordination and it's no surprise that this reflex disappears at around six months – the time when solid food is recommended to be introduced. If this reflex has not been integrated into the body when you introduce solid food, can you imagine how frustrating it will be for your baby that whenever they hold food in their hand and reach to look at it, their arm moves away from them? Of course, historically, spoon-feeding purées has been the solution to this problem, but if you wait until your baby is developmentally ready, this reflex will be inhibited and they will successfully be able to bring food to their mouth.

Brain development

How solid foods can help brain development

Solid foods come in all shapes and sizes and have a myriad of different textures and layers to them. The experience of peeling a banana is different to peeling a satsuma, particularly if you've never done either before. Each fruit has several different textures involved, which can give your child several different touch sensory experiences that help to encourage their development. When you're weaning initially, you don't have to worry about your child's nutritional intake from solids, so take your focus off trying to get your child to eat. Instead, think that you're simply giving your child different kinds of toys to play with – in this way, you can use foods to encourage your child's psychological and cognitive development.

Children need simple, hands-on experiences for their brains to develop, involving touching, talking, listening, tasting, smelling, playing and looking. Your child's brain is developing rapidly and they are laying down and strengthening new neural pathways every day. Keeping their brains active is key for rapid brain development and food provides a great opportunity to engage their brain in multidimensional new experiences. Frequent new learning experiences and challenges are like nutrients to their brain that encourage growth, and you have on average five opportunities a day to provide these using food. Imagine the difference for your child's brain between experiencing bland, and similarly coloured and textured foods every day, and encountering different tastes, shapes and textures in terms of how each may stimulate their cognitive development. Which do you think will better facilitate their brain's development?

During the first year, the natural focus of a child is on what they can do. This refines their motor skills and increases their independence.

Practice makes perfect

Allowing children to repeatedly practise simple tasks and movements improves the development of cognition, confidence and independence. Repeated practice is required to strengthen cognitive pathways and it increases learning and development speed. Children's brains are 'wired' to encourage the repetition of sounds, patterns and experiences because this helps them to develop strong neural pathways in the brain – these are the highways of learning and they help your child to understand (and therefore feel more secure within) the world around them.

The focus on doing

During your child's first year of life, their natural focus is on what they *can* do. The reason for this is that it helps develop motor skills, which are important to help children get around in the world and become more independent. Using food, you can help them to develop these motor skills by allowing them to 'do' things with safe objects. This will aid them in their journey to make sense of the world and navigate around it.

Stress and sensory overload

If your child becomes stressed when they're eating, it can be for many reasons; for example, perhaps they're frustrated or maybe they sense anxiety, impatience or irritation in others. However, stress can also come from sensory overload, which is one reason to not offer your child too many different foods to choose from. Some top-of-the-range educational toys can be over-stimulating with too much choice, and your child often shows this by rejecting the toy, preferring a more simple toy: the box it came in. During weaning, food presents an opportunity to expose your child to a new experience while keeping it simple. You can also provide several different sensory experiences with the same food – for example, mashed banana is different to half a banana or a whole unpeeled banana, in terms of the sensory experiences each offers your child.

Sensory overload is another reason to keep toys and books away from the table at mealtimes. The sensory exploration should be coming from the foods and cutlery that may be on offer and introducing toys and books can overload a child and reduce their desire to 'play' with the food.

Memory

A baby's memory capacity is developed by repeated everyday experiences, so if they repeatedly play with food with you, it will enhance their capacity to remember and become familiar with different foods. Your brain holds a database of foods and experiences and you are helping your child populate that database with different smells, textures and tastes.

Recognition, categorization and problem-solving

Children naturally use colour, texture and shape to work out what things are by grabbing, mouthing or reaching for them. Through experimentation with different foods and through trial and error, children begin to make sense of the world by recognizing things and putting them into categories. Foods provide a wonderful opportunity to promote recognition in your child and also to help them to begin to link their own actions and consequences. For example, if you do things with food together (e.g. make a game out of peeling bananas with your child), it will enhance their ability to recognize that, when they pull banana skin, it comes off. This will also promote problem-solving skills – how does the peel come off the banana?

Shutterstock

Recognition, categorization and problem-solving skills are relevant for whatever your baby encounters, be it toys or food. Their function is to help your child to start making sense of the world around them, understanding what things are and how they 'fit' into the world.

Do the foods eaten in pregnancy affect a baby's taste preferences?

Before your baby was born, they were swallowing. By the end of the first trimester, your baby had developed the swallowing reflex and swallowed plenty of amniotic fluid during their nine months *in utero*. The amniotic fluid has been shown to reflect the flavours of foods the mother has eaten, thereby impacting on the child's behaviour when they start weaning. In one study, children who were exposed to carrot flavours in either amniotic fluid or breast milk behaved differently when encountering the carrot flavour again when weaning[66], reflecting that they had experienced the flavour before and it was already familiar to them.

There isn't yet enough quality evidence out there to confirm whether or not the tastes

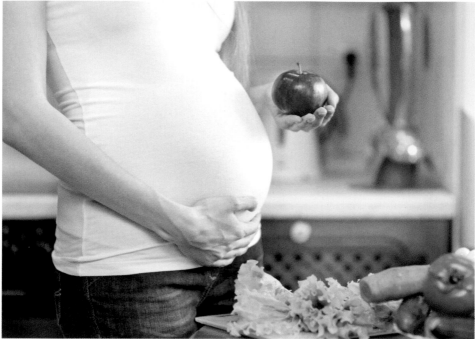

Familiarity to taste begins in pregnancy with the amniotic fluid reflecting the flavours of foods the mother has eaten.

a baby experiences *in utero* is a good predictor of food preferences later. However, one trial encouraged a mother to consume garlic and another aniseed during pregnancy. The newborn babies, when exposed to aniseed and garlic smells, would turn their heads towards the potentially 'familiar' smell, which was taken as a sign of recognition[67][68]. In another study, mothers who drank carrot juice throughout their pregnancy had babies who were less likely to make negative faces when fed carrot-flavoured cereal when compared to mothers who drank only water[69].

Does breastfeeding help prevent a fussy eater?

Breastfeeding may prepare your child for flavour changes and new experiences when they start to eat solid foods. Studies suggest that being exposed to a variety of flavours[70] at the early stages of development makes children more accepting of different flavours. The foods a breastfeeding mum eats will alter the taste of the breast milk for a couple of hours on average, livening up your child's meal. A few points on this:

- The taste of any food you have eaten will have disappeared from the breast milk within eight hours
- The taste from most foods you have eaten will disappear after approximately two hours
- Banana will remain in the breast milk for approximately one hour after eating[71]
- Menthol flavour can remain in breast milk for up to eight hours[72]

How can I expose my child to more flavours if I'm offering infant formula?

With infant formula, your child will be exposed to the same taste each time they have their milk. This makes it difficult to expose your child to new tastes. However, each formula recipe is different, so if you think it's appropriate, it might be worth changing the brand you use.

Is it okay to do that? Well, in most cases, it's fine to change formulas provided that you stick with the same type. For example, the ingredients in all cows' milk-based, iron-fortified infant formulas are essentially the same but the taste may vary slightly. If your baby is on a formula such as a soy-based, iron-fortified formula, switching to a different brand of soy-based, iron-fortified formula should have a similar effect. However, if your GP or paediatrician has prescribed a specific formula, such as hydrolysate formula, or if you're considering switching types, then discuss with your health visitor, GP or paediatrician first.

There is some evidence to show that the type of formula milk supplied affects the later acceptance of similar drinks, although it has little effect on the acceptance of foods[73]. For example, serving a soy-based formula may provide greater acceptance for soy-based beverages.

Shutterstock

Infant formula exposes your child to the same taste at every feed.

Cathy and Matthew

Over ten years ago I stopped eating chocolate for Lent. Not a single chocolate has passed my lips since the moment I gave it up and over time I have grown to detest the smell of chocolate, even that of cocoa butter makes me feel nauseous. My husband, however, loves chocolate so our house is full of the stuff. Interestingly, my son also hates chocolate. He will accidentally put a piece in his mouth on a cake or something and spit it out in disgust. Why is this? It could be wanting to be like Mummy or it could be due to the limited exposure because he would never have experienced this flavour *in utero* or in his early years, never having had a bite of Mummy's brownie. It will be interesting to see if this aversion continues beyond childhood – he is now four years old and still resisting.

Chapter Five

Social and Behavioural Development

You can promote good eating habits, while bonding with your baby and nurturing their psychological development and motor skills. When you understand the social and behavioural principles behind your baby's development and the defining role that your relationship plays in the process, you can maximize your child's development at every mealtime. As time goes on, you will probably realize that you have three opportunities a day to offer meals to your child and two opportunities for snacks – these are five potential learning opportunities every single day. You can teach your baby to develop a healthy relationship with food from the moment you start weaning, which will stand them in good stead for the rest of their life.

Eating is not just about hunger; it is a complex psychological experience.

The psychology of eating

It is generally accepted in contemporary research literature that eating is not just about hunger, but is an extremely complex psychological experience. In fact, one's relationship with food can be intertwined with negative self-image in a very powerful and entrenched way. A crude example of this is to think of someone with an eating disorder – food and eating have taken on an extremely complex and unhelpful psychological role for that person. However, the relationship with food is a complex one for all of us and eating is a complex experience. Our relationship with food is, of course, established as we grow up and can be based as much on what we see others around us doing as on what we experience ourselves – that's all part of the child's need to copy adults and to fit in. For example, if you routinely cope with emotions by eating, you'll unwittingly be teaching your child to do the same – that might just be the best reason you could have to sort out your own food issues!

As well as the habits we learn from others, the food and eating experiences we have as children unsurprisingly play a huge part in how our relationship with food develops. An easy example of this is to think back to your own childhood – was there anything you loved and weren't allowed a lot of? Do you eat a little bit too much of it now? Were any foods forbidden? Do you still get a kick out of eating those foods now? Were any foods particularly associated with a special person (e.g. your grandma's Sunday roast or chicken soup)? Do you particularly love them now or do they cheer you up? Are any foods associated with a particularly horrible experience (e.g. being forced to eat them at school)? Do you still hate them now? Have a think for a moment about your relationship with those foods – you'll understand that it's almost certainly been shaped by those early experiences.

The context we are in affects us a lot when it comes to food, even when we are adults – the time of day, who is with us and where we are all affect how we react to particular foods. For example, is there anything you love that you couldn't face at breakfast? Some people can't face eating at all at breakfast. This concept may partly explain why eating out at a restaurant with a toddler can feel like such uncharted territory. The restaurant pasta and tomato is a 'new food' to your toddler, even if you make them pasta and tomato at home, because the context is different. There may be different people eating with you at your table (not to mention all the other people in the restaurant!), you may be eating at a different time of day than your child is used to and you'll be in a completely different environment, where nothing is familiar (even the cutlery and crockery and their high chair are different). There are also lots of distractions.

The psychological aspect of eating plays a big part when it comes to obesity, which is why it is vital to help your baby to have positive experiences – weaning is a golden opportunity to start things off in the right way. Eating habits are extremely powerful, psychologically speaking. Eating habits have been found to overwhelm preferences and intentions when it comes to guiding what we eat on any given day. That's one of the reasons why it's hard to change eating habits when we're used to eating in a particular way. In Western society, we also eat mindlessly, and research has shown that over-eating happens much more often when people are distracted while eating[74] and that food is enjoyed less. At Yummy Discoveries, we always encourage eating together as a family and not having the TV on or any electronic gadgets at the table while you eat – these encourage children to be distracted from eating and to focus on a game/programme instead of bonding/listening to their physiological cues regarding hunger/satiety. Even when you're weaning, we encourage you to eat with your baby, or to have a cup of tea even if you don't feel like eating. It's about creating a positive social experience from the very beginning.

Eating is very complex and food is never *just* food. That's why how you wean is so important – it's the starting point from which you can give your baby the best chance of developing a healthy relationship with food and healthy eating habits for life. Of course, weaning involves exposing your baby to hundreds (if not thousands) of new food experiences. Experiencing a new food isn't a simple process for a baby, so understanding what that's like for them can help with the process. As adults, we haven't done it for a long, long time.

What's it like to encounter a new food?

When's the last time you encountered a food that was actually new to you? By this we mean a food that you knew *absolutely nothing* about before you tried it? We venture that that hasn't happened since childhood. You might be thinking: 'Ah, well that's where you're wrong – I encountered something new

As an adult, you rarely encounter a new food that you know nothing about – you can often relate at least one feature to some other food you have experienced before. Children often have nothing else to relate it to, making them more naturally suspicious of it.

the last time I was on an exotic holiday.' Well, yes, you might have encountered a new food, but it's probable you knew *something* about it; in fact, you used your knowledge of other foods to help you decide whether to try that food.

In short, the thousands of sensory memories your brain has created in its enormous file entitled 'food' helped you make the decision about whether to try something new. You can see this in the fact that, as adults, any time that someone suggests that you try a new food, a first question is often: 'What's it like?'

If the person can tell you: 'It looks a bit like a strawberry, but squishier and with more juice, and it doesn't have as many seeds' then you already know a *lot* of information about that food before you even come into direct contact with it. Just think – you have approximate information (and certain expectations) about its colour, its shape, what the skin looks like, what the texture is like, how wet or dry it is, what the inside and the outside are like, and whether it has bits, seeds, pips or a stone. In an instant, your brain uses all of the information it has already stored about the world of food to guide you into making a decision about whether to try that food or not. If you love strawberries, you might give it a go; if you hate them, you might be less keen.

Can you imagine what it might be like to know *nothing* about that food, including whether it's poisonous or not, and having to decide whether to try it? Well, that's the position your child is in, every time they encounter a new food or a familiar food *in a different form* than they know. Let's take a moment to imagine what it might be like for them.

If you have seen the television programme *I'm A Celebrity … Get Me Out Of Here!* you will be familiar with the concept of celebrities living in the jungle and having to, as part of a 'bushtucker trial', eat foods that are unusual to them. These foods resemble no other food they are used to eating. They are immediately fearful of the food, despite knowing it can't be dangerous as the TV executives would never allow them to come to harm. This is quite similar to what your child goes through when they encounter a new food.

Once the celebrity has seen their opponent take a bite and confirm it is okay, somehow they are more reassured and more likely to feel able to eat it also. It is so important that you show your child the food you are serving is safe for them to eat.

Meet your child where they are

Imagine you've been given a completely alien substance, some kind of strange-looking stuff with an unfamiliar texture, smell and colour. You have no way of knowing for sure whether it's safe to eat or not. If it's not safe, it could poison you, so you feel naturally suspicious of it. You don't have your adult powers of reasoning or your knowledge about food to fall back on – you really know absolutely nothing about it. Someone you know is telling you it's nice and you should try it, but you have none of your own experiences to fall back on to help you decide.

What would you do? Well, if you knew and trusted the person who was suggesting you try the food, that might help you to make the first decision and pick it up, smell it, feel it or even put it in your mouth once – as an aside, if they were pressuring you to try it, how much less appealing would it seem? In any case, you'd be likely to take some time smelling, touching and examining it before you tasted it. If you found, when you tasted it, that the food had a completely and utterly unknown texture or taste, you'd be very unlikely to say: 'Ooh, yummy!' and keep eating it straight away. You'd be much more likely to make a bit of a face, put it down and

perhaps try it again later, once you'd worked out what you thought of it. To work out what you think, you'd probably become very slow and cautious about how much of it you ate, the speed at which you eat it, and you might spend more time smelling or touching it, for example.

Now imagine if the person encouraging you to eat that unusual-looking food was someone renowned for playing practical jokes on people. You might be less keen since the trust between you isn't there – your relationship is different to that of a parent and child. Trust between a parent and their child is essential to creating a secure environment which gives the child the reassurance that the food is safe to eat. How you are in your relationship outside of food impacts your relationship with food so if your child feels they cannot depend on you they are less likely to feel the security they need to explore

Shutterstock

Trust is one of the most important things in your relationship with your child. They rely on that trust when trying a new food – they trust that you won't allow them to eat something poisonous.

a new food. Remember, it all comes back to a basic human need for survival. Eating an unfamiliar food could mean it is poisonous, resulting in death – this may not apply so much to supermarket-bought goods on the table today but evolution hasn't quite adapted that far ahead yet.

So why is it that we expect our children to pick up an unknown food and put it in their mouths first time? Why do we expect them to try and then (often) finish something new that we *tell* them is nice, the first – or even the fifth – time? Why should we expect them to eat it when we aren't?

Going back to the previous example of a new food that wasn't completely unfamiliar but was like strawberries, it would probably not take you that much time to decide whether to try it or not. That's because you would have so much information about it based on what you already knew. Your expectations could be set and they would be likely to be met … if the other person was telling the truth, of course! In fact, that's also an interesting idea – what would your reaction be if the food was described as being 'like strawberries', which you loved, with all the detail written above, but when you tried it, it was like beef? Would you take another bite or would you be likely to put it down? You would have had somewhat of a negative emotional experience (more if you dislike beef) because your expectations (and your wish for something strawberry-like at the moment you tasted it) would have been completely dashed. A negative association would probably have been created with that food on some level – what would happen next time you were offered it? Might you be less likely to try it or quicker to dismiss it?

Even the idea of a food being 'like' another food is quite hit and miss. There may be a few foods that are very much like other foods, but if you were trying to describe a banana to someone who had never encountered one, it wouldn't actually be that easy. Of course, you could say that it's yellow and sweet and you could describe its curved shape, but how could you describe its texture in any way that describes what it's like to eat it? What is its flavour like? Or its smell? It's actually not like any other food, is it? This is worth thinking about because it's very easy to say to your child: 'Try this – it's like x, y or z' when, actually, your description won't do much to prepare them for the experience of eating it. They'll still have to encounter that food as if it were *completely* unknown, because it will be, to them.

Mindful eating – put yourself in your child's shoes

As adults, it can be very difficult to imagine what it might be like if you'd *never* encountered a particular food before, because we *do* have that huge catalogue of sensory and intellectual information about food mentioned previously. Our brains don't consciously notice everything about a food we already know well, because we use categorization as a tool to navigate the world. Our brains naturally assign categories to things to help us organize the world around us, so that we can keep our attention on necessary tasks, instead of on the details of the things we know backwards already. This means that we often do not pay close attention to the details of everyday items and experiences and food is no exception to this.

In our workshops, we do an interactive exercise called mindful eating that helps parents to realize how many sensory experiences their child has to process every time they encounter a new food. You can do it with a friend, where one of you is the narrator and

Most adults have forgotten what it is like to encounter a truly new food. Mindful eating will help you to understand how many sensory experiences your child has to process every time they are faced with a new food. Try it!

one of you is doing the exercise; then you can swap roles. You can use any piece of food for this exercise, but we like to use a strawberry. It only takes a few minutes and the parents at our workshops have found it to be really useful.

Start with one of you holding the strawberry with your eyes closed. The person holding the strawberry follows the directions of the narrator. If you don't have a friend there with you, you can take a quick look at what you need to do and try it on your own. The key to this exercise is to do it at a very slow pace – take your time with each instruction. The narrator, speaking slowly, says:

1. Open your eyes and look at the strawberry. *Really* look at it, as if you'd never seen it before. What colour is it? Is it opaque or translucent? Vivid or muted? What texture does the skin have? Is it smooth or rough? What do the different parts look like (e.g. seeds and leaves)?

2. Close your eyes again and feel the strawberry – pay attention to what it feels like in your fingers. Is it wet, smooth, squishy? Really pay attention

3. Bring the strawberry to your nose and breathe in slowly, smelling it. What does it smell like? Is it a sweet aroma? Is it strong or faint? Does anything else happen when you smell the strawberry; for example, does your mouth water? What does it make you think of? Does it make you want to smile or pull another face?

4. Keep your eyes closed. Touch the strawberry onto your lips but don't take a bite. What does it feel like against your lips? Is it room temperature or cold out of the fridge? Is the skin wet? What texture does it have? Is it smooth or bumpy? Do the various parts feel different?

5. Keep your eyes closed. Now take a bite of the strawberry and hold it in your mouth for a moment. Then begin to chew extremely slowly, noticing every aspect of what that experience is like before you swallow it. Is it juicy? How different is that juiciness, compared to what the strawberry was like on the outside, before you bit into it? How cold is it? How sweet or sour is it? What do the seeds feel like in your mouth, compared to the flesh? Again, what memories does it evoke? How does it make you feel? Do you experience pleasure eating it? Are there any associations that pop into your mind as you're eating it (e.g. jam, cream, pavlova)?

Shutterstock

Shutterstock

Shutterstock

Your child has an enormous amount of sensory information to process when they encounter a new food. Give them permission to explore it in their own way and at their own pace.

6. Now open your eyes and look at the strawberry you have just taken a bite from. How different does the inside of the strawberry look to the outside?

Now swap roles.

If you've done this exercise slowly enough, you'll have focused on the strawberry using each sense and really paid attention to it from several different perspectives. Your baby has to deal with all of this sensory information coming at them at once, every time they encounter a new food. Your baby's brain has

to process a *lot* of sensory information every time a food is presented to them. They need to be allowed to explore each food at their own pace.

Social confidence

You are your child's main social focus at the moment, so weaning them in a way that focuses on your relationship means that you're meeting their needs at every mealtime. It also enhances opportunities for 'face time' and bonding, which helps your child to feel more secure. This is required for the development of independence and confidence, which they will need as they grow up and begin to interact more and more with other children. Weaning is therefore a valuable time for you to help your child's cognitive and social development.

+ + + **Tip** + + +

Allow your child to explore food at their own pace.

+ + + + + + + + +

Joint attention

Joint attention is very important for your child to learn so that they develop social skills. Joint attention means that you and your child are focusing together on something, another reason to eat with your child and not give them food on their highchair tray while you tackle the laundry. Mealtimes are a good example of when you and your child can engage in a focused activity together; the more you eat together and engage with the food with them, the more your child will learn how to interact with other people.

Your baby will want to copy you – use it!

Your baby wants to copy you. If you smile, they smile. If you poke your tongue out, they are likely to do the same. Your baby wants to copy you because you're modelling – showing them what's safe in the world by your own behaviour. Another reason your baby wants to copy you is that mimicking is likely to increase bonding and will therefore help your baby 'fit in' to society (i.e. your family unit) to survive.

You may be surprised at how much they want what is on your plate! When you're introducing solids, you can use this knowledge to get your baby to engage with new foods, and it's always a good idea to go with their natural interest. After all, food should be fun, so they need to be interested in it. For example, you might have decided to serve your baby purées, but then you notice that they show interest in something you're eating. If this happens, go with it (provided it's safe for them to eat – see p.111 for more on this).

Caroline and Ruby

When it came to weaning Ruby, I puréed my carrot and got my baby rice ready. Excitedly, I brought the spoon to her mouth and she spat the baby rice out. I tasted it, thinking it might be too hot, and realized that it tasted bland. I got the carrot ready and tried again, but she slammed her mouth shut. I figured she wasn't ready to wean, so got her out of the highchair. An hour later, I peeled a banana for myself while balancing Ruby on my hip and, before I could stop her, she leaned over and took a big bite with her gums. I watched in amazement as she chomped it up and went in for another bite. I sat her down in her highchair, mashed up some banana and gave her some big pieces too, to see what happened. We must have spent an hour squidging the banana in our hands and across our faces, eating, laughing and exploring it together.

What a positive first experience of food! It was about fun and discovery at Ruby's own pace, rather than about tasteless baby rice controlled by a parent. Caroline followed her baby's instincts by following her lead and allowing her to explore the food but within a framework she felt comfortable with. This has set them both off on a path for happy mealtimes.

'When I grow up, I want to be like Mummy/Daddy'

Research has shown that in the period from birth to two years, your child will adopt the eating habits of the family[75]. This period is a crucial time for establishing eating habits for life. Dietary habits established in childhood are shown to persist through to adulthood[76]. You have the power to shape the development of your child's eating behaviours and this isn't just down to the nutrition but how the foods are introduced, as well as eating styles, behaviours at the table, management around food and how food is seen in your family.

If you have struggled with your weight or if you are an emotional eater, you may be worrying that your own child will grow up with similar issues, and you're right that this is the time when you really need to carefully consider your own behaviour and think about trying to change it (with help, if need be). Your child will pick up whatever you model, so if they see you getting upset and reaching for a chocolate bar, for example, they will want to do the same and you'll probably have even more trouble when you won't allow them to do something that they see you doing all the time.

This means that it's not fair to sit at the table with them and eat something they can't have, neither is it fair to refuse vegetables, for example, because you don't like them, yet expect your child to eat them – it's all about modelling the behaviour you would like to reinforce. We have consulted with many families where one parent is a fussy eater and refuses to eat broccoli in front of their child. Not surprisingly, the child is copying that behaviour. If you or your husband/wife are a fussy eater, you really need to try to model different behaviour if you want your child to eat a wide range of foods.

Janine, David and Miles

Janine came to see us, unsure about how to get Miles, aged two, to eat vegetables. Janine worked long hours and sometimes David fed Miles, while other times she cooked for Miles or for the whole family. When we had an in-depth conversation with her, it emerged that David, her husband, was a fussy eater and, despite being a good cook, he didn't eat what he prepared when Janine wasn't around, preferring to eat ready-made food while serving Miles up something 'healthy'. It also emerged that Janine often ate something different to Miles when she cooked for him, preferring a sandwich at that time of day to a 'proper meal'. The other issues that came out of the consultation were that David didn't like vegetables and wouldn't have them at Sunday dinner and that the family didn't eat together that often due to both parents' work patterns. Every time Janine offered vegetables to David, he would say: 'No thanks, I don't like X, Y or Z'. Janine said that Miles used to be a good eater, but that over the past year his palette had become narrower and narrower and he was now refusing to eat any green vegetables, saying 'I don't like X, Y or Z' every time he was offered a vegetable. Janine, not knowing what to do for the best, either took it away or tried to persuade him to eat it by bribing him with dessert.

We helped Janine and David to create a framework around eating that took advantage of Miles' natural desire to copy them. David stopped saying: 'I don't like ...' and instead took a small amount of vegetables, eating them at family mealtimes. He didn't make a big deal of it or say 'Ooh, how yummy', he just ate the vegetables.

Why is a false proclamation of deliciousness not a good idea? Because this could easily slip into trying to persuade Miles to eat vegetables or trying to label them as particularly 'yummy' or 'healthy' — it's an easy slip from there into insisting: 'eat your broccoli, it's good for you'. Plus Miles had been watching David refuse them until this point so it just wouldn't make sense, and children aren't stupid. There's nothing wrong with expressing that you love something if you genuinely do and it's not part of a strategy to persuade your child to eat it, but steer clear of behaving in a false way.

Janine and David also stopped eating different things to Miles. They made a point of eating with Miles whenever one parent was at home, and eating together as a family as much as they could. Whenever Miles said: 'I don't like ...' they just responded with, 'That's okay, you just haven't tried it enough times yet' but they didn't take the food away and got on with eating their own food without making a big deal of it. One day, Janine noticed that Miles picked up a piece of broccoli after watching David eat it and, over time, he began to eat some vegetables again. Mealtimes became much less stressful for everyone!

Miles' eating improved because he was given a food-related framework that he could understand. Mummy and Daddy both ate what he ate, which allowed him to copy them and to feel less suspicious of the food that was put in front of him. Also, he was not seeing food being rejected by his parents and thus learning to do the same. These changes took time and repetition and it wasn't until almost twelve weeks later that these small adjustments began to show in Miles' eating behaviours.

It is common for older children to regress and demand to be spoon-fed when they see a younger sibling being spoon-fed.

Avoiding eating issues with siblings

If a new baby comes along who is being spoon-fed, it is common for the older child to demand to be spoon-fed too, to get attention. By allowing everyone at the table to self-feed, everyone feels included, with nobody getting special attention. Occasionally, self-feeding children become fussier eaters when a new baby enters their home in an effort to get attention, but if you're used to doing things via A-B choices (see p.182) and you react by allowing your child to make and live with the consequences of their own decisions, you'll be able to handle it. At least if you take spoon-feeding out of the equation, you will be removing the most common way that children regress where food is concerned.

It is normal for older children to feel insecure when a younger one comes along and to regress or become increasingly needy. By recognizing this as a normal behaviour, you

Shutterstock

Children use their mouths to further explore and understand the objects they encounter. Whether the object is a rattle, your car keys or a chunk of cucumber, it is treated the same by your child.

can expect it and prepare for it, enabling you to respond in a way that makes your older child feel more secure, while continuing to parent them through situations where they may have difficulty managing their emotions.

Food and toys are the same

Babies use their mouths to explore the world, including the objects they encounter – that's why your baby grabs everything and puts it in their mouth. You want them to be interested in the world, so you probably spend your time finding toys with new colours, shapes and textures for them to explore. Babies aren't born being able to keep their 'attention' on something – this skill develops as your baby begins to engage with the world, and is important for cognitive development.

Plain toys, plain baby rice

Have you ever wondered why there aren't many beige baby toys for sale in shops? Well, they probably wouldn't look particularly interesting to you as the buyer, for a start – would you buy something featureless, shapeless or colourless for your baby to play with? Toys are designed to be noticeable, both in their colours and textures. They are designed to attract your baby's gaze and interest – gaze

Shutterstock

A pile of bright, colourful food is not too dissimilar to a pile of bright colourful toys.

It's interesting to note how baby rice manufacturers package their products with bright and eye-catching colours, despite the bland colour and texture of the product inside. They know what parents want and what engages children – but do their products actually provide it?

development needs to happen before attention can develop.

Beige things don't grab a baby's attention or trigger their curiosity to reach out and explore, so why do we think that beige food would be interesting to them? Many parents are encouraged by well-meaning friends and family (and the baby rice manufacturers) to serve up baby rice as a first meal, and don't give a second thought to what it looks like, or whether it's important for children to be interested in the foods offered. If you've ever tasted baby rice, you'll know it not only looks boring, but it smells and tastes completely bland, too.

So the question is, if you wouldn't choose to eat it, why should your baby? Perhaps the assumption has historically been that milk is bland too, but we now know that it isn't, and that the taste of breast milk, just like amniotic fluid, varies according to what the mother

has eaten (see p.57). A breastfed baby is therefore being introduced to a wonderful range of flavours before they are even born and this continues as long as mothers continue breastfeeding.

Baby rice bears very little resemblance to the taste experiences a baby will have had so far through breastfeeding. If your baby has been formula fed, you may also have varied the brand of milk, thereby giving them a few different taste experiences (see p.59 for more on this). Introducing baby rice does not build on these taste experiences. In fact, by introducing baby rice as a first food to formula-fed babies, you are taking a baby who has only experienced one flavour, whom you now wish to introduce to a world of food with hundreds or even thousands of flavours in it, and giving them a bland and tasteless introduction to it. Your child will already be less used to experiencing different flavours than a breastfed baby, so you logically need to encourage the experience of a range of flavours, rather than giving them one bland taste via baby rice.

The fact that breastfeeding exposes your child to hundreds, if not thousands, of flavours before they even pop a cucumber stick into their mouth could be the reason that one study showed that babies who are breastfed for at least six months are less likely to be fussy or picky eaters in toddlerhood[77].

> **Key point:**
>
> **Formula-fed babies will have received fewer taste experiences than breastfed babies. Exposing these children to flavoursome first foods is therefore even more important.**

Everything your baby comes across should be interesting for them to engage with, and your little one can't tell the difference between food and toys, as everything they grab is worth exploring. The only thing that counts here is how they see the world so, effectively, this means that there *is* no difference between food and toys. In fact, food has the potential to be even more interesting than toys, because it has even more dimensions – it has taste, smell and temperature, too! Your baby is concerned with exploring everything they come across, so make the food you offer appeal to their natural curiosity – consider shape, size, colour and texture. If you want your child to reach down and put something in their mouth then apply the same principles and attention to detail when choosing food to serve as you would when choosing toys.

Playing with food

When you introduce a toy to your baby, you probably initially interact with it in front of them. You may point out the features, such as showing them a button to push or a rattle to shake, all the time labelling the different parts of the toy and telling them what you're doing. They are likely to copy you then and you can both take great pleasure in the interaction. When you introduce food to your baby, behave like you would when introducing a new toy.

> ### Key point:
>
> **Consider colour, texture and dimension when choosing food. Variety is important.**

Firstly, show them what to do with it by putting it in your mouth, peeling it, licking it – whatever you would expect them to do. You might, for example, take a cucumber stick and say: 'Is this red like a strawberry? No. Is it green like a leaf? Yes'. It is helpful to give right and wrong answers so that it's fun for your child when they can take part, plus for many children 'Yes' and 'No' or shaking or nodding their heads are early ways of communicating so they can get involved, even with a limited vocabulary. It makes interacting with food a game, and they can see you getting things wrong too, which, as they get older, gives them the confidence to try and answer a question without being scared of making a mistake.

The tasks of being able to form and understand words use two different brain functions, so just because your baby can't verbalize doesn't mean they aren't processing the words you are saying. You may have encountered people who can translate a foreign language but not speak it – these are two different skills that each need to be learned and practised. Recent studies have shown that the ear and auditory part of the brain are formed even before your baby is born, at around twenty-three weeks of gestation, when they can even discriminate between different syllables[78]. There is evidence to suggest that babies become 'primed' for whichever language the mother speaks while they're in the womb by becoming familiar with her tone and intonation when speaking, so they're born predisposed to learning and understanding their mother's language[79 80]. So just because your baby isn't talking, it doesn't mean your words and one-sided conversations with them have no meaning for them.

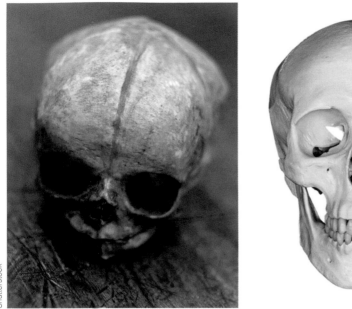

The proportions of a baby's skull are quite different to those of an adult's.

Many taste preferences form before a child learns to walk

This baby skull shows how a baby's eyes are initially much bigger than an adult's in relation to the size of the rest of their head. This isn't a coincidence – there is a developmental and psychological purpose behind it. The eyes are initially the main tool that your baby uses to explore the world. Their large diameter enables your baby to absorb as much information as possible about their surroundings.

Your baby's eyes are important for bonding. Bonding ensures your child's survival through their relationship with you – you will take care of them. Notice how your baby's eyes are also proportionally bigger than the rest of their facial features to make them seem more attractive to adults, to encourage us to naturally want to bond. Have you ever noticed how, in animations,

characters are usually drawn with bigger eyes so that they seem cuter and more vulnerable? Or how we use expressions like: making puppy eyes, or Bambi eyes, to mean gazing at someone in a way that says vulnerability or innocence? With your child's big baby eyes, you are more likely to be drawn into gazing at them and developing a deep bond with them, and to want to nurture them. Even as adults, we experience intimacy by looking into someone's eyes, so your baby's eyes represent their main tool for creating intimacy quickly – this is vital for survival.

Babies are programmed to recognize and respond to faces from birth, so that they can play their part in bonding by responding to you. Research showed us long ago that babies of just nine minutes old pay more attention to faces than other shapes[81] and that they engage with faces in a unique way. It's also been shown that babies of just two days old can distinguish their mother's face

A mother and baby gazing at each other strengthens the bond between them.

from a stranger's face[82]. By engaging with you and gazing into your eyes at the same time that you're drawn to doing the same with them, a reciprocal bond will form between you.

Your baby's eyes are vital for engaging with other objects in the world too. As we have discussed, babies are attracted to different colours and visual effects, all of which are designed to help particular areas of cognition develop at different times. This means that food needs to be visually exciting and interesting before your baby will want to engage with it. The things that *do* catch your baby's attention are going to become familiar more quickly because your baby wants to explore them and therefore spends more time in contact with them. To humans, familiarity often means safety, so your baby is programmed to develop preferences for familiar objects – if that familiar food is a sprig of broccoli rather than a purée pouch then that can only be a good thing.

As your baby grows, their nervous system develops and their mouth becomes another tool to help them to experience more dimensions of the world (now you know what the attraction is when your baby suddenly pops your car keys into their mouth!). The eyes continue to be important but the mouth has become more important as a sensory tool to allow your baby to interact with the world. Finally, hand control develops, giving your baby yet another tool to understand and interpret the different dimensions of the vast array of objects that they encounter. Your baby can now use their eyes, mouth and hands to explore and learn about any new object. However, before they will start exploring, an object needs to spark their interest and baby rice just isn't going to cut it on that front.

Textures and tastes that become familiar via your baby's mouth will contribute to taste preferences, which develop before your baby can walk[83]. However, it is worth noting that it is normal for your baby to accept certain

This baby may change his mind about whether he loves vanilla ice cream!

foods more willingly (e.g. sweet flavours) and to reject sour and bitter flavours initially. This is arguably another developmental survival mechanism, going back to caveman days. Most berries that are fresh and nutritious will taste sweet, yet old fruit starts to sour. Many berries that are poisonous to humans taste bitter, so these instinctive preferences make it less likely that a 'caveman' toddler would pick up and eat old fruit or poisonous berries. It's nature's way of keeping us safe and ensuring that the human species survives by filling up on nutritious foods. You can't change it – it's part of how all humans develop, but being aware of it ensures that you don't let it lead you into feeding your baby according to their instinctive taste preferences. Instead, you can aim to broaden their horizons by introducing new foods patiently.

It's worth mentioning here that taste preferences are *not* the same as true likes and dislikes. Taste preferences mean a general willingness to accept flavours such as preferring something sweet over something savoury. Likes and dislikes refer to particular foods, such as liking carrots or disliking broccoli.

Likes and dislikes are unstable until five years old

While taste preferences may be more stable, likes and dislikes are generally unstable in children aged under five years. Research backs this up – one study asked two groups of children (under- and over-fives) to choose

> **Key point:**
>
> **It takes time for your baby to develop true likes and dislikes. Bear this in mind when offering foods you 'think' they may not like.**

their favourite flavours of ice cream over several different days. Those under five years old chose different flavours every time they were asked, whereas those over five kept choosing the same flavour. So if your 3-year-old says that strawberry ice cream is their favourite and you buy a tub of it, don't be surprised if tomorrow they prefer chocolate. They aren't being contrary or difficult; their brain is still developing and they haven't yet stabilized their true likes and dislikes[84].

The fascination with car keys

Many babies like to put car keys in their mouth, much to their parents' despair. A trip to the toy shop to buy some plastic keys often follows but they don't seem to hold your child's interest in the same way. What is going on? Well, there aren't many toys in your baby's toy-box that are like car keys. Metallic, pointy, jagged, cold, heavy – all words that might describe keys, and all words that are not associated with children's toys. It is because they are so different that your child is attracted to them and they are popped into the mouth to explore using a child's primary exploratory tool. Food is viewed in a similar way and your child will initially be more likely to explore foods that are unusual – but this opportunity and urge won't last forever. You have a small window (usually up until the cruising/walking period) to introduce as

Shutterstock

Your baby's mouth is an important exploratory tool.

many weird and wacky things as you can before neophobia kicks in (see p.117) and your little one rapidly becomes fearful of new foods rather than curious of them.

Now you know this, don't be surprised if, when you visit Great Aunt Judith, your little one wants to touch all the knick-knacks and valuables. They are simply seeing something unfamiliar and wanting to explore it – they don't understand that it isn't a toy and is not to be touched. Your baby learns through seeing, touching and tasting and every object in the world initially falls into the same category as 'toy'. This urge to explore is part of a child's natural development and saying 'no' to their curiosity is suppressing this urge. Encourage your child to explore the world and objects around them and move those valuables out of the way.

> ### Key point:
>
> **Key point: Keep offering your child new foods to try in the early days of weaning. This is a golden opportunity before neophobia presents itself!**

Shutterstock

The small bumps on the surface of the tongue are your child's taste buds.

I don't like carrots, nor does my baby. Coincidence?

Research has shown that there is a genetic element to the flavours humans prefer. The small bumps covering the tongue are the taste buds. The chemicals from foods stimulate them and send the signal off to the taste centre in the brain to be processed. The density of these taste buds on the tongue is down to genetics, so individual babies will each experience the same taste differently. However, before you go off blaming genetics for your bad eating habits, consider that studies of twins suggest early exposures and social interactions outweigh genetics when it comes to food preferences. In fact, we can even say that 85% of our eating patterns are down to non-genetic factors, such as learned behaviours[85], so you have an enormous amount of (non-genetic) influence in shaping your child's eating habits. Regardless of genetics, from the moment your baby was born their experience has modified their genetic predispositions.

In early tongue development, the nerves connect together with the taste buds, wiring tastes into the nervous system. When a child learns a new skill, such as walking, they do so through repeating and practising to make the skill hard-wired, so those neurons are firmly connected. It is very easy to see how, through the same process, repeatedly exposing a child to the same foods will hard-wire the taste buds to 'know' those flavours. If those foods are processed foods then, before your child is even two years old, those eating preferences are formed and hard-wired into your child's brain and nervous system.

The nervous system is malleable and can be altered, but once a connection is made it is harder to change it than it is to get the connection right to begin with. Think about an established habit you have, such as holding your pen the wrong way – once established it is harder to break, but it is certainly possible. It just might take a few more times and a little bit more effort on your part as a parent.

+ + + **Tip** + + +

Taste buds are more sensitive when they are warm, so an easy way to get your child trying new foods is to serve the same recipe warm and cold. You will be impacting their ability to accept and experience a new 'taste'.

+ + + + + + + + +

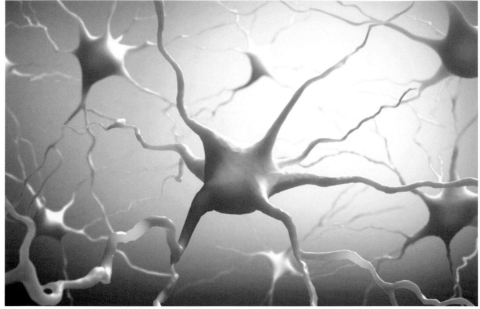

Shutterstock

A neuron connects to another neuron, creating an enormous web of pathways inside the brain. These pathways reflect the cognitive structures behind our learning and repetition helps to form these.

Adult perceptions of likes and dislikes

It's a common story: you serve a plate of food to your child, sit down to enjoy it and watch in horror as they swipe it with their arm, pushing it onto the floor. You wouldn't be alone if you presumed, from this act, that your child doesn't like the food and is sending you a message. Another time, you may have watched your child make a face, start arching their back to get out of the highchair, repeatedly shake their head or say 'no' – these are all common actions that may lead you to presume your child 'doesn't like' something.

As already mentioned, your child's food likes and dislikes are not stable until the age of five, as a general rule[86], and even then there is still plenty of potential for change. So if your baby tastes something and pulls a face, remind yourself that their expression represents a lack of familiarity, rather than a 'dislike' of the food offered. It's important to remember that there is a big difference between unfamiliarity (which generally leads to rejection of a food – see neophobia on p.117) and dislike. Maybe they didn't choose to accept that food there and then, but that shouldn't put you off serving it again. Familiarity takes a while and requires repeated exposure, so that's what you need to provide for your child.

Don't jump to conclusions about what your baby is trying to tell you. Your child's ways of thinking and communicating are a lot less sophisticated than yours are, as an adult. Toddlers often say the word 'no' because it's a word they hear often rather than because they mean 'no'[87]!

Your child might know a food by one name and say they don't like the same food when you use a different word. This shows

Preparing food gives children more opportunities to become familiar with it, encouraging curiosity and conversation. It's also something fun you can do together.

you just how many dimensions of a food need to be familiar for a child to recognize it as the food they know – even the name needs to be right!

Christine and Seth

Seth loved eating chunks of meat. One day when he was served his dinner he asked what it was and Christine replied with 'beef'. Seth immediately responded with: 'I don't like beef!' and pushed it away. Christine knew Seth loved this dinner. He had eaten it many times before, but she realized that the title she had given it was new. Seth was used to eating 'meat'. She quickly worked out what had happened and replied 'Oops, sorry — Mummy got it wrong, it's meat.' Seth smiled and happily tucked in.

Remind yourself what your child is capable of and use that knowledge to interpret what they're trying to tell you. That way, you can respond to what they are telling you, rather than what you assume they are telling you from your adult's perspective.

Once a child has tasted a food, to help limit the knee-jerk reaction of 'yucky' which often follows, implement strategies to portray the food in a positive way. This is the thinking behind having your child prepare the food with you. The fun and joy in preparing the food helps to create a positive association with the food and research shows that foods

> **Key point:**
>
> **Pressuring your child to eat can increase neophobia.**

with a positive association are more likely to be accepted[88 89 90].

With this in mind, the opposite also is true, in that when a negative association is created with a food, rejection is more likely. This is where your role as a parent in the weaning relationship is more important than ever, since if you become frustrated and angry, and pressure your child into eating a food, a negative association is highly likely to be formed, as your child starts to associate that food with your displeasure, and a new neural pathway in the brain is created. In fact, research shows that when a parent pressures a child to eat or try a food, their resistance increases[91 92].

Chapter Six

Weaning and Emotions

Your emotions affect your baby

Your baby will always pick up on how you're feeling – they are designed to do this because they need to take their cues from you about how the world works. That means that they learn how to feel about outside situations from you. This is a basic survival mechanism. In caveman times, if your child didn't learn to feel fear when danger approached, they wouldn't try to run away. On the other hand, if they felt scared all the time and didn't learn when to feel safe, they wouldn't get the opportunity to discover the world and develop. On a more complex (but no less of a survival) level, your child needs to learn how to fit in with other people, so they need to learn how to operate and how to feel about what happens when other people are around. They learn that from you, too, so it's important that you know how you're feeling and that you manage your emotions when you're sitting down at mealtimes with your baby.

Some key things to remember:
- Become aware of your feelings about weaning and mealtimes *before* you sit down to eat
- If you feel anxious/annoyed/frustrated (or any other unhelpful emotion), then you need to take some time out to manage this before sitting down with your child
- Remember that this is only one meal. Weaning is a gradual process and all

you need is for your baby to engage with what you're doing together. Food is for fun and exploration at this age – your baby is getting all their nutrition from milk feeds initially (see p.26 for more on this)
- Manage your child's emotions *for* them by empathizing, being loving and helping them to calm down. Remember that there is no point forcing the issue if your child gets upset. Their appetite will have gone, the blood will have gone to the muscles in their legs and they will need to get rid of the energy
- Help them to calm down by cuddling them in their chair or bringing them onto your lap for a cuddle whilst you remain seated at the table. Forcing your child to stay in their seat and eat their dinner is going against their physiology since the stress response will send the blood to their leg muscles away from their digestive system
- Try again around twenty minutes after they have calmed down, once the hormones have left the system and the appetite has returned

Food as a comforter

The simple action of food-giving is not necessarily a comforter in itself; it is all the other things that accompany the act of feeding your baby that comforts them. Babies need to be held and engaged with when feeding, so the

Shutterstock

This baby isn't having the bonding experience of being in his mother's arms and gazing into her eyes while he eats.

combined effect of all of these elements helps a baby to relax as they eat. You may see that your baby has a relaxed, spaced-out look about them after drinking breast milk – this is also due to the relaxing hormones it contains.

Allowing a baby to hold their own milk bottle or allowing your baby to lie in a bouncer means you're removing the bonding experience your child would get if they were to breastfeed, or if you held them in your arms while you supplied their milk feed. The experience of being breastfed is acknowledged to be associated with improved cognitive development in babies[93] – although the mechanisms that underlie this outcome are still unclear. Who's to say that the bonding process and the baby's opportunity to tune in to its mother's heartbeat during feeding, for example, or for their body's systems to be regulated by their contact with their mother,

doesn't contribute to this? For you as a parent, getting used to feeding your baby while they are not being held can lead you down the road of encouraging your child to eat alone, which isn't ideal with regards to milk feeds or solid foods. Leaving a baby alone with a bottle is similar to leaving them alone with a meal while you wash up – it takes you physically farther away from your baby and means you're not attending to them as intensely as you would otherwise be, just when they should be given the opportunity to bond with you.

As you probably know by now, eating is a social activity. Your baby doesn't need to learn how to hold their own bottle – their physical development will take its own course, and there are plenty of other things for your baby to grab and hold (often your hair!). Allowing your baby to feed while you prop the bottle up for them means missing out on all the other factors including bonding, engagement and positive associations with food that otherwise accompany a milk feed.

Self-soothing

The term 'self-soothe' can be a confusing one, as is the hot debate regarding what it is and whether it is something that infants can do on their own. When we talk about self-soothing, we are referring to the idea that an infant, with no contact from its parent when distressed, can comfort themselves emotionally. We strongly believe that this is not possible. On the contrary, it is well accepted that babies are not born being able to regulate their own emotions and it's your role as their parent to teach them how to do so[94 95]. It is suggested that children learn how to regulate their emotions through observing, parental modelling and social referencing (i.e. looking at parents' faces for cues about what to do when they aren't sure – children are already using social referencing by between ten and twelve months old). A family's 'emotional climate' is also important in this regard; for example, one's general parenting style affects a child's capacity to regulate their emotions. There are considered to be four parenting styles:

Authoritarian – what we would now call Victorian, in common parlance – with little warmth and lots of strict rules. Authoritarian parents don't give children choices and they don't explain their actions, punishing when they see fit or demanding obedience 'because I said so'. These parents do not teach children that they are unconditionally loved and accepted or that they are heard and nurtured when experiencing negative emotions. Instead, they teach them to follow the rules 'or else'. As adults, these children may associate success or obedience with love, have low self-esteem or have difficulty in social situations.

Authoritative – this style involves warmth but with firm boundaries. These parents listen to their children, encouraging choice and independence. They allow their children to express themselves and administer discipline fairly and consistently, explaining what's happening. These children learn that there are certain guidelines but that they are loved and accepted, no matter what. They are taught to feel safe expressing negative emotions and they learn how to handle them, being able to reassure themselves things will be ok. As adults, these children tend to be happier and to have good social and emotional skills, together with good self-esteem. This is currently considered by Western psychologists to be the 'healthiest' parenting style.

Permissive – involves warmth but a lack of boundaries. Rules may change and these parents may be more like a friend than a parent, bribing children to get them to behave. These children are not taught to manage themselves or that their parents provide them with a reassuring framework to fall back on when things go wrong, which can encourage insecurity. As adults they may become self-involved, demanding and lack self-discipline, sometimes with poor social skills because they don't know how to function within the frameworks of social relationships.

Uninvolved – these parents are emotionally distant, offering very little guidance and showing little love. They have few expectations and are often absent during important events. They may be too overwhelmed with their own problems to be there for their children. These children are not taught that they receive support and love when they experience negative emotions – no one is there to listen when things go wrong. As adults, they can be afraid of intimacy or becoming 'dependent' on others, feel stressed or anxious because they don't have family support and may be unable to manage these emotions healthily. They may become 'loners', believing that they need to provide for themselves as no one else will.

Attachment relationships also affect emotional regulation, as does whether a family expresses and talks about emotions. The kind of relationship the parents have with each other (i.e. warm, distant) is significant too[96].

Babies are born without the ability to understand their emotions (in the way that we can reflect on, be aware of and understand our emotions as adults). As mentioned previously, they learn these skills through our modelling. Part of that involves showing how 'feeling better' works, by soothing them. You should aim never to leave your child to regulate their own emotions without your input – learning to manage negative emotions is a childhood-long endeavour and you need to be there to continually reinforce and teach them throughout this period.

Even as adults, we use other adults to help us soothe ourselves when things get tough – if you're close to your parents, who do you go to when you need reassurance and support? If you're not, then that's what your partner and/or friends do for you – comments like 'It'll be okay' represent others helping us to self-soothe. The difference is that, by the time we reach adulthood, we will ideally have learned how to manage this on our own for the most part, as our parents will have been helping us to learn how to manage negative emotions from birth. Having these skills means that if no one is around when things go wrong, we can tell ourselves 'It'll be okay'. But your child *cannot* do this alone. Comfort them and be there with them when they are upset; this helps to 'contain' (by which we mean manage, rather than 'not show') their distress.

'Ah, but controlled crying works for babies … doesn't it?' you might be thinking, as you read this. Of course, every parent needs to make their own decisions about this, but it does not 'work' in the way many parents are led to believe it does. Yes, the crying may stop eventually, so from that perspective it 'works'. However, it teaches your child that no one comes when they're upset, so from the perspective of parenting in a way that always aims to help your child to feel more rather than less secure, you can imagine the effect this might have on them in that moment. There is much debate on this matter, but attachment theory[97], which is still one of the most prominent parenting theories – and with good reason, we would suggest, as it makes sense from an evolutionary perspective, among other things – recommends that responsive, appropriate and timely caregiving is paramount for a child's healthy development. Therefore, when your child is an infant (as well as throughout childhood), we strongly recommend that it is beneficial to support their emotions and respond to their needs by always going to them when they are distressed and soothing them.

Have you ever noticed that if a toddler is left alone to cry, they can become more and more hysterical, to a point where you realize that they aren't capable of calming down? Some even begin to exhibit their distress through behaviour such as head-banging. At that age, leaving them alone to cry doesn't help because they don't yet have the cognitive skills to understand anything other than what they're feeling in that moment. This is particularly true when they're emotionally overwhelmed. As an aside, current thinking suggests that feeling heightened negative emotions (e.g. fear/anxiety) actually affects our ability to think in a task-focused way and to perform well while we are experiencing them. A good demonstration of this concept is exam anxiety, shown to significantly affect task-focused thinking and performance[98]. This remains true even as adults – if you're panicking about something, how clearly are you thinking, when it comes to getting something achieved? Toddlers are developing their identities and independence, but they don't have the negotiation skills (or the sophistication of thought) to try to gain control through positive self-talk. They often become frustrated, distressed and overwhelmed if things don't go their way or when you tell them they can't do something they want to do. Your toddler therefore needs you to:

- Stay with them. Do not leave the room. If they don't want a cuddle, don't force them to be held as this can make things worse. Instead, stay near them, at their level (e.g. kneeling or sitting on the floor) and keep telling them you're there in a calm and loving voice
- Ask them at different points if they want a cuddle but don't pester them if they say no (with toddlers)
- Empathize – tell them: 'Oh I know you want to X, Y or Z, it's horrible when we don't get what we want'
- Ask them to tell you when they've finished crying: 'You let me know when you've finished crying, I'm here'
- Ask them to tell you all about it so that you are encouraging them to express themselves when they're feeling distressed
- Maintain a soothing tone in whatever you're saying
- Reassure them it'll be okay

Using this technique, you're teaching your child how to regulate their own emotions. You won't have to move the boundaries or give in to hysterical demands just to stop them crying. It may take a while the first time you try it, but over time your child will learn that you're always there for them when they're upset and that things are always okay, but also that they can express themselves. An important lesson within this is to teach them that feeling upset is normal. Many children whose parents couldn't handle negative emotions and either ignored them or did anything to make them 'go away' find that later on in life they repress negative feelings and don't state their own needs because they find it extremely uncomfortable.

Catherine and Louis

Louis was two years and two months old when Catherine came to see us. Louis had not slept through the night in all that time and she was exhausted. She had tried various sleep training experts and read numerous sleep training books but all insisted she leave Louis to cry it out and she just couldn't do it. From the food diary, it showed that Louis was having an 8 oz beaker of cow's milk in the evening at 6.30 p.m. and waking up crying out for milk at around 3 a.m. or 4 a.m. most nights – she would respond and he would drink around 2 oz before falling back to sleep. He would take ages eating his breakfast in the mornings, leading Catherine to become increasingly impatient as she had to get to work. What was she to do? She couldn't refuse her son food if he was hungry, yet she had returned to work and needed to sleep. At this age, milk feeds are meal replacements, so the 8 oz can be classed as a meal. Louis had begun to associate milk with comfort and the key was to teach him to associate cuddles with comfort instead, so that this knowledge would be there for him later in life. At this age, very small changes need to be made with longer adjustment times in between modelling or teaching different behaviours. The first step was to remove the middle-of-the-night milk feed so, when Louis cried, Catherine would go in and cuddle and comfort him until he was not crying. When he asked for milk she replied, 'Mummy's here, I love you. I understand what you want and Mummy's here'. An offer of water in an open-top cup was also made (not a beaker or bottle since it takes more effort to drink *from an open-top cup). The first night was rough with Catherine comforting and cuddling for eighty-six consecutive minutes (she timed it) before Louis fell asleep with exhaustion in her arms. The following night she repeated the same and it was twenty-seven minutes. On the third night he did not wake at all. Not surprisingly, the breakfast eating speeded up because Louis was hungry and more eager to eat and now everyone is getting more sleep.*

It's okay for your child to cry. Many parents become upset and distressed at their child's tears, which is understandable since nobody likes to see the person they love upset. The problem arises when the parental goal becomes 'I need to stop the crying' rather than 'I need to comfort my child'. Giving in to your child's request for milk will, of course, stop the crying, but what lesson are you teaching your child? A healthy 2-year-old has the stomach capacity to not need a milk feed in the night, so rather than trying to solve the problem for your child by giving them what they want, see this as a learning opportunity, a chance for your little one to be assured that Mummy or Daddy will comfort and soothe them when they are upset, but that that doesn't change the situation.

Your emotional regulation

The ability to regulate (manage) our negative emotions isn't something that we are born with. This is why the idea of babies self-soothing is a myth. In order to regulate your emotions, you need to have quite a sophisticated understanding of what's happening as well as being able to understand that things will be okay. We do have the ability to soothe

ourselves as adults, but how well we can do this depends partially on how our parents responded to us when we were upset as children. Our adult self-soothing takes various forms; for example, telling ourselves everything will be okay or doing something like taking a hot bath. However, don't we all have times when we need someone else to tell us everything will be okay? Aren't there still times when we need a hug and to be comforted by someone we love and trust?

How you manage your own emotions also teaches your child how to regulate their emotions. If you demonstrate that you can't manage your own emotions and you lose your temper or take their behaviour personally, for example, the message that life is unpredictable and full of emergencies is conveyed. It makes it harder for a child to learn how to calm themselves down and an aroused child finds it much harder to control their behaviour or their feelings. Obviously, all parents lose their tempers sometimes and we're all human, but it's worth bearing in mind that the most important thing you can do to help your child learn how to regulate their emotions is to show them that you can regulate your own and respond kindly and compassionately when they are distressed. Anxiety is an emotion that every parent feels and how parents manage it is particularly important. For example, if a toddler climbs up a climbing frame and gets scared, how the parent responds will teach them how to manage their emotions and self-soothe. If the parent can soothe them and help them find their way down with support, then the child is learning how to control their emotions and self-soothe when they feel out of their depth or scared. The neural pathways are being created that will help them to talk to themselves soothingly and calm themselves in the future, although again it should be stressed that this is a childhood-long endeavour – don't expect them to 'know how to do it' next time, for example! If the parent also becomes anxious and intervenes in a shot, over time, the child learns that they can't handle situations on their own and also that anxiety is 'bad' and needs to be avoided at all costs. They then begin to learn how to manage anxiety in this way rather than via self-soothing, and this can set a child up to be an 'anxious' person later in life.

To sum up, emotional management is taught to your child by you, and this begins in infancy. Self-soothing is learned by behavioural modelling and responsive parenting rather than by leaving a child alone to self-soothe – they don't possess the skills and are likely to experience this as abandonment.

'Crying it out'

The idea of leaving a child alone to 'cry it out' when they are distressed is rooted in scientific thinking that goes back at least as far as the late eighteenth century, when the preoccupation was with preventing infection and the spreading of bacteria. Parents were therefore discouraged from touching their babies unless absolutely necessary. This attitude wasn't softened in the twentieth century, when the field of psychology was dominated by behaviourism, which focused on changing behaviour rather than valuing experience or emotions.

John Watson[99] was an influential advocate of behaviourism and even warned mothers that being too loving was dangerous, suggesting instead that children whose parents were too 'soft' with them would end up being dependent and clingy. At the time, parents or grandparents were presumed to have little valuable knowledge of parenting in comparison to scientific 'experts'. The idea

was that 'training' your child to be independent would ensure you produced a self-sufficient adult with minimal difficulty. Parents were told that they should be in control of the relationship between them and their baby, and that they should not allow their babies to learn that crying = attention.

From an anthropological point of view, this might also have been related to the fact that extended families began to live together less, so parents had less support and therefore had to work out ways to cope with caring for their babies all day, every day without the help of other adults.

The impact of 'crying it out'

Recent neuroscientific research[100] shows that babies have a calming response that is activated by being held and carried in their parent's arms. The study suggests that it's literally biological; that carrying a baby when they're distressed activates a co-ordinated set of central, motor, and cardiac calming processes. The researchers argue that these are part of the parasympathetic nervous system and that an automatic calming response ensues when it is activated. This reaction may have been preserved through evolution to ensure babies' safety and survival (the idea being that the safest place for a baby to be is in their mother's (parent's) arms). This may help to explain why infants who seem perfectly happy may start crying when they're put down and it also suggests why swaddling can help – it might recreate part of the feeling of being held.

Nowadays, we also have neuroscientific research to tell us that allowing babies and young children to cry alone damages their brains and can negatively affect their ability to have stable relationships with both themselves and other people in the long term. Damage to cognitive pathways and brain

Shutterstock

When babies cry, they need their parent to comfort them.

synapses becomes more likely, as does damage to the 'network', which is being built extremely quickly in the infant brain. Stress hormones (e.g. cortisol) are released and increased stress as a baby can have a life-long effect on health[101]. For example, stress and anxiety are related to conditions like irritable bowel syndrome and heart disease. One study[102] showed that although babies who were left to cry themselves to sleep cried for shorter periods as the days passed, the levels of cortisol in their saliva remained high. This suggests that they adapted their behaviour but that ceasing crying didn't mean that the babies were feeling less stressed; in fact they felt just as stressed but had simply given up on trying to attract their mother's attention through crying.

We therefore now know that trying to force your child to be 'independent' may well impede their development and make them anxious and insecure, which can manifest as either withdrawing (because they've learned their needs won't be met) or becoming whiny and demanding/aggressive in order to get attention. Teaching children that their emotional needs will not be met when they are upset teaches them to physically and mentally shut down in the face of severe distress, which impacts on growth, trust and self-esteem among other things[103]. From a psychological point of view, it all comes back to attachment theory – if the child learns that their needs will be met by a loving parent, they form a view of themselves as important and a view of the world as a nice place where things are going to be okay. Through having this repeated experience over many years, they learn how to soothe themselves.

What might the effects of crying it out be on you, though, even if you're conceptually on board with it? You and your baby are an inter-connected duo, where the relationship is paramount. Ignoring your child when they're upset can also arguably negatively affect your relationship with them. It may desensitize you to their cues and signals, which means that you may become less likely to pick up on them at other times. A scientific review in 2011[104] suggested just that – that it could prevent parents from responding consistently and sensitively to their child and lead to long-term adverse effects on child-parent bonding, child stress regulation, mental health and emotional development.

What does leaving your baby to 'cry it out' have to do with eating?

When babies become toddlers and are therefore a bit older, some parents may feel overwhelmed if they get distressed or hysterical and may think that leaving them to calm down might help, therefore trying to ignore the behaviour (or even putting them in another room) to give them time and space to do this. However, if you're at the table and your child is upset at not getting fish fingers again, leaving them to self-soothe is unlikely to help matters. In fact, toddlers can become more and more hysterical if left alone when distressed and become physically incapable of calming themselves down. Offer your child cuddles, comfort and reassurance to support them through this moment of disappointment as they start learning that, sadly, just because they want something, they won't always get it. It's not an easy concept to get to grips with, even as adults, but supporting your child through their grief, frustration and disappointment will help. Even as adults, if you see a friend crying do you leave them alone or are your instincts to comfort, cuddle and reassure? Your bond with your child is far greater than that with a friend, so why would a different approach be either appropriate or helpful?

Controlled crying?

Many parents can't tolerate leaving their children to 'cry it out' when they are distressed, but the idea of controlled crying (where the baby is not left alone until crying stops but is instead left alone for controlled periods) is still reasonably common and certain well-known childcare figures advocate it as part of a routine-focused approach to parenting. The debate on the efficacy of this continues. A recent study[105] suggested that using controlled crying as a behavioural technique does not cause longstanding damage or adverse effects over a five-year period; however, the researchers said that this is an ongoing debate among scientists

and that researchers are calling for rigorous studies over time to help resolve it.

The views are, therefore, as is often the case with scientific research, very much split. However, this approach very much contrasts with the attachment parenting approach of attending speedily and appropriately to your baby's needs as they arise and prioritizing the bond between you. At the end of the day, only you can decide what feels right for you and your family.

Waking and crying at night may be unrelated to what your child is eating

Waking in the night could be due to a developmental spurt and nothing to do with hunger. Sleep regression is common at eight to nine months, as babies start to mobilize and learn to crawl, walk, pull-up to standing or are teething. You may find your child standing up in their cot in the middle of the night, crying, as they haven't yet learned how to lie back down. They may kick or fling their arms around in their sleep as their nerves myelinate and they rehearse their new moves, embedding these actions into their neural pathways. You need to help older babies to learn how to settle back down when they wake up – they need reassurance and your presence, not always food. If they begin to rely on milk feeds to settle, then you may be setting them up for a pattern of needing food to calm themselves – this can start a child on the road to emotional eating.

Only you can decide whether that call for you in the night means hunger or comfort and only you can decide how to respond, but if you do decide to respond with a milk feed be sure to adjust your expectations around eating solids to allow for this (see p.24 for further details).

Why do *you* feed your child?

We often ask why *we* eat. Is it boredom, tiredness, anxiety? But have you asked yourself why you feed your child? Previously, we talked about it not being a good idea to resort to food when your child is upset, but have you ever thought about why you might be tempted to do it? Do you hate to see them upset? If so, why is that? Does the idea of them being upset feel uncomfortable to you? Would you do anything to stop them crying? Do you use food to cheer them up? Or is it a distraction? When they wake up in the night do you presume their tears are hunger rather than distress? Many people *hate* the idea of upsetting anyone, let alone someone they love, and therefore will do anything to 'make things okay' because they feel guilty if they think they've upset someone else. If this sounds like you and you think that you might be using food to make things okay when your child gets upset, it's useful to take a moment and have a think; become aware of it as it's not a helpful strategy.

Many people feel guilty when people they love are upset because, when they see the distress, they quickly assume that *they've* upset the other person. That's one of the reasons why they hate it and want to try to stop it as quickly as possible. People who struggle with this may also find it difficult to set boundaries or tell other people when they've done something that isn't okay because if the other person becomes upset then they immediately think it's their fault. This can translate into parenting, as parents can find it difficult to set boundaries with their children or to correct their behaviour because when the child becomes upset they feel like they've caused it, so they back down. This can turn into a real problem,

particularly where food and eating is involved but, actually, it often becomes a problem across the board.

If this sounds like you, try to take a step back and realize that when your child becomes upset, let's say because you've asked them to do something they don't want to do, it's nothing *you've* caused. They are upset because they can't get their own way, but that isn't of your creation; that's just how life works and it's an important lesson for children to learn. If you can take the focus off yourself as the cause of the upset and realize that it's the task or the situation that has upset them (you're simply communicating what it is), then it may feel easier to keep those boundaries in place and their distress may feel more tolerable, allowing you to soothe them through cuddles and containment rather than through reaching for anything in a desperate attempt to stop them crying. (Please note that containment here means helping your child to tolerate their negative emotions – it doesn't mean 'containing oneself' as in the common expression – i.e. not manifesting or pushing down one's emotions.)

Tara and Charlie

My 4-year-old son was at a party and another child squirted some ketchup down his top. My son was naturally upset and so I quickly attended to him and soothed him and comforted him. I was surprised to hear the other child say 'shhhhhhh' to my son when he was crying. This made me think that maybe this child was used to his tears being responded to in this way, which is a shame. I'd rather my son was encouraged to express his emotions with me alongside him to support and help him manage them.

Managing a child's upset through soothing is far more beneficial than ending the tears quickly with food. It's okay for your child to become upset; in fact they *need* to become upset because it's a part of feeling a range of emotions as a human being. It's just your job to teach them how to manage it, so make sure that your own unhelpful knee-jerk responses to distress don't get in the way of that.

Rachel and Lewis

From the moment Lewis was introduced to solids, we ate breakfast at the table every morning. Then one day out of the blue Lewis said 'I want breakfast watching TV'. I naturally said 'no' and was greeted with a barrage of tears and upset. This completely threw me. As a working parent, I'm on a timetable and needed to get out of the house but I knew I couldn't give in else he will want the same tomorrow. So I cuddled him and comforted him, soothing him with phrases such as 'I know, it's hard when we don't get what we want' and 'Let me know when you're ready to go to the table'. We were there for twenty minutes, and I was texting my husband asking what on earth I should do. I hate being late and I had a long list of patients needing to see me (I'm a GP). My husband replied with two words which summed it up for me: 'Family First'. After twenty minutes of this, Lewis pulled his head from being nuzzled into my chest and announced, 'I'm ready to go to the table now, Mummy'. And that was that. We went to the table and ate breakfast as if nothing had happened and it's not happened since (touch wood). I still have no idea what prompted that behaviour but I now manage all other resistance to doing something in the same way: with cuddles, comfort and lots and lots of patience.

Chapter Seven

When to Wean and How to Do It

How do I get started with weaning?

Our philosophy of weaning isn't prescriptive. Weaning is a process which is all about learning as you go. We hope to empower you to tune in to your baby and yourself and make the decisions that are right for both of you.

When should I start weaning?

Before four months?
Studies detailing infant development have established that infants are not ready for food (puréed or finger-foods) before four months[106]. Weaning before four months (seventeen weeks) is not advisable for a number of reasons. Babies weaned early have been shown to have higher rates of diarrhoea and to see their GP more often during weaning than babies who are weaned later[107].

The DH guidelines state that solid foods should never be introduced before the age of four months (seventeen weeks)[108]. Certainly, weaning earlier than seventeen weeks should only be commenced under the guidance of a paediatrician (for example, in a case of severe reflux).

Only after six months?
There are two approaches regarding when to wean: follow the recommendation from government organizations or listen to the cues your baby gives you that they're ready.

Currently, the UK DH recommends introducing solid foods, on top of breast or formula milk, to your baby at around six months of age. Before this, your baby's digestive system is still developing, and weaning too soon may increase the risk of allergies or infections. However, each child is an amazing, unique individual and your child might be ready to wean at a different date. Watch for signs that your child may be ready. These include:

* Sitting up with little or no support
* Wanting to chew, putting toys and other objects in their mouth
* Grabbing a handful of your food and popping it in their mouth

Parents often say 'I've decided to wean at x months old'. However, this is already going against the ethos of weaning together, which is about responding to your child's signs and starting the process when *both* of you are ready. Weaning is about tuning in, allowing your child to self-feed and make choices, so if your child chooses to scoop purée into their mouth over that lump of broccoli you've offered, then that is a brilliant thing. Your child is gaining independence, making choices and developing their hand-eye co-ordination.

Can I delay weaning?

There is evidence suggestive of a 'critical window' for introducing 'lumpy' solid foods: if these are delayed beyond ten months of age, it may increase the risk of feeding difficulties later on. Research has found that babies introduced to lumpier textured food after ten months of age had greater feeding difficulties at fifteen months than those introduced to them between six to nine months old[109].

If lumpy solid foods are introduced late, sensory issues may ensue[110]. The feeling of solid, lumpy, textured food around the tongue and mouth begins to desensitize it – an action necessary for more textures and tastes to be accepted later. Let's look at how tongue desensitization is necessary. If you are sitting down reading this, you're probably not feeling your back leaning against the chair or your legs being crossed, instead you're focusing on reading this. Now, imagine if your brain didn't dampen down those messages coming from your body and whilst you were reading this you were also thinking about the feel of your clothes on every part of your body, the seat against your legs, the pressure on your bottom, the tilt of your head. You would be so overwhelmed with this information that you wouldn't be able to concentrate on these words.

Through you spending hours and hours exposing your body to different textures and positions, your brain has desensitized the feedback to these areas in the brain so you aren't constantly alerted to them. It's as if your brain has worked out that these things are 'normal' so it doesn't need to bother your consciousness with them. The same 'dampening down' needs to happen with the messages coming from the tongue and the inside of the mouth – the window of opportunity for this is between six and ten months. If this milestone is missed or introduced late, it is possible that a sensory issue of 'oral defensiveness' can occur. For a child with this issue, textures in the mouth are not dampened down and can be overwhelming. Later,

these children are often called 'fussy eaters' and often:

• Avoid certain textures, temperatures and flavours
• Gag/choke easily
• Have difficulty sucking, chewing, or swallowing
• Avoid/dislike brushing their teeth or washing their face
• Dislike going to the dentist
• Avoid/dislike getting their hands or face messy
• Exhibit inappropriate tasting or mouthing of non-food items

How to deal with these problems is a matter for a different book, but weaning your child with a variety of textures will help desensitize the inside of the mouth and tongue to hopefully reduce the chance of your child developing oral sensitivity difficulties.

If you offer your child foods of different textures from the moment they are weaned, then they are being 'introduced' to them. It may take some time before they get to grips with actually eating them but you've started the process and have begun enabling them to learn for themselves what they need to do with these foods in order to eat them.

One thing that allowing your child to self-feed can do is help improve the awareness of their mouth, preparing them for speech. A technique we often use with children with oral aversion is 'wakening up the mouth', which involves very lightly brushing different textures around the cheeks, lips and mouth. This improves the brain's connection with and awareness of those areas, giving greater control. It's easy to see how allowing your child to self-feed and letting them experience different foods and textures all over their mouth will have a similar effect.

There is no 'right' time to stop offering milk feeds to your baby

Wondering how many millilitres of milk your baby should be having brings us back to the problem of parents worrying about how much their child is eating. Your baby is unique and may be smaller than another person's baby so why should we presume they should consume the same volume of milk? They may be going through a growth spurt and need more milk to sustain these changes or have mastered eating solids so they need less milk. Giving you a measure of how much milk your child 'should' be drinking will serve no purpose but just give you something else to worry about. If you are a breastfeeding mother you will already have no clue as to how much you're offering so, whether you are bottle-feeding or breastfeeding, continue to offer milk feeds on-demand (without pressure to finish the contents if bottle-feeding) and you won't go too far wrong (if you feel you do need a little more advice, contact your health visitor or GP).

Remember, from twelve months old milk is viewed as a meal so if your child is still having a night feed you should consider this when it comes to your expectations about their intake of solids. And remember, all children are different so twelve months should not be seen as a hard and fast deadline, more as a guideline to assist you in making a personal choice.

Fran and Lola

At twelve months it was time for me to return to work. I continued to breastfeed Lola in the evenings before bed and in the mornings before I went to work. For me, this was important bonding time for us so I spoke with the childminder and let her know that Lola will have had breakfast before she arrives each morning and will have supper when she gets home so to not be surprised if she wasn't hungry.

For Fran and Lola, their time together feeding was important and worked for them. Fran simply had to adjust her expectations about how much solid food Lola ate during the day. Speaking with whoever is caring for your child during the day can help ensure that they are not pressured to eat.

Ready for solids

You don't need a calendar or book to tell you when you are ready to introduce solid food – look to your baby for signs that they are ready. Seventeen weeks is the absolute earliest that solid food can be introduced but this is not recommended (unless under the guidance of a paediatrician) since it is unlikely that your baby is developmentally ready. Offering milk feeds on-demand for six months (ideally with breast milk) is preferable. This applies equally for babies with reflux – there is no reason why they shouldn't show signs of readiness or be delayed.

It's the maturity of the digestive tract and your baby's developmental readiness that determines whether your baby is ready to explore solids – not their weight, their size or their age.

It's no coincidence that your baby's digestive tract matures to a level where it can accept solid foods at around seventeen weeks, which is the same time that their taste perceptions change to accept sour and bitter. This is not a recommendation to introduce solids at seventeen weeks – your parents or grandparents probably did, but more research has been conducted since then, and just because the average is seventeen weeks, it doesn't mean that your baby's digestive tract is going to be ready at exactly that date. Plus, we aren't just dealing with the digestive tract development here – your baby is so much more than that.

Signs your baby might be ready to explore solid food

Self-feeding takes effort, not only on your part as the parent but also on your child's part. It is important that a self-feeding baby has sufficient physical stamina to self-feed with enough food to keep pace with their rapid growth. It obviously takes a lot less effort to sit back and allow the food to be dripped into your mouth than it does to actually reach, pick it up, chew it and swallow it. However, if food is introduced to your child when they are developmentally ready, there will be no issue with this. Research has shown that children have the skills for self-feeding by around six months[111][112] but, as we know, all children are unique, and they all develop at a different pace.

So what are these self-feeding skills and what are the signs to look out for in your child that suggest they might now have them?

Motor skills:
- Sitting up with little or no support
- Being able to reach for an object to put it in the mouth

Psychological skills:
- Interest in food and mealtimes

Some babies may sit up sooner, some babies may crawl sooner – they are all individuals. The same applies to the development of the digestive system. Interestingly, it has been observed that children who reach out for food later also tend to achieve other developmental milestones later[113]. It is important to know that it's completely normal for children to develop at different rates, so don't feel disappointed (or affected by any competitiveness of those around you) if your child seems to be reaching for food (or reaching any other milestone) a little later than other children. When your child sits, crawls or rolls over is out of your control and when your child is ready to explore food is, by and large, out of your hands too.

Sitting up

The principles of child motor development are 'big to small' and 'close to far'. This means children will develop and gain control over the larger, chunkier muscles of the trunk before they gain control over the smaller muscles of the lips and tongue – a control which is necessary to manipulate and manage food.

Self-sitting is one of the first major milestones of motor development. Children on average gain this trunk control at around five months of age[114][115] or five-and-a-half months of age[116], but remember this is an average based on statistics and may not reflect your own child's developmental pace.

The pictures on p.96 show the process that a baby goes through to self-sit. Picture one shows a child who has little postural control – notice the way her postural muscles are not working to hold her upright and she is falling into a banana shape. This child is unlikely to have the motor skills needed to master solid food.

Picture two shows a child who has gained more postural control over the trunk muscles but still relies on the hands to

Shutterstock

This baby can use his trunk muscles to sit up but needs his hands for support. He is also unlikely to have the skills required to master solid food.

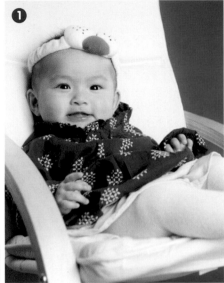

Shutterstock

This baby can't sit upright on her own and is unlikely to have the motor skills to master solid food.

Shutterstock

This baby can sit upright on his own. He can use his hands to feed himself so will be more likely to be able to master solid food.

support himself. You may be surprised to read that this child is also unlikely to have the motor skills to self-feed because he is relying on his arms for balance and, so, being able to use those arms to pick up food to self-feed will be a challenge.

Picture three is an example of a child who is self-sitting. His trunk muscles are strong enough to hold him upright without relying on the arms and he can freely put his hands in his mouth; a motor skill necessary for self-feeding. Self-sitting is necessary for self-feeding so that your little one can use their arms to reach for food rather than for balance[117][118].

Reaching for an object and putting it in the mouth

It's no coincidence that at around the same age that self-sitting develops, so does the

Fig. 1 Two babies using a two-handed approach to reach for an object. This is a common reach in babies yet unable to self-sit.

ability to reach for an object and put it in the mouth. Postural development and infant reaching are both key to self-feeding.

Before a child is able to self-sit, they will reach out with both hands to pick up an object (see Fig. 1) and explore it further. In many children this action of bringing both hands together across the midline to grasp an object occurs at around two to three months[119]. As the child's motor skills develop, they become single-handed and will reach with one hand only (see Fig. 2). Research has shown that non-self-sitting children have symmetrical, synergistic use of both arms and hands when reaching for objects (when sitting) yet self-sitting children show asymmetrical and one-handed reaches (when sitting)[120]. Interestingly, when children are lying on their tummies or on their backs they will often use one hand only but this is possibly because the torso then has the added

Fig. 2 An example of a more advanced one-handed reach.

Key point:

For children to have the hand-eye co-ordination needed for successful self-feeding they must have the postural control to self-sit.

support of the ground. The key is for your child to be able to reach with one hand when sitting because all eating should be done in the sitting position and the postural muscles are therefore less supported.

From this, it is clear to see that postural control is needed for early hand-eye co-ordination, which is necessary to be able to bring food to the mouth to successfully self-feed.

Hand co-ordination begins to develop at a similar time to self-sitting[121]. This allows the child to use their hands in a co-ordinated way to manipulate and explore objects – exactly the same skills they will need when introduced to solid food.

Interest in mealtimes

At the same time as self-sitting develops, children also begin to differentiate between size, shape and different physical attributes that objects have and will adjust their reach to suit the object[122]. It's because of this ability to notice differences between objects that an even greater urge to explore food becomes apparent since food is the same as toys!

When your child becomes interested in food and mealtimes, you may notice because they start reaching for what's on your plate (if they're on your lap, for example). When they do this they're also beginning to want to copy you using food, which is a great way to start weaning – by using a naturally

occurring behaviour, which, if you think about it, seems like an evolutionary trait designed to ensure that children eat safe foods by copying their parent.

Julie and Oliver

Oliver's mum Julie brought him to see us because she was concerned that he wasn't interested in food. Oliver had reached seven months and Mum said that all of his peers had begun to at least show interest. She was beginning to worry that he wouldn't get the right nutrition if she couldn't get him to start eating solids. Julie had tried various different things to get him to try food, such as leaving food in front of him when playing and sitting with him on her lap during mealtimes and she was beginning to wonder whether she should spoon-feed, even though she had wanted to do baby-led weaning with Oliver. She had tried once or twice but he had shown little interest and became upset when she kept trying. Julie felt like she was getting it wrong before she had even started and she was beginning to feel anxious about weaning altogether.

It emerged that Oliver was developing a little later in other ways too. When Felicity examined him from a biomechanical point of view, it became clear that he still retained a number of reflexes which would hinder his ability to interact with food. For example, the gag reflex was still very anterior and his Asymmetric Tonic Neck Reflex (ATNR) would make it very hard for him to bring food to his mouth (this reflex causes the arm to extend when the head turns to look at it). Felicity gave some exercises to encourage movement through and beyond these reflexes.

Anna spoke with Julie, who admitted feeling a little pressured by what her friends' babies were doing. She also said that she had wanted to lessen the amount she was breastfeeding and was beginning to feel a little frustrated that things didn't seem to be changing. Together, she and Anna thought about where these feelings were coming from and Mum realized that they were more to do with her expectations of herself and comparing herself to others than to do with Oliver. Once Mum understood that Oliver wasn't 'behind' and realized that he would show her specific signs when he was physically ready for solids, she felt more able to go with the process and allow Oliver to take things at his own pace. We suggested a few activities that she could do together with Oliver to allow him to begin handling certain foods without any pressure or expectation that he might eat them. This helped Mum to feel like she was making progress and taking active steps towards weaning with Oliver while allowing him to set the pace. Within a month, Oliver had begun to show interest in food and weaning began, helped by the fact that he was already familiar with touching certain foods — these became his first foods.

Ideal positioning

Kicking feet and elbows on the table

Does your little one kick the table when they're sitting in the highchair? You might be tempted to think they are being a bit of a pickle, but maybe there's another reason. Your child's body position can drastically impact on their eating skills. If their body isn't stable then it will naturally strive to find stability, using energy and working hard

Children can eat in all sorts of positions once they have mastered motor control.

along the way to do just that. You may notice the shoulders and arms being lifted up higher than necessary and the feet flinging around, trying to find their position in space.

As an adult, if you sit with your feet dangling, you also strive for this feedback. You might find yourself putting more force through your upper body to gain that support through your torso. In the images on p.101, and the one above, you can see how adults and children of all ages use their arms to gain this stability. At the table, this might involve you leaning on one elbow while you eat with a fork.

If your child's body cannot get the stability and support it needs, or if there is insufficient proprioceptive feedback to the brain to tell it where a limb is in space, they may have diffi-culty controlling the movements needed to self-feed. Regardless of age, the position of

Shutterstock

Allowing this child to kneel to eat their food might be beneficial.

the body when feeding is important. Even with breastfeeding babies, positioning the baby on the breast is key to a successful latch and when introducing solid food the same applies. Eventually, your child's motor control will be so great that your little one will be able to eat in all sorts of positions (see the picture of a child eating upside down on p.100) but, until that time, your child needs to be able to sit with a stable base and have the freedom to align their head and neck properly so they can eat, drink and swallow efficiently, rather than being in the situation where they are fidgeting and focusing on discomfort.

Pre-schoolers might find it more comfortable and easier to eat if they are kneeling than if they are sitting in a chair that does not allow them to secure their feet on a surface. At this point, you are not teaching bad manners – you are helping to make eating easier. Once they have finished eating then you can request that they sit normally, but placing pressure on a child to eat without adequate lower limb support is unfair.

Wedged in

Parents are often tempted to prop their child up and wedge them into the highchair to prevent them lolloping to one side, but this can quickly create a round-shouldered, slouched position. In this slouched position, the head is naturally positioned more forward and downwards, which makes it harder to swallow. Try tilting your head downwards to drink and then upwards to drink and notice how much more difficult the former is. The position of the shoulders impacts on the position of the neck, which finally impacts on the function of the throat, lips, tongue and all the other structures we need to swallow. A slouched position is unlikely to prevent your child from swallowing but it will make it more challenging and less enjoyable.

To prevent this slouching, some parents try wedging a child into a sitting position with pillows and other props around them but this prevents the head from moving, which is necessary to allow the jaw and other structures to move. Some parents, however, do find that supporting their child around their torso can be helpful – under the arms along the sides of the body or behind the back. Just

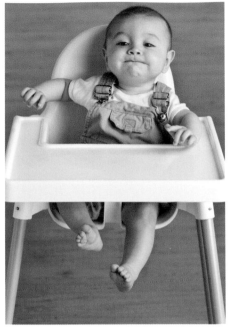

Notice this child kicking feet and shifting around to try and gain some stability.

An example of sitting in a more stable position.

Sitting with dangling feet while leaning on arms aids stability.

Notice this child leaning on one elbow for support while eating.

---- Key point: ----

Look at how your child is sitting. How is their body positioned? Is there enough stability to allow them to freely move their arms to be able to bring food to their mouth (with hands or cutlery) and is there enough movement to allow their head and neck to move for successful chewing and swallowing? Are they sitting straight or is their spine curved round in a banana shape?

remember that having free-moving head and neck control is essential for children when they eat.

Many parents find it fascinating to realize that the position of their child's pelvis when they're sitting can have an effect on their head control, breathing and mouth. If the pelvis is tilted, the spine curves to compensate for this and it will impact on oral motor control.

Jen and Poppy

'Baby-led weaning isn't working! She's just not interested in the food. She just messes with it and becomes upset.' This isn't the first time we have heard this and Jen is certainly not alone. Poppy was six months old and Jen was watching all her NCT mummy friends feeding their babies purée while Poppy was just messing around, not eating and ending up breastfeeding instead. At home she was fine — but out and about it was a disaster. Following an osteo-pathic examination, it was clear Poppy's postural muscles did not have the motor control necessary for easy self-feeding. We observed her lying on her front in the tummy-time position, happily reaching with one hand to grab her giraffe but, sitting on the treatment table, she would remain in a banana-shape and reach with two hands. When perched on her mother's hip, her postural muscles engaged fully and she was able to single-handedly reach. Poppy had not quite gained the postural control needed to self-feed when sitting in the coffee shop high-chairs since she was still relying on her shoulders and arms to hold her in the sitting position. It would be easy to say 'wait a week or two' but Jen knows her daughter better than we do and she was confident Poppy was ready — showing interest in food, eating well at home and reaching and eating happily when propped on her mum's hip. What was going on? The difference was simply the stabilization of the pelvis. The highchair Poppy was using at home had a footrest — the Costa Coffee one didn't. (See p.100 for a reminder on why this might have an effect.) It was important for Jen to continue to see her friends and she wanted Poppy to eat with her peers. We wanted to ensure that Poppy was able to be included in the social eating and fun that happened at Costa, so the answer was simply for Poppy to sit on her mother's lap to explore her solid food for a few weeks until she had done some of the postural support games and gained the postural control necessary to self-feed with her feet dangling in space.

Absolute 'do's' and 'don'ts'

When it comes to practical guidelines for weaning, before you give your child the opportunity to explore solid food, bear these things in mind:

- Do make sure your child is developmentally ready before introducing solid foods
- Do make sure you are introducing solids for the right reason (i.e. not to stop them waking in the night)
- Do make sure your baby is sitting upright
- Do sit with your baby and eat with them
- Do have two or three things available to enable your baby to make a choice
- Do cut small fruits such as grapes and cherries in half and remove any stones
- Do cut foods into good-sized chunks that your baby can easily hold in their fist
- Do be prepared for a mess
- Do be prepared to have some fun!
- Don't let anyone, except your baby, put food in their mouth
- Don't leave your baby alone with food
- Don't offer your baby any salt, sugar or whole nuts
- Don't offer your baby any raw honey until they're twelve months old

What's wrong with raw honey?

Many parents question the 'no honey until twelve months' rule. So why is it important? Well, the stomach produces hydrochloric acid (HCL), which kills off most bacteria, but babies naturally produce less HCL than adults. Before canning and other modern preserving methods were developed, foods were often stored in honey since the low water and oxygen content meant many bacteria couldn't grow[123]. But bees often brush against botulinus spores as they collect pollen to make honey. In adults it is fine if we swallow the spores as the HCL in our stomach kills the bacteria, but because of the low volumes of HCL in babies, there isn't enough to kill the spores and so ingesting raw honey before twelve months may lead to the botulism bacteria attacking your baby's muscles. So this is the reason you should wait until your child is twelve months before introducing raw honey.

Worried they might go hungry?

Self-feeding certainly takes a lot more effort and therefore more energy than spoon-feeding. Some days your child will be full of beans and engaged with the food; other days they won't be interested. This is normal and fine – just continue to offer milk feeds on-demand and, if bottle feeding, don't get hung up on the volumes. Your energy varies too, as an adult – some days you might feel you have enough energy to cook a meal from scratch, other days you might not have the inclination and you choose freezer-food instead. It's normal for your energy levels to go up and down, just as it is for your baby's. Daytime activities, growth spurts, teething and tiredness all have an impact and the beautiful thing about this approach to weaning is that you can relax and follow your baby's cues without stressing that they didn't finish the purée pouch.

It is common for parents to be concerned about their baby's energy intake when they introduce self-feeding with solid foods, but research has shown that, as children become more practised and skilled at handling foods, parents realize that their child is happy and healthy and this anxiety quickly reduces[124]. Are you concerned about your child's self-feeding? Well, just know that it's normal to be worried, but here are some things you can do to help calm your fears:

- Be sure to offer milk feeds on-demand. In the first nine months, a child's prime source of nutrition and energy is from milk so avoid the routine and analysing what you think your child 'should' be having and let them feed on-demand – this will give you confidence that they are happy and not hungry
- Introduce easier foods. Chomping on robust foods can be hard work, so take this opportunity to serve up more sloppy meals such as spaghetti bolognese, cottage pie and other easy-to-eat dishes. Remember, if you're worried about them chomping away on solid pieces of food, it's okay to purée up that steamed broccoli, pre-load the spoon and let them feed themselves
- Once your little one is getting the hang of eating, be sure to offer energy-dense protein-based foods such as meat, eggs or fish. This isn't as necessary before nine months because during this time milk feeds should be filling your little one up more than solid foods. In the United Kingdom, meat consumption was found to be positively associated with psychomotor skill development (e.g. learning to perform actions that require coordination) in children up to twenty-four months of age[125]. Further-more, a study performed in the US city of Denver demonstrated that the acceptability of beef as a first comple-mentary food by exclusively breastfed infants at age five to six months is iden-tical to that for infant rice cereal[126].

Try our Meaty Menu below, which is iron-rich, easy to eat and multi-textured.

Meaty Menu

Preparation Time: 5 minutes
Cooking Time: 15 minutes
Serves 1 little person

Ingredients
Single steak
Oatcake
Beef stock (optional)

Method
1. Pan-fry or grill a single steak
2. Cut it in half and serve one half whole (the bigger the better to lessen the chance of choking)
3. With the other half, blitz it in the food processor so it becomes mushy. If necessary, add some beef stock to make it even more gloopy
4. Spread some of the gloopy steak on an oatcake
5. Put a dollop of some of the steak on the plate

You have now offered the same food in different ways, both of which are going to be experienced differently. Both options are high in iron and you have given choice: the big chunk if your child is up for chewing and munching and the easy-to-eat stuff in the form of the gloopy mixture if they aren't.

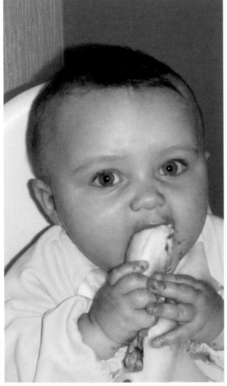

David Bertin

An almost 7-month-old child exploring a chicken leg.

Energy

Young children have sensitive self-regulation skills[127] when it comes to food intake. Provided that you have watched for the signs that they are ready and have the motor skills to self-feed, and that you offer a range of foods and continue to offer milk feeds, their energy intake will match their needs for growth. If any of these components are missing, then there is a risk that your child's energy levels will be affected.

Checklist
To ensure your child has their energy requirements met:

- Does my child have the motor skills necessary to self-feed?
- Am I serving up a variety of foods over the week?
- Am I continuing to offer milk feeds on-demand?

Because each child is unique, grows at a different rate and spends their days participating in different activities, there is very little research around the amount of energy a child needs. As long as they continue to grow, it is accepted that there is a positive energy balance[128]. It's interesting that research that has looked at energy levels in spoon-fed children compared to energy levels in self-feeding children found that spoon-fed children were more likely to be overweight or obese as they got older[129].

One last check before lift-off ...

You're now armed with all the necessary information, but before you get started with weaning, make sure you have a look at this checklist to ensure you have everything you need in place:

- Is my baby ready to wean (see p.94 for details)?
- Am I comfortable and relaxed with the food I am serving (see p.43)?
- Am I serving at least two different foods at each meal (see p.184)?
- Am I allowing my child to self-feed (see p.171)?
- Am I sitting and eating the same foods with my child (see p.106)?
- Am I continuing to offer milk feeds and

not worrying about the volume of consumption (see p.26)?

There's a whole world of exciting food flavours, colours and textures awaiting your baby, and weaning in a way that views it as a journey that you and your baby are taking together gives you the tools to bond with your baby and enhance your relationship with them through food. You're the one who can encourage their cognitive, biomechanical, emotional and social development through weaning. So what are you waiting for? Let's get started!

Let's do it!

Now it's time to have some fun and introduce your baby to a wonderful new world of food. Here are some quick tips for getting started:

- Position plenty of wipes and kitchen roll nearby
- Have all your child's food and drink to hand before you start
- Have something for yourself at the same time – ideally the same thing. You may be sitting there for a while and your baby will be more inclined to copy you and tuck in if you are eating
- Lay some cheap PVC matting or news-paper on the floor around the highchair
- Dress your baby in a long-sleeved bib – you may choose to put a crumb-catcher bib on top
- Place at least two different food items on the table and watch them explore
- If you choose to offer purées, dollop some on the highchair tray and let your baby use their hands or a spoon to self-feed
- Allow your baby to choose whether they want to use a spoon or eat with their

Overly-focusing on your child's eating at mealtimes can be counter-productive.

hands. If cutlery becomes a problem at some point (e.g. your baby is throwing it or banging it on the tray and this bothers you) then remove the cutlery and let your baby eat with their hands
- Don't hover and praise your baby for eating something, or focus attention on whether your child eats x or y. Instead, focus on enjoying the process of discovery together (e.g. squishing, picking up and smearing food). Your aim is to act like eating is normal – it's not a big deal; it's natural!

Focus on eating together, *not* on your child's eating

When you introduce solids to your baby for the first time, it is a highly emotional event for all concerned. It's a big milestone, mixed with

Making eating a social occasion feels great, doesn't it? Your baby thinks so too!

anxiety and excitement; there are possibly cameras around and you might even be waiting for certain family members to be there to experience the event with you. Remember that your child is attuned to you and will pick up on all of these factors – this first bite of food therefore has huge emotional connections for your baby, as well as for you. Many parents find that their child's eating is an emotional issue in general and that's understandable because you care so much, on so many levels. Nourishing your child taps into your basic parenting instincts, not to mention that you understandably want your child to enjoy the food you provide; so it's not surprising that parents have a lot invested in how well their child eats, what they eat and how much.

Because of that, it's easy to really focus on your child's eating at mealtimes – putting all the attention on them and their eating, kind of like you would if you were spoon-feeding (i.e. all your attention is on them taking that mouthful of food that you're controlling). Put yourself in your baby's position. Imagine you're out for dinner with a friend; are you focusing on what they're putting in their mouth, in minute detail, and then praising them a lot when they take each mouthful? Are you sitting there, not eating whilst they eat? Probably not, and focusing on your child's eating process in this way can lead to fussy eating problems later on, for a number of reasons:

- Firstly, your child will soon pick up that you're invested in what they do with that food you are serving them. They will cotton on that you really want them to eat it. This may set mealtimes up as a

25

battleground, as your baby's identity develops and they want to take some control

- Secondly, eating is a normal thing to do, and you need to act like it's normal from the beginning – there's no need to praise excessively when your baby eats something. In fact, with older fussy eaters, you should ignore them when they try something new, but that's another subject altogether
- Thirdly, eating is a social activity and the reason we enjoy eating with others is that it's an opportunity to bond over a pleasurable activity. Eating together isn't an activity where each person is scrutinized or pressurized, and adding these experiences to mealtimes will undoubtedly make it less fun for your baby, just as it would for you. Have you ever been out for dinner with friends and everyone checks whether you're all having starters? We don't want to eat alone – it feels uncomfortable and goes against our need to feel included
- Finally, eating is a learned skill; your baby learns through seeing you doing something and repeating the action. Think about how your child learns to talk. It is through hearing you say 'Mummy' or 'Daddy' repeatedly. They try and mimic you, so why would this not be the case for eating? Does your baby watch you spoon baby rice into your partner's open mouth at mealtimes? Your child's need to feel connected and part of a group, with that sense of belonging, is overwhelming

When humans eat together their oxytocin levels increase and the digestion of the food becomes more efficient. A child eating with family members who create an atmosphere

+ + + **Tip** + + +

Eating with your child will increase their ability to absorb vitamins and minerals.

+ + + + + + + + +

of togetherness, love and patience will break the food down more efficiently and use those vitamins and minerals more effectively simply because they are eating a meal with people who love them[130].

Mark the occasion with a colourful feast

This is the perfect time to eat with your baby and work with their need to explore the world through the eyes and mouth. Mark this amazing occasion of your little one being developmentally ready to explore solid foods with an amazing feast of brightly coloured butternut squash or slippery avocado, instead of with a serving of bland, beige baby rice. Eat with your hands if that's what the occasion lends itself to and create positive associations with eating, rather than fear and anxiety.

Keep these ideas in mind when you're weaning and try to develop an atmosphere where you're sitting with your child and modelling how yummy food can be by eating/drinking something yourself. Talk to your child about all sorts of things while you're eating that aren't related to food – just as you would at a dinner party. Resist the urge to wash-up or do other jobs whilst your child is eating, as they will experience this as being left alone with the food, rather than you both being together at mealtimes. Grab a cuppa and sit down and enjoy this time with your child!

Why you should aim to eat with your child ...

- Your baby copying you encourages exploration of new foods
- It confirms to your baby that the food is safe to eat
- It promotes the association of food and togetherness
- It models to your baby how mealtimes should be
- It enables you to respond quickly should they choke
- It stimulates the release of oxytocin which encourages absorption of nutrients

Several studies have reported that the benefits of eating family meals together include healthier eating patterns and improved psychological well-being[131][132], and it is also true that the more people there are around a child eating new food, the more willing they will be to try it[133]. We are told that, 'For the greatest effect, every person around the child should be eating it at the same time'[134]. This isn't true for all ages since children aged three years and under are shown to be influenced by others eating more than children aged four years and over[135]. But when a child reaches adolescence peer pressure again has a greater influence on their eating[136].

Chapter Eight

Weaning Worries

Allergies

Unsurprisingly, there are lots of conflicting opinions and thoughts around allergies and when and how to introduce foods to prevent them. Dr Robert Wood, director of Pediatric Allergy and Immunology at Johns Hopkins University School of Medicine, commented that when it comes to introducing new foods when weaning: 'You can do whatever you want because we're not sure what makes a difference'[137].

So what do you do? This chapter is no different to any of the others in this book – we give you the facts as they are today and you make the decision on how to apply them to your own family. So with that said, here are your choices and the evidence backing them up as it stands at the time of writing:

Introduce high risk foods only after twelve months
Some institutions[138] recommend introducing high risk foods later and in a gradual manner. High risk foods include:

- Cow's milk
- Eggs
- Nuts
- Soy
- Wheat[139]

It is currently thought that introducing these high risk foods later, once your child's digestive tract is more mature, reduces the chance of developing allergies to them.

This is what the UK Department of Health and many health visitors recommend at the time of writing. The current guidelines were written in 2011; before that, it was thought that introducing high risk foods before twelve months was more likely to *create* an allergy, which is slightly different. However, recommendations change continually as more research is conducted. We wonder whether, by the time you are reading this, the advice will have changed again.

Don't delay introducing high risk foods
Much recent research is showing that delaying the introduction of high risk foods actually can *increase* the risk of allergies[140] [141] [142] [143]. Indeed, a research paper released in February 2014 supports the hypothesis that diverse foods under one means less chance of allergies such as asthma[144].

We often get asked at what age little ones can be introduced to seafood or nuts and parents are often astonished when we reply: 'Provided you have no family history of allergies, you can introduce these foods from six months, if that is what you feel comfortable with'.

Why do we feel this is the case? Well, we have a theory: during the first twelve months, your little one's immune system is developing rapidly. It is working out which things coming into the body are goodies and which are baddies. It's like a game of cops and robbers (but with food it's often a case of mistaken identity!). When a new substance (such as a prawn) is eaten, the immune system, which is like a big army of policemen, approaches the prawn to see if it recognizes it. If it's the first time it has seen its sort, it doesn't recognize it as a good guy, so it presumes it's the enemy (bacteria or a virus) and attacks it. It may take a few meetings for the cops to realize that the prawn isn't a baddie but, as this happens, it will slowly begin to be seen as a new friend, and the cops will begin to call off the attacks. However, it takes time for a true friendship to form and the attack to be completely abandoned. After twelve months, the immune system has matured and decides it's probably got enough new friends and there's no room for any more. This makes it more likely to continually attack new baddies that come in.

Now, we're not saying that *all* or even most new foods introduced after twelve months are going to be treated as baddies, but some foods just look suspicious and are more likely to be attacked. Peanuts, eggs and shellfish all look a bit suspicious and troublesome to the body because their molecular structure appears more similar to what the body recognizes as an antigen, so the immune system is more likely to attack them – hence they are common allergens. In contrast, the molecular structure of broccoli and cucumber, for example, look very innocent and are usually allowed to pass through without any bother. This sounds a lot like what might happen in society – people who are wearing hoodies may be regarded a bit more suspiciously than those who aren't, based purely on their appearance. Now, we know we've simplified this, but hopefully it helps you to understand why introducing these prime suspects before twelve months could help the body to include them in the 'friends' category and

not attack them – thus preventing allergies later on.

To all of you parents with medical knowledge, we apologize for the crude explanation but we're sure you get our meaning!

Interestingly, families with a history of allergies are often more hesitant to introduce high risk foods but 'Insufficient evidence exists for delaying introduction of solid foods, including potentially allergenic foods, beyond four to six months of age, even in infants at risk'[145].

THE EAT STUDY

At the time of writing, an interesting study called the EAT (Enquiring About Tolerance) Study is taking place. Funded by the Food Standards Agency and Medical Research Council, its aim is to find out whether introducing certain foods early in a child's diet alongside breastfeeding could prevent a food allergy from developing. The study has recruited 1,302 children; one group will be exposed to six allergenic foods from three months of age (alongside breastfeeding) and the other group will continue to follow existing recommended guidelines. The children will be monitored until they are three years of age to see whether the early diet has reduced the prevalence of food allergies[146]. We eagerly await the results of this study so that parents and health professionals may be better informed and new guidelines around food introduction and allergies can be created if necessary.

Introduce new foods one at a time

There are some health institutions that recommend introducing each new food to your child one at a time[147 148]. This is to enable you to spot a potential allergen or intolerance food quickly, not because the method will have any effect on whether your child will be

Shutterstock

Serving one food in different ways will give your child choice.

allergic to it. It makes sense that if you introduce lots of foods together (as in a spaghetti bolognese) you won't be able to spot the culprit should a reaction occur.

Choice is crucial to your child's eating – it expands the palate and their ability to accept new foods so introducing one new food at a time can make for a rather boring plate of food. If you feel this is the best approach for you and your baby then, when you introduce a new food, try and use your imagination to serve it in different ways. If, for example, you choose to introduce eggs then consider hard-boiling a couple of eggs (allow to cool and peel). Thinly slice one of the eggs and serve the other whole. This same food will now be experienced in two different ways (yes, introducing 'different' food experiences, as far as your baby is concerned, can be as simple as slicing or leaving whole the same food). You may serve up scrambled egg, poached egg, just the white, just the yolk – all will go a small way to help your child expand

their palate whilst also giving you the comfort that you are monitoring which foods are interacting with their digestive system.

What are the signs of an allergic reaction?

- Skin reactions: a red rash, a blotchy and/or itchy swelling of the mouth, itchy eyes
- A stomach upset
- A runny nose
- Breathing difficulties

If *any* of these occur, talk to your GP. If you think your baby is suffering from a severe allergic reaction, always call 999 and ask for a paramedic.

Felicity and Lucas

When my little munchkin was eight months old he developed a reaction to a food. I still have no idea which food (I tried to establish this without success) but it began by my noticing a small rash on his cheek which within a few minutes had spread to his eyebrows and forehead. We went to urgent care, the GP prescribed antihistamines and that was that. I hadn't introduced anything new that I had known about but I guess that's just the way it goes.

Gagging

While your baby is working out how to swallow food, they may occasionally gag and may even vomit. Gagging is what happens when the 'gag reflex' is triggered and your child's mouth ejects the food. This is normal and means that your baby's gag reflex is working correctly. Choking involves food getting stuck in your child's airway, blocking or partially blocking it, and is very different to gagging. With choking, food has gone beyond the gag reflex.

The gag reflex is there to prevent things being swallowed that shouldn't be. It prevents children from swallowing toys and other objects that often go in their mouths (babies put things in their mouths as a way of learning about objects and the world around them and 'mouthing' is an important part of child development).

In adults, the gag reflex is often triggered voluntarily as a way of trying to induce vomiting. You may have heard this referred to as 'sticking your fingers down your throat'. If you've ever had to do this, you will know that the reflex in adults is quite far back (roughly the length of your middle finger). However, in younger babies, the 'trigger zone' for the gag reflex is a lot further forward in the mouth. Again, this may well be related to survival – your little one's digestive system can't cope with solid foods or foreign bodies at first, so the body has put a mechanism in place to eject them if they find their way too far into the mouth.

With the gag reflex initially being so far forward, it is natural that spoons, little fingers and first foods will trigger this reflex, so gagging is likely to occur when you first start weaning. The first time it happens, you will probably be more alarmed than your little one. Chances are, they will just spit out the food and carry on without being bothered by it at all. Remember, children are very in-tune with your body language and emotions so, even if you are panicking inside, try and remain calm. Gagging and choking are not the same thing.

It takes time and trial and error for that reflex 'trigger zone' to recede. Your baby is working on that throughout the weaning

Key point:

Gagging and choking are different. The first is a normal part of exploring food and the second requires urgent medical attention.

process and most children, by eight to nine months, will have little or no gag reflex when self-feeding[149] provided that they have had the opportunity to explore food. This is the reason nutrition plays no part in the solid-food eating process until around nine months – your child has been practising eating until this point.

In one qualitative study, it was found that 30% of parents reported one or more episodes of choking with baby-led weaning. However, all parents who reported choking also reported that their child independently dealt with the choking by expelling the food from their mouth through coughing, and that parents did not have to intervene with first aid. The majority of these parents blamed raw apple as the food responsible for the choking event[150].

It's worth considering that babies are likely to cough when food even slightly feels like it might go down the wrong way; they are more sensitive to these sensations than we are as adults. However, even as adults, we'd see a significant difference between something 'going down the wrong way', when we would cough and drink water in an attempt to help calm it down, and 'choking', where someone's windpipe is blocked by food and which could prove fatal (in this instance, someone often performs the Heimlich manoeuvre to dislodge the food). One is a reasonably regular occurrence, showing how we still misjudge the eating process as

Children interact with toys in the same way they do with food. By having toys at the table your child may focus on 'playing' with those and not the food.

adults, and the other is a potentially life-threatening event that never occurs for many of us. For your child, it's also pretty common that they'll misjudge the handling of food in their mouths and cough to expel it. Parents may also be extremely sensitive to signs that their child is having difficulty with foods and label an episode choking when it's simply one of these minor occurrences. This can needlessly increase anxiety – real choking is much less common.

Choking is more likely when hard foods such as raw apple or round, coin-shaped foods, including slices of sausage, are offered to children, or when the child is distracted while eating[15]. This is a good reason to ensure that the television, toys and books are kept away from your child at meal-times. However, just because research has shown choking is more likely to happen with foods such as raw apple, this doesn't mean

it *will* happen. We always recommend halving spherical or coin-shaped foods, such as grapes and cherry tomatoes, just in case though. If you are nervous about raw apple, why not try grating the apple, which will offer your child a new taste and texture experience while ensuring you feel comfortable with the situation.

Avoid offering food to your child also when they are lying back in a car seat or in a bouncer. Feeding in the correct position will help you to avoid the dangers of choking. To ensure the gag reflex is triggered, your little one needs to be sitting upright, so that when food hits the trigger zone, it can be moved forward – either to be chewed some more or spat out. There is no reason that your child should be more likely to choke when eating 'real' foods (as opposed to purée), as long as you follow the basic guidelines on p.103.

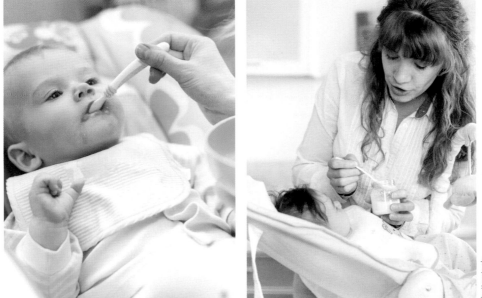

Serving food in a reclined position may increase the chances of choking.

If I skip purées, is my child more likely to gag or choke?

Many parents are put off serving their baby family foods because they are concerned about gagging or choking. Choking can happen to anybody, including adults. It is very unlikely that a baby would choke when eating family foods because, initially, only large pieces of food should be served. If your baby isn't developmentally ready to swallow then they are unlikely to be able to bite off a choke-size chunk and move it to the back of their mouth to swallow it – this is a sort of natural protection. It could be considered that choking is actually more likely when feeding a child with a spoon or putting small finger-foods into their mouth for them, because you are not allowing them to control the process or allowing their body to protect them as it was designed to do.

Serve foods in a way that you feel comfortable with

For some parents, the idea of following baby-led weaning and serving their baby a large piece of steak or a sprig of broccoli as a first food doesn't feel quite right, yet neither does the idea of parent-led weaning, involving puréeing carrots and shovelling them into their little one's mouth. You may love the idea of serving your child real, home-cooked food but find yourself resorting to purée pouches

> **Key point:**
>
> **Always sit and eat with your child to ensure a quick response should they choke or get into difficulty whilst eating.**

Children may initially eat a food readily and then suddenly stop eating it. This is far from uncommon.

because someone tells you there is a risk of choking or because you believe they contain all the vitamins and minerals your baby needs (this is actually not true – see p.127).

You may have heard the saying in the baby-led weaning world that 'Your baby eats what you eat' and many parents embrace this, while for others it doesn't feel quite right. So let's confirm this now:

~~'Your baby eats what you eat'~~

'Your baby should be offered a range of foods in forms you feel comfortable with'

Likewise, if you're worrying about choking while you're weaning, it will definitely intrude on fun food time with your little one. So go with what works for you. Give yourself permission to serve food combinations that *you* think are suitable, rather than looking to your mummy-friends or family for guidance; but always allow your child to self-feed. Self-

feeding and the benefits it can bring to your child are discussed in more detail on pp.170–75. Remember … you don't need to label yourself. It's highly unlikely that you and your baby are going to fit exactly into either one of these moulds so instead form your own approach to weaning, armed with the information and facts to make valid choices.

Neophobia – the fear of new foods!

You only have a small window of opportunity when your newly weaned child will readily accept most new foods. Once your child begins to walk, a protective mechanism called neophobia kicks in, which may turn your once happy eater into a suspicious child who is fearful of new foods. Don't be surprised if you hear yourself uttering, 'I don't know what happened – he used to eat everything …'.

Neophobia refers to a fear of new things, and is a phenomenon that developed when our ancestors were hunter-gatherers. Try to picture daily life during the caveman era: once cave-babies could walk they would have been able to toddle around, picking and eating berries and leaves from branches that could be poisonous. So neophobia is a natural survival mechanism in all of us and it is normal for any young child when they start to walk to be suspicious of new food, or to refuse it initially. It doesn't mean they're being difficult or that they don't like what you're offering – it means they don't know it well enough yet.

You've probably heard more people say they don't like brussels sprouts than potatoes. This is no coincidence since research has found that neophobia is more commonly directed at cabbages, broccoli and brussels sprouts – plants whose leaves contain poisonous compounds which are difficult to digest[152].

In a survey of almost 600 2–6-year-old children, neophobia was significantly negatively associated with fruit, vegetables and meat[153] but not starchy foods, cakes and biscuits[154]. Why is this? One idea is that children are biologically wired to be attracted to calorie-dense foods because when food was scarce and humans didn't have three square meals a day, we needed to ingest as much high-calorie food as possible, whenever we found it. Neophobia would have hindered that. Another idea is that things like cakes and biscuits were not part of our diet back in caveman times, so we didn't develop an instinct to 'avoid' these foods. Another theory for an aversion to meat is that it bears no similarity to any toy. The colour, texture, shape and sensation in the mouth is not like anything that has been experienced before and so the newness can be scary for a child. Of course, if a child has been allowed to self-feed real food from the beginning then meat

may pose less of a problem but for a child who has only experienced puréed meat it will be frightening. The same goes for all foods – allowing a child to see a food in its natural state, looking like real food rather than mixed in with a cheese sauce or blitzed in a food processor, will increase familiarity. Experiencing foods in different ways will help build a child's food database so experiencing carrots growing in the garden or picking strawberries from the plant, seeing pictures in books and playing with real-looking foods, will all help build familiarity and when the time for neophobia comes around, your child will not be scared of these foods since they are already familiar.

Another theory as to why sprouts may be a problem but cakes are not is that children are predisposed to reject foods with a bitter taste. As well as the caveman instinct to avoid sour and bitter foods in case they are poisonous, approximately 70% of humans have been found to be especially sensitive to bitter tastes and this is down to genetics. Studies of pre-school children have shown that children who are genetically predisposed to be sensitive to bitter tastes are less likely to eat green vegetables (e.g. sprouts and broccoli) and say that they're 'yummy'[155]. Being one of these 'bitter-sensitive' people might have been an evolutionary advantage for survival if you and your baby were foraging for food in the wild, which is what we used to do. A bitter taste is one indication that a plant may be poisonous, which explains why toddlers may be particularly keen to avoid anything with even a slight bitter taste. For example, most children don't like olives, yet as adults many of us love them. How did that happen? We *learned* to love them, after trying them again and again because so many people around us eat them all the time and seem to enjoy them so

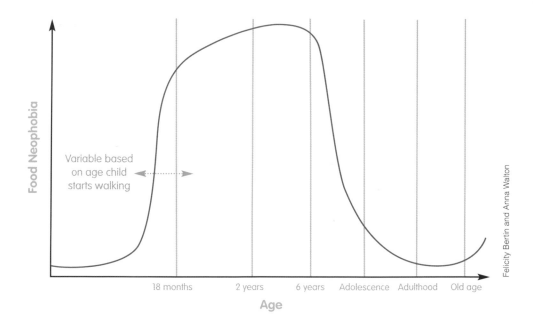

A potential lifespan model for food neophobia.

much. We may not have realized that we were exposing ourselves and our taste buds over and over again to their flavour in response to the social cues we consistently received from other people, but that's how it works[156]. Is there anything you hated as a child but have now learned to love? Then you've overcome neophobia too!

The good news about neophobia in children is that it appears to be age-dependent. It is at its lowest during weaning, starts to increase as a child walks and then peaks from two to six years[157][158]. It then starts to decrease until adulthood where it appears to stabilize[159], presumably because fewer foods are truly new to us and we have established our likes and dislikes. This decrease in neophobia can again be traced back to how our human race has survived: humans have diverse nutritional needs and these nutrients can only be gained from eating a varied diet[160].

(Interestingly, neophobia is often seen to recur in elderly[161] people, possibly because they are reluctant to try new foods for fear of it making them ill – a protective mechanism, perhaps, to prolong their life.)

Eat the same foods as your child to counter neophobia

Neophobia has actually helped the human race to survive – this fear of new foods and the need for you (or whoever is the caregiver) to show that a food is safe before your child puts it in their mouth are completely normal. That's another reason why, when eating with your child, you should also eat the same foods, as this reassures them that the food is safe to eat. You may not naturally want to eat at the same time of day as your child, so you might take a tiny portion of your lunch or dinner and eat it with them, saving the rest for later.

Historically, kings, queens and other people of importance would have had a

Children often eat better together due to their need to feel included.

'taster' sample their food to prove it wasn't poisonous. Your child looks to you as their taster and when you're not around, maybe at nursery, they may look to their peers. Your child may infuriate you by being fussy at home but eating well at nursery – there, not only do they have their tasters proving the food is safe to eat but they also have the social pressure to feel included and fit in with what everyone else is doing. The drive to fit in is a powerful force, again because at the most basic level fitting in means survival.

> **Key point:**
>
> **Your child looks to you for assurance that the food is safe to eat. Give them this assurance by eating with them.**

New taste, smell, texture, shape, name = new food

Be patient with your child's neophobia. Remember, you have decades of food experiences to draw on (think back to pp.63-6) when trying something new and yet you will *still* do everything you can to minimize the element of surprise in a new food. If someone tells you that its texture is just like semolina, which you dislike, you might think: 'Ugh, I won't like it' and you might then not even try it.

Gemma

I grew up not liking peppers. I don't think I'd ever actually tried one but because of the name I thought it was like the pepper my parents would shake over their food and I didn't like the smell of. It wasn't until I was well into my twenties that I actually tried a pepper in chicken fajitas

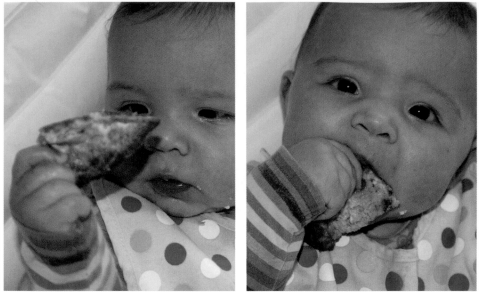

Jules McEachran

This child visually assesses the food, confirms it is safe to eat and puts it in her mouth to explore it further.

and realized they tasted nothing like pepper seasoning!

I also never liked olives as a child or coffee as a teenager. I tasted one olive once and then would never try one again, even though I saw adults eating olives throughout my childhood — my mum would put them out as a snack whenever we had visitors. Everyone had coffee after family dinners or lunches, and my parents drank it in the mornings. I clearly remember, when I was older, consciously thinking that olives can't be that bad because so many people seem to enjoy them, and making an effort to try them a few times. Once I became accustomed to their flavour, I loved them!! The same thing applied to coffee — people were always telling me: 'I can't do without my cup of coffee' and I couldn't work out why because it was so bitter! Nevertheless, I concluded over a period of years that it must be something delicious, from the way

people behaved. So I started trying it from time to time in my late teenage years and found a way to make it palatable for me — I sweetened it. I still don't drink it that much but, when I do, I genuinely like it! In hindsight, I think I must be one of those people who are predisposed to be sensitive to bitter tastes, as I still enjoy it less without sugar!

At the moment, for your child, *anything* different about a food makes it a completely new food (e.g. a roasted carrot is different to a carrot in a casserole). A new texture, a new appearance, a new temperature, a new name – all of these elements make foods different. Your child is also not yet able to cognitively categorize objects, so that includes food. That's why many toddlers might accept one pasta shape and not another – they haven't yet developed the ability to categorize.

Over time, your child's categorizing will improve and they will stop putting things in their mouth which aren't intended to be eaten. The categories that your child will form may start to affect their eating. They may then create a category for 'foods I like' and 'foods I don't like' or 'things that are disgusting' and 'things that are okay'. These categories aren't fixed and food can be moved between them, so don't stop exposing them to any foods, just because they tell you they're in the 'disgusting' category!

Facilitating your child to enjoy different flavours

It's very simple: keep offering different flavours to your child. Children under twelve months old need, on average, only one exposure to a food in order to add it to their repertoire of 'safe foods'[162]. You have a limited opportunity during this period to have almost every new food you introduce tried (as long as you follow the steps of eating it too).

For children over twelve months, on average an unfamiliar food needs to be experienced between sixteen and twenty times before it is accepted. (Remember, this is an average and some foods will be accepted immediately, while others may take longer[163][164].) Your child's database at the time of eating

---

> **Key point:**
>
> **Repetition is paramount when it comes to facilitating your child to enjoy new flavours. Research shows that new foods are routinely offered sixteen to twenty times before they are accepted.**

---

has a big effect on this. For example, does the new food smell like something they have experienced before? Does it resemble something they like? Is the name familiar?

There are so many external factors that come into play here that no two children are the same, which is why we cannot tell you exactly how many exposures it will take before your child will try something. All we can do is assure you that if you continue to offer the same food over and over again and model eating it then it will gradually become a 'safe' food and your child will be more inclined to taste it.

One study conducted showed that children aged over seven years' repeated consumption of an unfamiliar food led to an increased liking for this food. This wasn't limited to sweet-tasting or bland foods, but also included foods that many adults are reluctant to eat such as liver, mustard and cabbage[165].

Hesitation and wariness around new foods is a protective mechanism to avoid those bitter and sour foods that are more likely to be poisonous (see pp.116–18 for more on this). This principle is fairly logical – would you eat an old, sour-smelling piece of fruit or would you throw it away and eat a fresh, sweet-smelling one? It is interesting, therefore, to consider that the rejection of the food doesn't occur during tasting, since that would risk poisoning, but happens primarily on what your child sees. So foods that do not 'look right' will be initially rejected based on vision alone[166]. With this in mind, you can see why offering foods in their 'real' state from the beginning is so important. If your child is only used to carrots hidden in a cheese sauce or puréed into mush, when it comes to experiencing a carrot in its true form, they are more likely to reject it. So don't be tempted to hide the veggies – you are simply delaying the problem for another day, and as your child gets older, those neural pathways become harder to change. Tackle the problem today. Below is a summary of how a new food is experienced in a child over twelve months:

Step 1: the food is recognized and accepted visually
Step 2: the food is tasted
Step 3: the taste is assessed subjectively (is it yummy or disgusting?). This step is strongly related to familiarity (is it 'like' anything else I already know?)
Step 4: the visual image is associated with the taste and this new taste begins to have its own set of associations which create familiarity as neural pathways are created in the brain
Step 5: repeated positive experiences lower the reluctance to eat it – a stronger sense of familiarity is created as neural pathways are strengthened

It's worth noting that likes and dislikes are unstable until a child is roughly five years old, so just because the taste in Step 3 is considered 'disgusting', that doesn't mean it will stay that way. (See pp.75–6 for more on this.)

With the visual domain being the foundation for food rejection, consider HOW you serve a new food. Each time you offer the same food in a different way, it is experienced differently. So the experience of grated carrot and carrot in a casserole should be

> **Key point:**
>
> **It is your job as a parent to give your child the opportunity to populate their database with a wide range of foods.**

treated as two separate food experiences since that is how your child will experience them. For more on this see pp.78–9.

Spoon-feeding your child prevents them from going through the natural developmental process of recognizing and accepting a food visually, which enables them to feel secure enough with it to put it in their mouth. This is potentially why children who self-feed are less likely to become fussy eaters, since they are rehearsed and practised in following this process.

Taste and texture are symbiotic. Studies have shown that if you increase the range of textures a child will eat then they will naturally accept a wider range of flavours[167][168]. This

> **Key point:**
>
> **Each time you offer the same food in a different way, it is experienced differently.**

+ + + Tip + + +

It may sound like bad manners and behaviour you want to discourage, but allowing your older child to spit things out when they don't like them can be helpful when it comes to introducing new foods. Many parents find the approach of 'we try everything once but we don't have to swallow' makes trying a less frightening experience. Follow with a big drink of water if necessary.

+ + + + + + + + +

works the other way too, in that if you offer a wider variety of tastes then more textures will be accepted. This is another reason for home-cooked food to be served to your baby since no two attempts at the same recipe are going to be exactly the same. Serving plates of food with a variety of tastes and textures will be beneficial to your child in so many ways.

It's contaminated!

As categories start to form regarding likes and dislikes (which aren't stable under the age of five but are definitely experienced by children in the moment), there can come a point for the older toddler or child where they perceive that a 'liked' food has been contaminated if it's touched a 'disliked' food. Research has shown that children as young as twenty months will downgrade a food that was previously 'liked' to a 'dislike' category if it has touched a disliked food – but that doesn't mean it will stay there[169]. It also doesn't mean that the disliked food will continue to be disliked forever. If your little one is showing signs of going through this phase it can be helpful to serve a new food on a separate plate and resist the urge to hide foods – if your child finds you out, the trust between you is potentially rocked and it's simply not worth it.

If your child rejects the new food, tell them that's fine, they just haven't tried it enough times. Instead of taking it away, just leave it there (wherever you put it originally) so that your child doesn't get used to you removing foods the minute they say they don't like something. If you go down that road of removing foods, then before long your child may not even tolerate the presence of a 'disliked' food near them – you can imagine how difficult it would be to go from there to trying it again, let alone accepting it!

If you remove the food, it also prevents your child from changing their mind, or trying it later on in the meal – although this may not happen often, it is worth at least leaving the door open for things to change. For example, a 'disliked' food that has been repeatedly left on their plate (so at least your child is familiar with it) may be encountered in another situation (e.g. at a friend's house) where they may decide to copy their friend, who happens to love it, and try the food on their own.

It's worth noting that, if you, as a parent, are extremely anxious or see elements of Obsessive Compulsive Disorder (OCD) in yourself, your child will pick up on this and they may manifest your anxiety about cleanliness by thinking that foods are 'dirty' if they are touched by other foods. In this case, it's really best to seek professional help to manage your anxiety or OCD. Under these circumstances, concerns about contamination may represent more than your child going through a food-related phase, reflecting instead that they are beginning to feel anxious or develop obsessive ways of thinking themselves (see the case study on p.173 for how this can manifest in bigger issues).

OCD is characterized by having uncontrollable intrusive and unwanted thoughts that can lead you to feel compelled to perform certain behaviours. You will probably know that they're irrational but feel unable to stop yourself performing them. Examples of common areas of compulsive behaviour are:

- washing or cleaning, underpinned by feeling anxious about or afraid of contamination, lack of cleanliness or bacteria
- checking things several times that you associate with danger; e.g. repeatedly checking that the door is locked or the oven is off, or checking loved ones are okay

Shutterstock

Grated carrot and whole carrot are experienced by your child as two different foods.

- extreme perfectionism, often under-pinned by a fear that if things aren't done perfectly something terrible will happen
- arranging/counting things, and feeling obsessed with order or symmetry. You might feel extremely superstitious about certain colours, arrangements or numbers or you may repeat certain words obsessively
- hoarding, characterized by feeling too anxious to ever throw anything away, being afraid that something terrible will happen if you do
- having a lot of intrusive and uncontrol-lable thoughts or ideas (these can be extreme and violent/sexual in nature and a lot of people who have these feel ashamed and embarrassed, so will never tell anyone about them but instead think they must be 'abnormal' – they aren't)

These points are not intended to 'diagnose' in any way, but rather to share with you some signs to look out for, because having OCD is nothing to be ashamed of and it can be very isolating if you don't get help. OCD is often rooted in an overwhelming sense of anxiety, fear and responsibility and many of the symptoms above become ways to manage that anxiety that may feel like they work in the moment but don't actually work in the long run. If you experience any of these symptoms to the point where you feel troubled by them, we would strongly recommend that you go and see your GP so that they can help you. Please don't suffer alone; there are many ways to treat OCD and therapy can really help.

Don't give up!

Remember: studies show that a new food needs to be offered between sixteen and twenty times on average before it is accepted visually and tried [170]. This probably sounds like you'll have to deal with a lot of rejection! All that precious time spent lovingly cooking and preparing food, only for it to be refused, can be disheartening but remember you are working with a primitive response in your baby – they aren't rejecting you. This repeated offering of new foods will not guarantee your baby is going to like all new flavours, but it is a necessary part of helping them to develop a broad palate.

Recall the categories your child will form. If the name, shape or appearance of the food changes, it will be experienced differently and as a new food. Don't be surprised if a carrot chopped and included in a stew is eaten yet a carrot presented as a side-dish is refused. It's unfamiliar and they are naturally hesitant.

Jo and Imogen

Imogen will happily eat tomatoes. She will eat them raw, cooked, as cherry tomatoes or beef tomatoes, and she loves spaghetti bolognese. But when it comes to meatballs, she painstakingly scrapes them, removing all trace of the tomatoes before they go in her mouth. I have explained so many times that the sauce is tomatoes and she likes them but it doesn't get us anywhere. I guess only time will help her move on from this.

Jo is absolutely right to take this approach. It is Imogen's prerogative to choose which of the foods presented on her plate she wants to eat and if she doesn't want the tomatoes then that is her decision. One day, the connection and categorization may be made

to bring tomatoes under the meatball category (or maybe it won't), but either way this is not Jo's decision and taking a step back and allowing Imogen to make this decision herself is a stress-free approach.

Increasing familiarity is key

Your baby needs to become familiar with a new food so that the suspicion can wane and a positive association can be created, and this takes time. If you miss this step, you will not stimulate the taste buds or the neurons that enable your child to connect a new flavour with pleasure.

Research conducted in 2007 [171] took a group of parents who were anxious that their 7-month-old babies were refusing a certain vegetable. They had offered the same vegetable three times and each time it had been rejected. The parents continued to offer the same vegetable every other day and, after eight offerings, over 70% of babies had not only accepted the vegetable but were then eating it in the same quantity as other foods. From this, it was concluded that they 'liked it'. Nine months later, 75% of the babies (who were now toddlers) were still eating that vegetable when offered.

Offer a rejected food to your child every other day

As a parent, you are frequently going to experience your child rejecting food. It is part of their normal development. However, just because your child didn't choose to accept that food then and there, that shouldn't put you off serving it again.

A study in 2004 [172] showed that 25% of parents give up after serving a refused fruit or vegetable once or twice. Only 1–2% of parents persevere more than ten times. Why is it that many of us are happy to serve baby rice more than a dozen times before moving on to another food, but not happy to commit to the same with fruits or vegetables? Ask yourself: which foods would you want to feature several times a day in your child's diet in ten years' time? It's unlikely to be baby rice, or even rice pudding – a grown-up equivalent!

Have you considered why as a parent you might not persevere with serving those foods repeatedly? Do you feel rejected? Maybe you don't like waste? It's important to make sure that your behaviour around food is not dictated by your own emotions, which are not related to what your child is experiencing. For example, your child is not trying to reject you by refusing a food – it's because they don't feel familiar and 'safe' with that food.

It's inevitable that your child will reject food at some point in their early years and, as a parent, it's your job to manage that rejection so that your child doesn't become a fussy eater. So *when*, not if, your child rejects food, you should continue to offer it, but rotate it with other foods. You don't want to establish a pattern of rejection of a particular food, and you don't want to pressurize your child with any one food. The most important thing is to understand that food rejection is a normal part of familiarization with that food.

After you offer a new food, allow at least a day or so before offering it again. Food rotation is an important part of preventing food habits. Serve a small portion (perhaps a teaspoon), so that your child feels that they only need to eat a small amount of it. If your child is talking, a claim like 'I don't like it' or 'bleugh' should be met with 'That's okay, you've just not tried it enough times yet', then move on to talking about something else. As your child gets older, introduce statements into daily life like 'We try everything once', which can easily be transferred to food. So if

your child is about to ride a scooter, go to nursery or water the plants in the garden, a reminder of the statement 'We try everything once' will soon become familiar and when it's mentioned around a new food you may find they are more willing to 'try'.

Gemma and Clara

We have a rule in our house that we 'try everything' and that applies to everyone in our family. In the past, Mummy has had to try riding Clara's new bike and Daddy has had to try doing a roly-poly but this is what we do. Of course, it also applies to food — everyone tries everything. It's okay to spit it out, have a big gulp of water afterwards and not eat any more, but this is how our family unit works. We often say things like 'We are Frasers and this is what Frasers do' (Fraser is our last name), which gives us a sense of being included in the family unit. Being pregnant, this 'try everything' rule hasn't been easy for me — some days I really do not fancy trying the banana-mushed porridge, but Clara tells me 'try everything, Mummy' and I always try a tiny bit because I know it's paramount that I model what I'm teaching her.

What looks like 'I don't like it' is often 'I'm not familiar with it'.

Shutterstock

James, Iona and Beatrice

My husband hates broccoli, but it's important that my daughter sees him eating it so whenever broccoli is served he has the smallest floret he can find on his plate. As time has gone on, my husband has started having a single larger floret. My daughter nibbles the bushy part and my husband eats the stalk, which she finds hilarious!

I want to know how much my baby is eating

If your baby is self-feeding, it can be worrying to think that they aren't eating enough to get the raw materials to grow, and it's hard to tell exactly how much they've eaten as so much ends up on the floor or in their hair! Your friends might tell you to spoon-feed because then at least you will know for sure that enough has gone into your child's mouth. This concept of 'not knowing' can be quite worrying and is one of the most common reasons we hear as to why parents resort to spoon-feeding their children.

Let's look at the reality of this. In an ideal world, you would have exclusively breastfed until this point – but you would not have had the faintest idea how many ounces or millilitres of milk your baby had consumed. Together you would have established an understanding whereby your baby gave you cues that they were hungry and you responded with the breast for them to take as much or as little as they wished. They then would have given you another cue that they had finished. If you have been breastfeeding, this has worked successfully and allowed your baby to thrive and grow until now. So why mess with this system? It is as old as the

human race and has been thoroughly tried and tested.

Why, at the introduction of solids, do you suddenly think that you know how hungry/full your child is? The short answer is 'You don't'. Why would you stop trusting them to know when they're hungry and when they have had enough food? You don't know if they're teething and the food on offer today is irritating their gums, just as you don't know whether they are improving their efficiency as a feeder and accessing more of the fatty hindmilk and so are feeling less hungry. You *can't* know these things. An exclusively breastfed baby has an amazing gift of being able to self-regulate – don't come along and switch off that innate knowledge by believing the myths and hype that the baby food corporations would have you believe, that finishing off a jar or purée pouch is what your baby needs.

Another reason many parents turn to jars and pouches when introducing solid food is to ensure that their baby gets adequate nutrition. With meals advertised such as 'chicken and parsnip bake' it seems like a great way to get both protein and vegetables into your little one. Yet research has shown that many of the most popular brands contain less than a fifth of a baby's recommended daily supply of calcium, magnesium, zinc, iron and other crucial minerals[173].

Managing uncertainty

Many people find it difficult to handle uncertainty in life – it makes them feel more secure to think that they can control what's going to happen. Have you ever met someone who needs to plan everything and gets upset if they don't know in advance exactly what's happening during a day out, or on holiday? That's just an example of someone who finds uncertainty particularly difficult to handle.

Feeding your baby is understandably something that any parent wants to get 'right' – your need to nourish your baby for their survival is as strongly programmed into you as their need to eat for survival is programmed into them. But in order to get it 'right' you need to have control over it, don't you? Well no, actually, you don't have to have *all* the control. You haven't had all the control right from the beginning, but you might not have thought of it like that.

The chances are that you may not have consciously thought of the 'eating relationship' between you and your baby in terms of who has control while you were breastfeeding, but actually you are sharing control – they ask, you provide; they decide when they've finished and you withdraw your breast. You may not have realized that your baby is regulating their own food intake successfully while breastfeeding but they are.

Formula-fed babies do not necessarily perform in the same way with regards to self-regulation of milk feeds. They typically consume more milk at each feed than breastfed babies. One large study of 16,755 babies compared feeding volumes in formula-fed and breastfed babies and found that the formula-fed babies consumed 49% more milk at one month of age, 57% at three months of age, and 71% at five months of age[174].

So why do formula-fed babies consume more milk than breastfed babies?

- Breastfeeding has a natural ebb and flow due to the let-down reflex. The let-down reflex occurs when the baby starts suckling at the breast, which triggers the milk to start flowing. In contrast, the bottle provides a constant flow, meaning that greater consumption is more likely

- Not seeing how much milk is in the breast makes a breastfeeding mother less likely to coax her baby to continue after the baby is full[175]
- One of the key things breast milk contains that formula milk is missing is a hormone called leptin[176]. Leptin helps provide a feeling of fullness. It's interesting that sugar has been shown to down-regulate the hormone leptin, one of the reasons why you can keep munching sweets even though you're full!

With this in mind, it's not surprising that one study found that between six and twelve months of age breastfeeding mothers gave their babies less encouragement to eat solid foods and were more sensitive to their babies' cues[177].

If your baby has been allowed to self-regulate their eating up to now then you can trust them to do the same once solids come into the equation. This applies irrespective of whether you've been offering the breast or bottle until now. But remember, weaning isn't about withdrawing milk and leaving your baby to regulate their food intake in a whole world of completely strange food items. It is about offering milk while introducing new foods so that your child can *learn* how hungry or satisfied they feel when they eat certain foods, and for how long.

Your child's relationship with food (and you) will thrive if you continue to share the power as you did if you breastfed. Power struggles start when the parent tries to take too much control away from the child, so you're much more likely to avoid these issues if you become aware of your own feelings about 'not knowing'. Are you preoccupied with getting it 'right' to the extent that not knowing exactly how much your baby is consuming feels very difficult for you? If this idea feels familiar then the best thing you can do is to acknowledge that those are *your* worries, and that if you just act on them (i.e. by trying to persuade or insist that your child eats a certain food or eats a particular amount) then it's about what makes *you* feel better; you're getting caught up in accommodating *your* needs rather than your baby's, instead of finding a balance where you're accommodating both. From your baby's perspective, you're suddenly taking away their half of the control, which they've always had, and so they are, of course, going to resist it.

The truth is that the amount of uncertainty you have to handle once your little one starts eating solids isn't any different to the uncertainty many breastfeeding mothers encounter. Even if you feel like you didn't handle that uncertainty very well and you were worried about your child's intake initially, you managed, and you and your baby coped together, because as long as your body was producing enough milk and your baby could physically feed well, you couldn't consciously control their eating. Even now, whilst they are learning to eat, there's little chance that the average child isn't getting enough nutrition as long as milk is still available for them while they learn (see p.131 for information about vitamins and minerals).

> ### Key point:
>
> **Weaning is about offering milk while introducing new foods so that your child can *learn* how hungry or satisfied they feel when they eat certain foods, and for how long.**

So just try to bear your baby's perspective in mind and remind yourself that the most important thing is to keep sharing control, just as you have for so many months. That way you're doing what's best for your baby and, together, you'll figure out the rest.

Should I feed on-demand or follow a routine?

It's a battle that has raged on for years – whether to feed on-demand or follow a routine. As with most things, when you become a parent, it's up to you, but it's useful to have as much information as you can before making a decision. There will be lots of factors affecting your decision such as siblings, work and sleep but choosing to feed on-demand has an impact on your child's developing eating habits.

Non-responsive feeding

Eating based on the time of day rather than whether we feel hungry is one problem with our Western 'three meals a day' tradition – it dulls our sensitivity to our body's signals and can encourage us to overeat or to eat when we aren't actually hungry.

The infant equivalent of our 'three meals a day' eating pattern is non-responsive feeding. This is thought to override the child's internal hunger and satiety regulatory cues, causing the child to lose the ability to accurately respond to their own physical hunger signals[178]. This means that instead of managing their eating through these signals, a child learns to eat according to external cues, for example, at set times or whenever food is available. Logically, a child may then regularly begin to make choices to eat irrespective of whether they're hungry, and their ability to self-regulate will continue to be compromised. An example of how this could manifest might be that a child continues to ask for more of a certain food at a meal when they are no longer hungry, simply because they like it. If this behaviour becomes established, it can lead to overeating. A recent review on the development of healthy eating habits early in life found that responsive feeding was one of the most important practices for encouraging healthy eating habits and should be encouraged to reduce the risk of obesity[179].

Responsive feeding

By feeding on-demand, your child is learning to self-regulate and eat based on hunger rather than on the clock. As a newborn, your baby's primary need and greatest pleasure is feeding. For your baby's brain to develop optimally, the emotional brain needs nurturing. Your ability as a parent to respond sensitively and appropriately to your child's needs and emotions plays a big part in your baby's development into a confident, independent child (and later, adult). Developing a feeding-on-demand relationship, where your baby understands that you respond quickly to their primary need when they express it and that this response brings them pleasure, is therefore one very simple way that you can nurture them emotionally and enhance bonding, right from the beginning.

Research conducted by Oxford University showed that babies fed on-demand had a higher IQ at five years old than babies fed to a routine, yet their mothers were less confident and more tearful[180]. So, as with everything in this book, it's about both of you, and you need to consider your own needs too. It could be argued that an unhappy, tearful mum is not optimal for a baby's development either, as this would be more likely to result in her decreased ability to connect and give energy to the baby. It's about creating a balance that works for you, knowing that there is no right and wrong and that you need to judge what works based on your self-knowledge and your knowledge of your baby's needs.

Does bottle feeding impact on self-regulation?

There is some evidence that bottle-fed babies (regardless of whether the bottle contains breast milk or formula) may lose their ability to self-regulate their appetites[181,182], predisposing them to obesity. Infants who exclusively bottle-feed before four months are more likely to be obese at three years old than those who breastfeed[183]. This is likely because a bottle-fed baby is more likely to drain the bottle (or cup at a later date) than a breastfed baby[184,185]. This can sometimes be due to pressure from mum to finish the bottle and also the fact that bottle-feeding allows an easier flow of milk into the mouth, meaning less effort is required on your child's part to continue feeding. This lack of appetite control can follow a child into adulthood.

Research showing that breastfed babies have improved energy and self-regulation at eighteen to twenty-four months of age[186] helps to support this theory. It is supposed by some that breastfeeding represents a child's first exposure to a baby-led style of feeding but for how many parents is this a purely baby-led approach? Many conversations between new parents and health professionals revolve around routines and, ideally, mother and baby will be coming together and finding a feeding and sleeping routine that works for both of them. This example of a combined approach to feeding, where both the parent's needs and feelings and the baby's needs and feelings are taken into account occurs long before solid foods are introduced because – as most health professionals recognize – the health of both mother and baby are essential. It is not good enough to simply focus on one or the other. It isn't helpful to read a book on routines and sticking to the schedule of four-hourly feeds irrespective of whether you find that it sits well with you, simply because that is what one person says is best. What is optimum is that mother and baby come together to find what works for them as a unit.

How much should my child be eating?

We've said it before but it's worth saying again as it is so important: food is initially for fun and exploration, as most of your baby's nourishment will continue to come from milk feeds. At approximately six months of age babies begin to need more nourishment and, by nine months old, your baby will probably be self-feeding well, so their nutritional needs will mainly be met by food rather than milk. As your baby eats more solids they will naturally take less milk. According to the DH, as a guideline, you should continue to offer 500–600 ml of milk a day up to the age of twelve months but, of course, if your baby is breastfed this number is pretty pointless, so follow your instincts (or if you do need a little more advice, contact your health visitor or GP).

At nine months, the DH recommends your baby should be eating (although we prefer the term 'offered') three balanced meals a day in addition to 500–600 ml of breast or formula milk. They should, on a daily basis, be enjoying:

- Three to four servings of carbohydrates
- Three to four servings of fruit and vegetables
- Two servings of protein

But what is a serving? A good guide is to think of a serving as 1 tbsp for each year of age. A rough guide might be:

Average daily intake

1 year old	2 year old	3 year old
3–4 tbsp fruit or veg	6–8 tbsp fruit or veg	9–12 tbsp fruit or veg
2 tbsp protein	4 tbsp protein	6 tbsp protein
3–4 tbsp bread or cereal	6–8 tbsp bread or cereal	8–12 tbsp bread or cereal

There's no need to place pressure on yourself or your child to eat this volume every day, as in fact the volumes should be averaged out over a seven-day period. Your child's appetite will change depending on how they're feeling and how active their day has been, just like yours, so if they don't want to eat much on one particular day, don't panic. Things will even out over the rest of the week.

When children are learning how to eat, many parents worry that their child undereats yet as children grow and start going to school the worry changes to overeating. Trust your child. Your job isn't to interfere and tell your child how much they should be having and deciding whether they are full or hungry but to teach them to self-regulate and tune in to their own feelings. Self-regulation starts from the moment your baby is born. You respond to their cries for more and wipe up the vomit when they overeat. When you start weaning, your child is learning that they can't eat what they want whenever they want and they start to pace themselves and learn what volumes to consume during meals or snacks. Allowing a child to graze all day removes that learning opportunity.

My child has barely touched their meal. What should I do?

You make the big decisions, your child makes the small ones. You decide which food is served and when and your child decides how much to eat. All parents are going to encounter at least one meal where their child refuses to eat, even those with the best eaters. When this happens, you should make your child aware that, if they decide that they have finished eating, then that is it until the next snack/meal. For example, if they refuse the evening meal then they should be made aware that there will now be no food until the morning. You must then follow this through. You will need to be sure to ask them several times and be very clear so there is no confusion. Your child may still be having milk before bed, which should continue to be offered if the child is under twelve months but any pleas for a banana etc. should be responded to with a reminder that food was offered at dinner and there will be no food until the morning. Some children may wake in the night complaining they're hungry – offering water is fine but don't offer food. Be prepared to serve up an early, hearty breakfast the next morning, as your child is likely to have a large appetite.

As a one-off event, offering a milk feed during the night to a child over twelve months of age will be fine; however, some children continue this pattern long-term. Milk is a meal for children over twelve months. If a child refuses dinner and knows a milk feed will appear before bed, they may start to under-eat to compensate. How you manage this is your decision since you know your family routine better than anyone. Some parents choose to switch this milk feed to water, others choose to move that feed to the morning and others are perfectly happy to offer milk feeds through the night. Whichever path you choose, adjust your solid food expectations accordingly.

Sarah and George

I returned to work and the breastfeeding at night-time was so important to me that I was keen to keep this going. I enjoyed the closeness and connection George and I shared at this special time but he was becoming so fussy at dinner-time. I recognized that my breastfeed in the evening was a meal and this was more important to me than him eating his dinner at nursery so we just carried on as we were. I told nursery that George wasn't to be pressured into eating his food – it was fine, in fact, if he ate nothing at all but he was still to sit at the table with everyone – I decided that he would eat if he was hungry. We were all so much happier and more relaxed. Over time, George started eating his dinner and the breastfeeds reduced – we stopped when we both felt ready.

Sarah and George are a true example of weaning together. Sarah's needs and feelings were just as important as George's. By adjusting the situation to fit their own unique circumstances, they were both happier and a food battle was avoided. It was positive that Sarah was able to find a nursery that listened to and accommodated her individual needs.

Surely purées wouldn't be on sale if they weren't best for my baby?

If most children are not developmentally ready to accommodate food until six months then why are there purées for sale and more and more companies popping up to sell them recommending 'from four months' on the packets? The purpose of a company is to 'generate profits for its shareholders'[187], *not* to look after the well-being of your child. Have you ever thought about how a product that says it contains apple and pear can have such a long shelf-life when those fruits only stay fresh in your fruit bowl for a few days? The answer is in the preparation. The food needs to be cooked at a very high temperature, which kills the bacteria, giving it a longer shelf-life. This process unfortunately also has the effect of killing off a lot of the nutrients and, with that in mind, the 'organic' or 'baby-grade' ingredient claims become pretty much redundant. A similar experience that you could recreate in your kitchen might be boiling your broccoli for an hour and then eating it – it'll be bland, mushy and devoid of nutrients.

My baby is waking at night – they must be hungry!

Waking at night can be for all sorts of reasons – it doesn't necessarily mean your baby is hungry. They may just want a cuddle, they may not know how to get back to sleep, or they may be hot or cold. You wake in the night occasionally and maybe just want to snuggle up to your partner for some comfort – your child can want the same thing too. Studies have shown no link between sleep patterns and the early introduction of solids[188 189].

The Infant Feeding Survey (2010) showed that 26% of babies were introduced to solid foods early because their parent found they were waking during the night and presumed they must be hungry. It was therefore assumed that solid food would encourage them to sleep through. If you are feeling the same, then let's reassure you ...

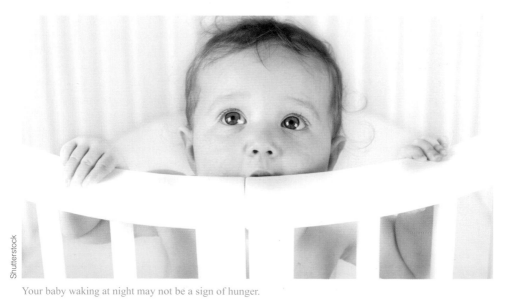

Shutterstock

Your baby waking at night may not be a sign of hunger.

Shutterstock

Children are able to self-regulate their calorie intake but not their nutritional intake.

So why is your baby waking in the night? Well, all babies are different. Some children sleep through from twelve weeks, some from twelve years! Some children eat tiny amounts and sleep consistently well, while others eat plenty and still wake up for one reason or another. Regardless of what your friends say: there is no link between a baby being weaned onto solid foods and their sudden ability to sleep through the night so using that as a justification to introduce solids isn't logical. In fact, introducing solids may mean they wake more, as they will be consuming less sleep-inducing, tummy-filling milk and more fast-digesting fruit and veggies.

When you start weaning, food is for fun, and your little one is trying to figure out how to eat efficiently. Children are not born knowing about food-related feelings and they have to learn to understand hunger and fullness and to regulate their food intake in response. Babies who are allowed to explore their food and feed themselves will probably eat less to begin with than those being spoon-fed, as they are trying to master a number of skills, such as self-feeding, which spoon-fed babies don't need to focus on, as their parents are controlling how food gets from the plate to their mouth. However, they will be drinking more milk to balance this out and so should be no more or less hungry than spoon-fed babies. As your child masters self-feeding, they will naturally reduce their milk feeds to accommodate the fact that they're eating more solid food.

> ### Key point:
>
> **There is no evidence to show that bigger babies benefit from early introduction of solid foods.**

My baby is big so needs solids

For breastfeeding mothers, there can be a sense that you won't be able to produce enough milk to satisfy your big baby. Typically, your breastfed baby will take 76% of the milk stored in the breast, even though there is more available – a sign your little one is already controlling and self-regulating their own food intake[190 191]. If you continue to allow your little one to nurse on-demand, your body will naturally make enough milk to accommodate your growing baby, regardless of weight. Don't be tempted to cut back on milk feeds or introduce solids to bring your baby down a centile or to reduce their weight. Your baby is already able to self-regulate their milk intake and will drink the appropriate volume of milk when allowed and self-detach when satiated. Remember, before nine months old, your baby is getting all the nutrients they need from milk.

My baby is small so needs solids

Breast milk contains more calories than most first foods that children are traditionally introduced to, such as mashed carrot or baby rice. It makes no sense, therefore, that weaning early will help a small baby to grow. The stomach, simplified, is much like a bag. If the bag is filled with solid food then there is less space for milk and your baby's overall intake of calories could, in fact, fall. Don't be tempted to wean early to fatten your baby up – it won't work. In fact, it could contribute to them waking at night and being hungry sooner, particularly if they've eaten something carbohydrate-heavy, energy-poor and easily digested, like carrot, which has left them with less space in their tummy for milk – which contains protein, carbohydrate and fat.

My baby has doubled their birth weight – it's time to wean

A certain weight doesn't mean your baby is ready to experience solid food. There is no evidence that doubling birth weight has anything whatsoever with your baby being ready to wean; instead, look for the signs on p.95 that your child is developmentally ready to explore solid foods.

My child will eat what they need … won't they?

You may have been encouraged to allow your child to eat whatever they like – in a belief that a child will naturally be drawn to the foods they need to satisfy nutritional needs. There is an element of truth to this in that research concludes that children who undereat at one meal will compensate at another, thereby taking in adequate calories[192]. However the quality of the calories is not proven and there is no evidence to date to demonstrate that children will, for example, naturally choose an orange over an ice cream because they are lacking vitamin C.

This self-regulation of calorie intake has been shown to apply when plain foods are introduced[193] yet when refined, sugary foods come into the diet it appears to disrupt the ability to self-regulate. This is likely to be due to down-regulation of a hormone called leptin, which affects our ability to feel full (see p.152–3 for more information on the importance of leptin in appetite control).

Chapter Nine

Weaning with Reflux and Premature Babies

Weaning babies with reflux

It is occasionally recommended by a health professional that babies with reflux are introduced to solids a little earlier than other children. One reasoning behind this is that gravity holds heavier food down more easily than milk. If you picture the stomach as a drawstring bag and you drop a heavy tin inside it then the bottom of the bag gets pulled down and the drawstring at the top comes together, closing the bag. It is this drawstring or gateway that may not fully close in babies with reflux, allowing the milk to bubble up.

It's interesting that reflux may cause some babies to *undereat* (if they associate feeding with the after-feeding pain, or if it hurts to swallow) or *overeat* (because sucking keeps the stomach contents down in the stomach and because breast milk is a natural antacid[194]).

If you choose to introduce solid foods earlier than six months under the guidance of a health professional, you may feel this goes against the ethos of baby-led-weaning, since you haven't waited for your child to be developmentally ready, and is very much a 'parent-led weaning' approach. But choosing to introduce solid food early to your reflux baby is an example of a combined parent-led and baby-led weaning approach if you are following your individual baby's needs as well as taking into account how you feel about this. If your baby has reflux and you

feel that the benefits of solid food outweigh the ethos of waiting for the developmental signs in their particular case, plus your paediatrician sees no issue with introducing solid food early, then you go ahead and follow your parental instinct and remember, you can always change your mind later.

However, there are a few things to be aware of:

Exclusively breastfeeding for six months is recommended by the WHO, the AAP and the DH because contemporary evidence concludes that it is the ideal approach for both mother and baby's health[195]. If you are an exclusively breastfeeding mother who is considering introducing solids before six months then be sure to weigh up the pros and cons of doing so before rushing into anything.

When your child has their milk feed or eats solid food, stomach acid is released to help break the food down. The stomach has thick, specially lined walls to manage the acid but the oesophagus doesn't, so there is a gateway between the two structures that makes sure that the acid stays in place. Reflux symptoms are often treated pharmaceutically with the aim of reducing stomach acid volume or with the aim of coating the oesophagus so it doesn't get irritated when the acid splashes – but neither of these treatments actually deals with the source of the problem. *Why* is this happening? Why is there too much acid? Why is the gateway between the stomach and oesophagus failing? The causes of reflux are many, which is why there

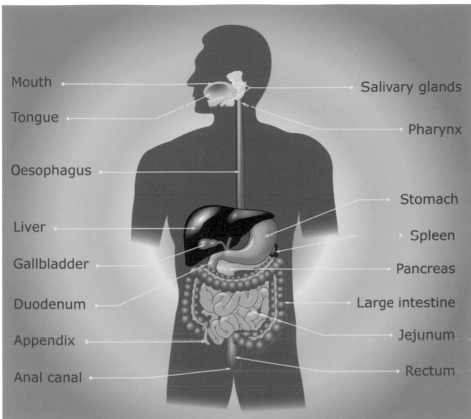

The diaphragm sits between the stomach and the oesophagus, ensuring the stomach acid remains in the stomach.

Shutterstock

is no one definitive treatment and the medications are aimed at generically relieving the symptoms, regardless of the cause. One way to consider reflux is as a biomechanical imbalance. The diaphragm closes the gateway between the stomach and oesophagus and is a muscle, just like your bicep. That means that it is modifiable and can be improved and developed and this may help it to keep the acid in the right place. In these instances a biomechanical assessment and approach may help so consulting with a manual therapist, such as a paediatric osteopath, may be beneficial.

How can reflux emotionally affect my baby's weaning process?

Many parents are advised that their child will grow out of reflux, but that doesn't make going through it any easier. For many parents it is heartbreaking to watch their child scream in pain following every feed. It stands to reason that if a child repeatedly experiences pain related to feeding then they will want to avoid it. This is likely to establish eating as an experience where their basic human need (and desire) to feed conflicts with their desire to avoid it; not only that, their brains begin to 'learn' that eating is associated with distress. Even healthy adults have an extremely complex relationship with food and eating – apart from anything else, eating should be associated with pleasure (both social and physical). Can you imagine how this relationship might be complicated even further for a child if its very beginnings are associated with experiencing repeated pain and distress?

Brenda and Erin

Brenda brought her 12-week-old baby, Erin, to be assessed at our clinic as she was suffering from reflux. Erin was breastfed and offered a bottle of expressed breast milk each evening as Brenda found it easier for the Gaviscon to be given in a bottle. When they came to see us, and as Erin was placed to Brenda's breast, she started screaming and howling. As soon as she was brought upright and away from the breast she was fine again. This happened repeatedly.

We are fortunate to run a multi-disciplinary assessment clinic where the expertise of Luci (a lactation consultant), Felicity (an osteopath) and Anna (a counselling psychologist) allows us to assess attendees from our own positions of expertise. In this case, it was clear that Erin had associated the breastfeeds with pain from reflux. A referral back to the GP was made to address Erin's medications with ranitidine also being prescribed by the GP. Osteopathic treatment was then started. On recommendation from Luci, mother and baby spent the following day at home, with no breastfeeds attempted but lots of skin-to-skin contact and closeness to the breast with cuddles and love. The goal was to re-associate the breast with

positive associations. The following day the breast was offered again and, although no suckling occurred, there was no screaming. Within the week, Erin had re-associated the breast with positive experience and not pain and was successfully breastfeeding.

It's easy to see how from such an early age a negative association can be made between feeding and pain. (A similar pattern can take place when solid foods are introduced too early to a child. If a child is not ready to experience solid foods they may experience pain from eating them and as a result a negative association can occur and fussy eating can begin.)

When children who have reflux develop anxious feelings about eating, they will not be able to recognize or understand their emotions or soothe themselves. As a parent, you are therefore likely to see your child becoming distressed around food.

How can I help my child?

You are a vital part of your baby's weaning process, which means that how *you* feel and respond to what your baby is going through is also a major factor that affects and helps to shape your baby's weaning process. This is because:

- You're the model for your child to learn how to respond to experiences (it's all part of learning how to survive in the world). Seeing you stressed when food appears will reinforce that eating is stressful
- Your job is to regulate your child's emotions for them when they can't do it for themselves

It's therefore *really* important, if you've been through reflux with your baby, that you take some time to recognize how *you* feel when your child experiences reflux and also how you're feeling about weaning your baby. Weaning is not just about your baby – it's about both of you. What should be a time for bonding, curiosity, discovery and fun can easily turn into a time of dread and anxiety. You can have a huge impact on whether it stays that way or becomes easier as time passes.

Having a history of reflux means that you and your baby may have a difficulty to overcome when the weaning process starts, because eating is already a negative emotional experience for both of you. A few tips are:

- Adjust your expectations and remember that things are likely to take more time and a lot more patience
- Make a point of noticing your feelings and take a few moments out to calm down if you're feeling stressed. Every time you can be calm around food, even if your child is distressed, you're teaching them that eating isn't stressful and that you can manage their emotions for them, which will make them feel more secure
- Be kind to yourself – if things feel difficult or they aren't going as well as you'd like, it's not a reflection on you. This is a unique journey that you and your baby are taking together and you're dealing with something that's really challenging
- Don't take any notice of what other children are eating or how fast they're progressing. Every child is unique and it's important to allow children to progress at their own pace

How can reflux physically affect my baby's weaning process?

In an ideal world, children would not simply be medicated to manage the symptoms of reflux but the root of the problem would be found and the causes of the reflux treated.

One problem with introducing solid food to a child for reasons such as reflux is that it is likely to happen earlier when they are less likely to be developmentally ready for solids. They may not have the motor skills necessary to manage 'real' food and self-feeding may be challenging. Your child could very quickly become frustrated with the food if they are unable to manage it successfully – repeated failure leads to increased frustration, unsuccessful mealtimes and more negative associations with food. Anxiety and distress also lead to stimulation of the sympathetic nervous system, which may aggravate the reflux further. We advise that you consider how things are going in your household and follow the path that is right for you and your child.

Reflux and food aversion

One trial found that a child may easily develop a food aversion if consuming it causes discomfort[196]. For parents of children with reflux this is worth considering because a food that causes pain or discomfort may be difficult to introduce again. This survival mechanism is there for an evolutionary reason – if a food causes discomfort it is likely to be harmful to the body. This is, however, an association that can be overcome given time and repeated exposure to the food, particularly if your child grows out of reflux and you can help them to associate that food with positive experiences that are pain-free.

Eating alongside a child with reflux is important as it enables you to spot signs of pain such as grimacing, fidgeting, coughing or body tensing. When these signs appear, acknowledge to your child that you understand they are in pain. Even if they are so young that they can't talk yet, reassuring your little one that you've understood their problem is helpful. Putting gentle pressure on the abdomen, gentle movement (like rocking) and popping on some calming music can all help your child relax and improve their levels of comfort.

There is no guarantee that a child will grow out of reflux, which is perhaps unsurprising, because if the underlying cause is not dealt with then the symptoms will persist. In older children it is key to encourage recognition of the difference between a hungry tummy and a tummy ache. Both sensations are similar, with stomach growling and stomach pains. You should teach your child to think: how long has it been since I last ate? On a scale of one to ten how much does it hurt? On a scale of one to ten how hungry do I feel? Recognizing the different feelings will help your child become their own problem-solver because how they solve their hungry tummy pains will be different to how they solve their reflux tummy pains.

Take responsibility for your decisions

For some parents, it can feel empowering to know that you are taking matters into your own hands and trying to do things for your child rather than passively leaving it up to the 'experts'. If your child has reflux, you feel that introducing solid foods early will be beneficial, and there are no medical professionals recommending otherwise, then you must go ahead and do what you feel is right for you and your family. However, it's important to know the facts – your baby may not be developmentally ready for solid food, so it isn't ever a straightforward decision. By not exclusively breastfeeding for six months your child won't receive the health benefits they otherwise would. It's something you need to weigh up so you can make an empowered decision. Don't forget; just because you try something, it doesn't mean you need to continue with it – you can always change your mind if you find that it isn't making any difference.

Elisa and Alice

Alice was brought to see us at eight weeks old, suffering from dreadful reflux. She had dropped a centile on her weight chart and her mum was exhausted from having to hold her upright for almost two hours in between feeds. She had been prescribed ranitidine and Gaviscon by the GP; however, as she was an exclusively breastfed baby, getting the medication into Alice was proving to be a bit of a fiasco. (Putting the Gaviscon in a bottle full of breast milk wasn't an option in this case as it was early days with the breastfeeding and mum didn't want to cause nipple confusion.) Everyone was sleep-deprived, and Elisa was being advised to use bottles of formula to top her up to ensure she got more food, which she desperately wanted to avoid. Three health professionals were involved in Alice's case – Anna (the counselling psychologist), Felicity (the osteopath) and Luci (the lactation consultant) – each looking at Alice from their own expert perspective. Alice had been a forceps delivery after mum had been pushing for almost four hours. Alice had been rotated with the forceps and that rotation was reflected through the thorax (ribcage), which is where the diaphragm attaches. One of the causes of this case of reflux was biomechanical — the gateway was failing to close because it was twisted. However, that wasn't the end of it. We watched her feed and addressed positioning and attachment issues with regards to the breastfeeding, with a poor latch allowing air to be swallowed, exacerbating the symptoms. We explained how to offer small frequent feeds. Contrary to popular belief, a lactating breast never truly empties. So by offering only one breast at each feed, Alice is rewarded with a slower flow of milk that won't overfill the stomach[197]. A strong rush of milk may cause Alice to gulp and swallow more air, which can trigger more spitting up. It's easy to see how bottle-feeding can aggravate symptoms of reflux, if the stomach is being overfilled and air is being swallowed during every feed.

From a psychological point of view, Elisa was becoming more and more stressed about feeding, which became worse as she became more exhausted. The birth had been traumatic for her and she had increasingly believed that she somehow wasn't feeding her baby properly. She felt guilty and anxious and often became tearful. She found it difficult to get Alice to settle and was feeling overwhelmed — she wasn't getting the good feelings and bonding during feeding and could only feel worried. The more this cycle continued, the more she felt like a bad mum.

Being advised to 'top up' with formula had increased those feelings of not being a good enough mum because she had been determined to breastfeed her baby. She felt so desperate not to resort to formula that she felt more and more pressured to make sure that Alice was taking enough milk, which of course increased her anxiety during feeding. And so the cycle continued, with Elisa getting ever more exhausted.

Anna explained to Elisa how her daughter was sensing her emotions and how, as well as the reflux, this may be contributing to Alice's difficulty settling. It emerged that Elisa was quite hard on herself and that she was finding it difficult to adjust to the idea of things not being 'perfect' or not happening as she had imagined they would for so long before Alice's birth. Mum learned some techniques to manage negative emotions and received some brief therapy to help her to be kinder to herself. This allowed her to relax and think in a less rigid way, allowing her to adapt her expectations of herself.

A holistic approach, where both mum and baby's needs were being acknowledged, addressed and treated, helped. Having Alice's biomechanical issues addressed and being advised that she could continue breastfeeding by offering small feeds helped Elisa to feel empowered, as she could feed her baby in the way she wished (and the way she believed was best) while managing her reflux. She was able to manage her emotions better and Alice began to settle more easily, allowing her to have more and more of the bonding time she desperately wanted. Using a multidisciplinary approach that addressed both mum and baby as equal partners in the process was vital.

Premature babies

It's often difficult for parents of premature babies to know when to introduce solid foods. Each child is different and babies born pre-term need special consideration based on their individual requirements because many have delayed motor development.

The British Dietetic Association recommend seeking the advice of a paediatrician or other healthcare professional for specific advice as to when to introduce solid food to your premature baby[198]. They comment that many pre-term infants may benefit from delayed introduction to solids to allow sufficient motor development. The charity Bliss recommends that five to eight months after the actual birth date is the best time to introduce solids to these children, commenting that few babies will be ready at five months or need to wait for eight months[199].

It's no surprise that the approach to solid food for premature babies is just like that for any other child – wait and watch for signs that they are ready. No specific age or date is suitable since all babies are different. It's interesting that the British Dietetic Association released this policy statement in 2013:

The British Dietetic Association recommends that each infant should be managed individually as they develop at different rates. Developmental signs of readiness for solid food, together with parental opinion, should be taken into consideration when advising on the ideal age to begin complementary feeding. There is little evidence that complementary feeding before 6 months is harmful and there is some emerging evidence to support the introduction of solid food before 6 months whilst breastfeeding, which may be beneficial for some infants[200].

Chapter Ten

Weaning and Nutrition

Vitamins

Adequate nutrition is a topic that worries many parents when it comes to weaning. Vitamins can be particularly confusing, and many parents are uncertain how to ensure an appropriate vitamin intake. So here's a little bit about what your baby needs when it comes to vitamins and why.

Vitamin D/calcium

Many parents are aware of the importance of calcium in their child's diet for maintaining healthy bones. However, without vitamin D, calcium can't be absorbed from the digestive tract and used. In other words, you can consume plenty of calcium but without vitamin D you might as well not bother. It sounds a bit unlikely in a developed country but, sadly, some UK children are now developing rickets due to a lack of vitamin D and/or calcium. In Southampton in 2010, Professor Clarke (an orthopaedic surgeon) assessed 200 randomly selected children and found that 20% required intervention for rickets, including children from middle-class backgrounds[201].

SOURCES OF VITAMIN D

The best source of vitamin D is the sunshine bouncing off your little one's skin as they play outdoors. (Continue to take the necessary precautions of using sunscreen and cover up your child appropriately before they show any signs of burning.) Vitamin D is a fat-soluble vitamin, which means it can be stored in the liver and fatty tissues so it doesn't need to be eaten as often as water-soluble vitamins. Vitamin D is, however, quite hard to come by and only occurs naturally in a few foods, such as:

- Oily fish (salmon, tuna and mackerel)
- Egg yolks
- Certain brands of fat-spreads and breakfast cereals

Sadly, vitamin D isn't present in the foods many older children seem to be drawn to and which are served in many child-friendly venues, such as sausages, beans and chips! In an age where pre-packaged meals are prevailing over home-cooked dinners and there is a dependence on technology (e.g. iPad apps and children's twenty-four-hour TV channels), many children dictate to their parents which foods they will and won't eat, therefore limiting their diet. It is therefore easy to see how vitamin D deficiency can easily occur in any child. However, by following the advice in this book, you are taking the first steps towards raising a child with a broad palate who is eager to try new foods that are rich in vitamin D.

Vitamin deficiencies

Vitamin deficiencies are generally rare in exclusively breastfed babies, but when mothers' diets are deficient, their infants may have low intakes of certain vitamins (such as vitamin A, riboflavin, vitamin B6, and vitamin B12). Vitamin D deficiency may also occur among babies who do not receive much exposure to sunlight. In these situations, improving your diet or increasing your child's exposure to sunlight, speaking to your GP about supplements, or administering vitamin D drops to your child are the recommended approaches rather than switching from breast milk to fortified formula or providing complementary foods to your baby before they are ready.

Vitamin drops

At the time of writing, the Department of Health recommends that all breastfed children from six months to five years old are given supplements, in the form of vitamin drops containing vitamins A, C and D[202]. But if your child is on more than 500 ml of formula milk then they don't need a vitamin drop as formula milks are fortified with these. If you are breastfeeding and didn't take a vitamin D supplement during pregnancy then you may be advised by your health visitor to give your child a vitamin drop from the age of one month.

Claire and Hannah

As a breastfeeding mum I was a bit surprised at the advice from my health visitor to give my child vitamin drops. I offer Hannah home-cooked food and a varied diet. We rarely eat junk food and we regularly have veggies from our allotment, so why on earth should she need these supplements? I think my friends were surprised when I told them that I was giving Hannah vitamin drops, because they held similar opinions. However, I chose to, just because the possibility of her not getting enough vitamins would play on my mind if I didn't. I wanted to avoid becoming anxious about her eating, and this helped me to, since I knew she was getting all the necessary vitamins in the drops.

Iron

Iron is an essential component of oxygen transportation, cell growth and immune system regulation so it is certainly important. Apart from babies who have a low birth-weight, are preterm or are born to mothers who have low iron levels, most babies are born with enough iron stores to sufficiently supplement the iron they get from milk feeds for about the first six months of life (although some will have sufficient iron up to twelve months[203]). Regardless, at six months, iron stores reduce and some parents fear the levels of iron in breast milk aren't enough to compensate for this.

The Institute of Medicine recommends that babies aged between six and twelve months should receive around 11 mg of iron per day yet breast milk contains around 0.35 mg/litre. Your baby's ability to absorb iron from breast milk is variable, ranging from 15–50%. With this in mind, your baby would need to drink 4–13 litres of breast milk per day to receive the recommended 11 mg of iron per day. It is impossible to know how much a breastfed baby has really had without expressing the milk into a bottle but on average research shows that babies of six months of age consume around a litre of milk per day. (It's useful to note that toddlers aged between one and three years need less iron than a 6-month-old – around 7 mg per day – because their growth is beginning to slow.)

Most baby rice cereals are fortified with

iron (for the issues with these see p.70) but by introducing your child to 'real' solid foods that are rich in iron, you can be confident your baby is getting exposed to this essential mineral. It's interesting to consider that the bioavailability of iron in iron-rich foods such as cooked beef or liver is actually much higher (~15.5%) than in infant cereals (~3%) . Bioavailability can be thought of as the percentage of the vitamin or mineral that can actually be absorbed and used by the body. With a lower bioavailability, one can suppose that a higher volume of baby rice will need to be consumed, compared to cooked meat, to get the same amount of iron.

It is also interesting to compare the bioavailability of iron in human breast milk to that of infant formula. It is estimated that infants can use up to 50% of the iron in breast milk as opposed to less than 12% of the iron in infant formula (although the high iron content of these formulas means that they do contain as much absorbable iron as a baby needs). This is because breast milk has high levels of lactose and vitamin C which aids iron absorption.

There is no evidence to show at this point that children who are exclusively breastfed and who go on to self-feed are more likely to be iron deficient than formula-fed children as long as a wide variety of foods, including those rich in iron, are made available.

Why do we see this drop in iron?

Historically, we have survived on breast milk without the need for formula or supplements so why have we evolved to lack such an essential nutrient after six months of age? Let's look to our ancestors for some ideas about why this might (since research is still inconclusive) have happened.

Six months is a key developmental age for babies – this is when they start showing the first signs of independence and curiosity. Sitting up, reaching for objects and popping them in mouths are common activities at this age so maybe we can look to this for a clue. Historically, babies would have been living in caves, spending a large amount of the time on the ground, rolling around in the earth and dirt. Soil is tremendously rich in iron. Is it possible, therefore, that we evolved to not take as much from our mother's breast because we could get our own from the soil? After all, our mothers would have needed that iron for their own health, so why deplete theirs when we could get our own from the earth? Even today, 'Some Indian tribes in the Amazon are known to eat dirt while pregnant or nursing'. Researchers suspect that this act of eating soil, called 'geophagy' could help animals get key minerals they need for nutrition[204]. However, it is not something that is practised in Western society.

Another question we have to ask is: if the gut is only just ready to receive solid foods at six months and your baby is only just starting to get their hand-eye control mastered to be able to get food into their mouth, why would the body reduce the iron levels so quickly? Wouldn't it make more sense to allow a transition period, of maybe a month or so, to allow eating to be established before reducing the iron stores? This brings us to a second hypothesis, which is to do with our Western culture of cord-clamping. The majority of umbilical cords are clamped and cut immediately after birth. However, this is a relatively new activity. The WHO recommend waiting two or three minutes after birth before clamping[205] since up to 50% more blood can then pass to your newborn, meaning they will get almost an extra four to six weeks' worth of iron[206]. So maybe the system is perfect after all, and our methods have interfered? It's certainly food for thought.

So with all this in mind, your baby might need a little help with iron at six months and they can get this in a number of ways:

- Many cereals are fortified with iron such as those made from whole oats
- Cook with iron-rich foods such as legumes, meat, egg yolks and green leafy vegetables
- Use spinach as a herb; sprinkle it into all your yummy dishes

To get you started, here are some iron-rich recipes from our book *Yummy Discoveries: The Baby-led Weaning Recipe Book*:

Chicken Liver Pâté

Preparation Time: 5 minutes
Cooking Time: 10 minutes
Serves 2 grown-ups and 1 little person

Ingredients
Packet of chicken livers (organic preferably)
1 tbsp unsalted butter

TO SERVE: toast or rice cakes

Method
1. Melt the butter and fry the livers for around 5 minutes or until the liver hardens
2. Pop into a food blender or mash with a fork

Tip: organic chicken livers may be better suited for your child. The liver is the body's factory, processing food and absorbing any toxins to which the chicken may have been exposed.

Adult add-on: liven this dish up for a grown-up starter by adding to the blender: 50 ml double cream, 1 tbsp brandy and a pinch of salt and pepper. Pop into ramekins, cover and chill in the fridge. Serve with hot toast and spicy chutney.

Health: chicken livers contain more vitamins, minerals and essential nutrients, gram for gram, than any other food.

Watercress and Spinach Pâté

Preparation Time: 5 minutes
Cooking Time: 10 minutes
Serves 2 grown-ups and 1 little person

Ingredients
Handful of watercress
Handful of spinach
1 onion (chopped)
1 tbsp cream cheese
½ tbsp unsalted butter

TO SERVE: toast, rice cakes

Method
1. Fry the onion in the butter until softened
2. Add the watercress and spinach and cook until they wilt
3. Stir in the cream cheese
4. Pop the mixture in a food blender, or mash with a fork

Tip: growing watercress is an easy and fun activity for your children. Pop to the garden centre, buy a pack of seeds and follow the instructions.

Leftovers: use any leftovers as a yummy filling for a baked potato.

Health: watercress is a superfood. Gram for gram it contains more vitamin C than oranges, more iron than spinach and more calcium than milk.

What's wrong with baby rice?

Baby rice (white rice flour cereal) has been recommended for decades as the ideal first food for babies, yet there is very little research and justification behind this. Evidence suggests that many taste preferences form during the window prior to learning to walk, so why are we insisting on giving our children large amounts of cereal made from processed white rice flour (baby rice)? Are those the taste preferences we wish to shape? What about the world of fresh food out there, where each food item is a different shape and colour to the next? No wonder that world seems strange, if a baby is used to eating bland, beige food.

Some parents are still encouraged to mix some baby rice with breast milk or formula when they wean. The problem with this is that, as the enzymes in your baby's saliva get to work on the baby rice, its conversion to glucose (sugar) begins and *bingo* – you have now created a positive emotional connection between eating sweet, processed foods and pleasure – is that really what you want to be hard-wiring into your baby's brain?

Why is baby rice so popular?

Well, the main reason for its recommendation back in the 1980s was its fortification with iron – lack of iron in a child's diet can have enormously negative health consequences, even today. Its popularity is actually nothing to do with the nutritional content of the rice itself; indeed, it seems just to have been a vehicle for adding iron to your baby's diet. So why don't we fortify foods we DO want our children to eat with iron? The problem appears to lie in the molecular structure of the individual food. For example, high-protein legumes, such as beans, peas or lentils, are

Your baby can explore food whenever they come across it – experiencing colours, shapes, textures and smells all help to build familiarity with foods.

Exploring foods in different ways encourages them to become visually familiar.

high in phytic acid, which inhibits their ability to absorb iron[207]. The authors from one piece of research conclude: 'Infant cereals are usually fortified with elemental iron powders, but this form of iron has extremely poor bioavailability and should not be used in complementary foods'[208]. Weaning is a time where small volumes of food are eaten. With the iron having low bioavailabilty, it won't be easily accessible to the body so the child will need to consume a large quantity to get an adequate volume.

As well as having poor bioavailability, baby rice could actually be harmful (and has been linked to bladder cancer in later life)[209]. A third of baby rice on sale in the UK has been found to contain so much inorganic arsenic, a human carcinogen, that it would be illegal in some countries[210]. This is because rice soaks up arsenic from the soil more readily than other grains do. Even when you read 'baby-grade' on a packet of baby rice, this isn't a government standard confirming the product is fit for your baby, but a marketing-manufactured statement. Sir Muir Gray, Chief Knowledge Officer to the National Health Service, commented that this is 'An important issue, with an urgent need for more research'[211].

Remember how babies are born knowing very little about the world and are therefore constantly populating their cognitive database with shapes, smells, tastes … etc.? Why not use the time before your child starts eating solids to help them become familiar with these foods? Allow them to wander around the allotment, sniff the cucumber when they're in the shopping trolley or hold a beef tomato. These objects, if firm and full-size, are far too big to be 'eaten' but they can explore them and become familiar with them.

Cow's milk

Cow's milk should be avoided as a drink for babies less than twelve months old because it lacks the necessary iron and vitamins found in infant milk feeds. Cooking with cow's milk is suitable for children of any age when they're weaning, but take into account your family history of allergies before introducing new foods. As a rule, only use full-fat milk as this will provide optimum calories for your baby.

If you choose not to offer cow's milk, there are lots of alternatives on the market today. Rice milk, goat's milk and almond milk are popular choices. There is a lot of debate about whether soy milk is suitable for young children because the soy isoflavones are seen as weak estrogens (this does not apply to soy-based formula milk, which is different to soy milk). One paper states: 'Given the limited evidence for the health effects of soy isoflavones in infants, pediatric and health organizations in several countries suggest caution in feeding soy to infants and young children'[212].

Processed food

Obesity is a relatively new epidemic, emerging in the 1980s – so what has changed to cause this? In the 1960s, children were weaned on 'real' food. Processed foods were expensive and they were not abundantly available, so babies and children didn't encounter them often and didn't get a taste for them. However, when these children became parents themselves in the 1980s, the trend for convenient, processed foods with additives and preservatives was snowballing, partly as the cost had come tumbling down. It's no coincidence that this was when childhood obesity figures began to rocket.

There is another way. What if the first food you served your child was a food that looked like the natural food that you wanted them to eat? What if the positive emotional association you create with food began with some

Shutterstock

There is no such thing as a bad food; it's how often you eat it that matters.

grated cucumber or broccoli florets? Wouldn't that be a fabulous first food association? It's easy to achieve – just skip the baby rice and serve up real food instead. There is a lack of research justifying the benefits of serving baby rice and, increasingly, evidence suggests that it leads to unhealthy eating habits later in life (see p.147 for more).

Sugar

Nutrition is the most inexact of sciences. There are no absolute truths or perfect diets and guidelines and recommendations are always changing. In the nineteenth century, sugar was a 'superfood' giving energy to families in poverty. Today, it is seen as the promoter of dental cavities and the real cause of the obesity pandemic, not to mention diabetes[213]. Certainly, today we know that processed sugar is nutritionally empty and that consuming too much sugar causes spikes and falls in blood sugar that aren't good for us at all.

Sugar acts on the brain producing a rush of chemicals including dopamine and serotonin. These have an opiate-like effect, which

Sugar has been linked to many health problems and is nutritionally empty.

makes us feel relaxed and content. The effects of sugar are so potent that, in Sweden, sugar solutions are used as anaesthetics for minor surgeries and they are frequently given to babies in the USA for minor procedures – when taking blood, for example. Sugar has even been used for alcoholics to help them fight the urge to drink – the effect on the brain is that profound.

Sugary drinks are processed differently to sugary foods because they are primarily populated with high fructose corn syrup (HFCS); the digestion, absorption, and metabolism of fructose does not stimulate leptin production[214] (leptin being the fullness hormone) and so despite consuming the calories in a sugary drink we do not experience the fullness. When we chew sugary foods, our body recognizes them as being high in calories – the caveman in us remembers that berries and fruit are sweet and contain lots of energy. As a result, over the course of the rest of the day, we are likely (unless we let social habits override these instincts) to consume fewer calories as we unconsciously believe that our bodies have enough to keep us going. However, a similar mechanism does not exist for sweet drinks, as these were not encountered in caveman times. When we drink (rather than chew and swallow) sugar, the body does not associate this with high-calorie consumption, so we keep looking for more calories to fill us up – even though we've already had them in liquid form.

As we have already said, there's no such thing as a 'bad' food – it's how often you serve something that's a problem. But consider those empty calories your child is getting by having that glass of squash – are you setting your child up to overeat?

How can we avoid consuming those unnecessary calories? It's simple – always

Drinking from a bottle is easier than a cup so higher volumes are more likely to be drunk.

Key point:

Remember, there's no such thing as a 'bad' food – it's how often you serve something that's a problem.

---

serve water and *only* water with meals and treat those sugary drinks as a snack. If you offer three meals a day with two snacks then each cup of squash, juice or smoothie drink counts as a snack and your child needs to know that – the plus point is that they may change their mind about having it if they know that they won't get the raisins or banana muffins that they hoped for if they choose the sugary drink instead.

We want more sugar when we are growing rapidly

With this in mind, you can understand why your child might go through phases of being drawn to sweet foods. During periods of rapid growth and development, more calories are needed and the search for sweet foods is therefore thought to intensify[215]. Think back to your teenage years – a period of rapid growth – you may have loved sherbet dip-dabs or flying saucers, which now, in your adult years, might seem unbelievably sweet and possibly even repulsive. Research has shown that desire for sweetness is linked to the periods of development – and those first two years of life are all about your baby's rapid development.

Camilla and Theo

When we notice Theo is going through a growth spurt we are a little more relaxed on puddings and may even allow a glass of pineapple juice with breakfast. You can see the attraction to sweet foods amplifies and so we accommodate it for a week or two until things settle.

Research suggests that we seek sweet foods during periods of rapid growth.

Babies naturally shy away from sour or bitter foods at first. Because the digestive system is only suitable for milk (which is sweet), this is a protective mechanism to prevent a food that may harm the gut from being ingested. This also makes sense from an evolutionary perspective – as we've mentioned before, part of what would discourage us from eating a poisonous berry would be its taste, which would be likely to be bitter and unappealing (see neophobia, p.116). Your baby's digestive tract is thought to be sterile until they pass through the birth canal. Then, through you kissing them, cuddling them and through encountering the billions of microscopic bacteria in our world, it matures and populates with 'good' bacteria, which are capable of breaking down different foods. You may find that a baby is 'intolerant' of a food until the necessary bacteria are in place – this is not to be confused with an allergy (see p.110). New enzymes are formed over time, as the digestive tract gets ready to be able to accept foods other than milk.

Refined sugar

Refined sugar should be avoided where possible. As the parent, you are the nutritional gatekeeper and for a short time you will have complete control over the foods available to your child. Given that you're shaping your baby's eating habits from weaning onwards throughout their childhood, you'll be setting them up to develop healthy habits if you minimize their exposure to refined sugar while you can control what they consume. Having sugar makes you crave more sugar.

Historically, humans encountered times of feast and famine, so when we came across high-energy foods we needed to take on board as much as we could. In these days of abundantly available processed foods, this has a downside. When you consume fructose, a hormone called leptin is down-regulated. Leptin is the hormone that makes us feel full and so without that circulating in our bodies telling us to stop eating, we keep eating and eating and eating, even when our stomachs are full. Excessive sugar consumption is therefore a huge contributor to obesity, but it also plays a huge part in the development of diabetes and other chronic health conditions, such as hypertension and heart disease. A recent study even suggested that sugar causes damage to the body similar to that caused by alcohol[216]. Avoiding refined sugar at this age is therefore one of the best things you can do nutritionally for your baby, in terms of shaping their eating habits and food preferences.

More sleep, less food?

For many parents, sleep is certainly lacking. The number of sleep-fairies, sleep specialists and magic sleep plans around today reflects this fact, but does your child's lack of sleep impact on their appetite, potentially causing them to overeat? Research from the Avon Longitudinal Study of Parents and Children in the 1990s in the UK has identified that short sleep duration at an early age of thirty months predicts obesity at seven years old[217] and one of the reasons could be down to the regulation of leptin[218].

Leptin works in partnership with another hormone called ghrelin. They oppose each other: leptin suppresses the appetite (so you feel full), ghrelin has the opposite effect of stimulating the appetite (so you feel hungry). Several studies[219][220] have looked at the effect of sleep on these two hormones and results show that reduced sleep led to reduced leptin and elevated ghrelin – with the end result of increased hunger, possibly explaining the increased body mass index observed with short sleep duration[221].

Smoothies often contain several pieces of fruit, yet they result in you feeling less full than if you had consumed the fruit in its natural form. This is because chewed food registers differently in the brain (see p.150 for more on this).

Another small study[222] was conducted in children aged between eight and eleven years to see whether the amount of sleep they had impacted on their food intake. Results showed that reduced sleep duration in school-age children resulted in lower leptin levels and higher ghrelin levels, higher reported food intake and higher weight. More research needs to be conducted in this area to prove the correlation but it's useful to consider the impact that disrupted sleep is suggested to have on hormone levels and the risk of over-eating.

The predisposition to sweetness

Even before babies are born, studies have shown that they are drawn to sweet foods[223].

At birth, there remains a preference for sweet tastes – all other tastes are experienced as neutral (a bit like baby rice!). The desire for sweet foods is hard-wired into us and, again, we look back to our ancestors for the reasons why. Imagine a time when sweet foods didn't mean junk food, artificial flavours or preservatives but, instead, naturally growing fruits and berries that were high in calories, nutritious and safe to eat.

However, more important to the weaning process than this predisposition to sweetness is the relationship between you and your baby. Some babies are born with a protein allergy and are prescribed a protein hydrolysate formula. The proteins in these formulas have been broken down (hydrolyzed) into smaller pieces and the result is a bitter-tasting formula. Based on developmental physiology it stands to reason that babies should reject this food because it will not have the sweet associations that they would naturally need in order to want to taste and ingest it of their own accord. However, the positive association created between a mother and baby during feeding, the nutritional drive to survive and the frequent exposure to the formula can actually ensure that the bitter-tasting formula is readily accepted. This just goes to show that you can facilitate your child to enjoy all kinds of foods, not just the sweet ones they naturally desire.

Purée pouches promote obesity

Many parents think that a pouch of apple purée is equivalent to an apple. This is not the case. Look at the ingredients of any smoothie and you will see that a small bottle contains several pieces of fruit, so you are actually eating much more than you would were you faced with the whole fruit.

Research by Flood-Obbagy and Rolls in 2009[224] showed that eating an apple stopped hunger more quickly than apple purée or apple juice. The whole apple retains the fibrous parts, meaning the body has to work harder to digest it. It also takes the brain approximately twenty minutes to activate feelings of satiety (hence eating fast can be linked to obesity, even in adults).

Purée or juice is unlikely to take twenty minutes to consume, so your child may say they're still hungry and therefore want to eat more. With an apple, they are likely to spend long enough eating it that their brain has time to activate the feeling of being full-up.

Offering the odd purée pouch now and then as a snack for convenience doesn't mean your toddler will become fussy or obese, but with the Plum brand conservatively estimating sales of pouches for babies,

> **Key point:**
>
> **Juice and smoothie drinks are high in sugar and energy. Count them as a snack! And remember, it takes around twenty minutes of eating for feelings of fullness to be activated. Drinking a smoothie containing three pieces of fruit is unlikely to satisfy your child to the same extent as eating a single piece of whole fruit.**

toddlers and children at $53 million in 2012[225], we can't ignore the impact this growing trend is having on our children's eating habits.

So what should I be serving my child?

The truth is, it is up to you. As we have said before, this is not a weaning-by-numbers book with first-stage and second-stage advice because every child and every parent is different. Our aim is to arm you with the facts to make an informed decision, not to dictate to you what you 'should' do. On the following pages are some suggestions for some first meals which we have found have worked well with many of the families we work with:

First Food: Cucumber Platter

Menu:
Grated cucumber
Cucumber sticks with skin on
Cucumber sticks with skin off
Cucumber & Mint Dip

Simply pop these on a plate or the highchair table and let your little one explore.

Cucumber & Mint Dip

Preparation Time: 5 minutes
Serves 1 little person

Ingredients
¼ cucumber (remove skin by peeling with a vegetable peeler)
2 tbsp full-fat natural Greek yoghurt
6 fresh mint leaves (chopped)

Method
1. Whizz the ingredients in a food processor and serve

Leftovers: *use the dip to cool down a hot curry.*

Leftovers: *whizz in a garlic clove and squeeze of lemon juice to make a tzatziki.*

Leftovers: *yummy served with Broccoli Nuggets (p.156).*

Tip: *sit down with your baby and enjoy dipping your own choice of raw veggies in this dip.*

Just to let you know …

- Cucumber is not a common allergen because it mainly contains water. However, that doesn't mean to say it *can't* be one
- Offering a single food at a time means that you can identify an allergen quickly
- The different textures encourage acceptance of different tastes
- A selection of food enables your child to make a choice about what to eat
- The different colours, with the dark green and the light green, will stimulate your baby's interest
- Cucumbers are not nutrient-dense and may not satisfy a hungry baby (if your child is nine months or over)
- For teething babies, cucumber sticks can soothe and cool the gums
- Cucumbers can cause some babies to become quite windy

David Polonowski

Cucumber is not a common allergen due to its high water content.

First Food: Broccoli Bonanza

Menu:
Steamed broccoli florets
Broccoli Nuggets
Broccoli Cheese
Broccoli Purée (recipe on p.157)

Broccoli Nuggets

Preparation Time: 10 minutes
Cooking Time: 25 minutes
Serves 1 little person

Ingredients
4–6 broccoli florets
2–3 tbsp breadcrumbs
1–2 tbsp grated cheese
4–6 tbsp full-fat milk

Method
1. Steam the broccoli until tender
2. Preheat the oven to 190C/180 Fan/Gas 5
3. Allow the broccoli to cool. Pop in the food processor to chop
4. Add the rest of the ingredients to the food processor and mix together to make a gloopy mixture (add more breadcrumbs or cheese to thicken and milk to make wetter)
5. Shape the mixture into patties or sausages
6. Grease a baking sheet and lay out your nuggets and pop in the oven for 20–25 minutes (turning after 10 minutes). They're cooked when golden and firm

Tip: try serving with our Cucumber & Mint Dip (p.155).

Tip: we find the microwave steamers are a great gadget – broccoli florets will take 2–3 minutes to tenderize in one.

Broccoli Cheese

Preparation Time: <5 minutes
Cooking Time: <5 minutes
Serves 1 little person

Ingredients
6–8 broccoli florets
1–2 handfuls grated cheese
Knob of butter (melted)
Ground black pepper to taste (optional)
Squeeze of lemon juice (optional)

Method
1. Steam the broccoli until tender and then tip into a microwave-safe dish
2. Pour melted butter, pepper and lemon juice (if using) onto the broccoli
3. Sprinkle cheese over the top and pop in the microwave for 1–2 minutes until melted

Tip: ensure the cheese is cooled thoroughly before serving.

Tip: this works as a yummy accompaniment to any meal.

Broccoli Purée

Preparation Time: 20 minutes
Cooking Time: <5 minutes
Serves 1 little person

Ingredients
1 small potato (peeled and chopped)
1–2 garlic cloves (peeled)
10–12 broccoli florets
250 ml low-salt chicken stock
4 tbsp cream cheese
1 tbsp parmesan cheese (optional)

Method
1. Steam/boil the potatoes and broccoli until soft (10–20 minutes)
2. Chuck all the ingredients in a food processor and blitz so it has a 'mashed potatoey' feel

Leftovers: add more stock to thin the sauce. Stir in with some cooked pasta for a lovely pasta sauce. Experiment with different shapes of pasta to give variety to the dish.

Leftovers: pop in a casserole dish, top with some breadcrumbs and cheese and put under the grill for 5–10 minutes until golden and bubbling to make a quick broccoli gratin.

Just to let you know …

- Broccoli contains iron and calcium and also vitamin C, which enables the iron and calcium to be absorbed
- Broccoli has the same calcium content as cow's milk
- Broccoli (the stems especially) can cause some babies to be quite windy – try adding a small piece of ginger when cooking to counter this
- The shape of steamed broccoli florets are perfect for babies to grab hold of and use as a dipper
- Adding 1–2 tbsp of natural yogurt to our listed recipes can also help with digestion and reduce gas, aiding good bacteria
- As broccoli ages, the sugars break down so the broccoli develops a woody texture and a less-sweet taste
- Washing broccoli before storing encourages rotting
- Store broccoli in the fridge in an open plastic bag for prolonged freshness[226]
- Variety doesn't have to mean completely different. Try cooking broccoli florets in chicken stock for a slightly different taste

First Food: Splendid Sweet Potato

Menu:
Baked Sweet Potato
Mashed Sweet Potato
Sweet Potato Pancakes (recipe on p.159)
Sweet Potato Wedges (recipe on p.159)

Baked Sweet Potato

Preparation Time: 5 minutes
Cooking Time: 45–60 minutes
Serves 1 little person

Ingredients
1 large sweet potato

Method
1. Pop the oven on to 200C/180 Fan/Gas 6
2. Run the potato under cold water and poke holes in it with a fork several times
3. Run under the water again and then wrap in foil and pop in the oven for 45 minutes
4. Allow to cool, then cut in half and serve

Mashed Sweet Potato

Preparation Time: 5 minutes
Cooking Time: 30 minutes
Serves 1 little person

Ingredients
1 sweet potato
Knob of unsalted butter

Method
1. Peel the sweet potato and pop it in the steamer for around 30 minutes until soft
2. Mash it up with some butter, allow to cool and serve

Leftovers: *use to make Sweet Potato Pancakes (see p.159).*

Leftovers: *use as a great topping for Cottage Pie (pp.86–7 of* Yummy Discoveries: The Baby-Led Weaning Recipe Book*).*

Leftovers: *use as a filling in Filo Fingers (p.59 of* Yummy Discoveries: The Baby-Led Weaning Recipe Book*).*

Sweet Potato Pancakes

Preparation Time: 5 minutes
Cooking Time: 15 minutes
Serves 1 little person

Ingredients
Knob of unsalted butter
Leftover baked or mashed sweet potato
1 egg
1 tbsp self-raising flour
Glug of whole milk

Method
1. Pop the butter in a small frying pan and warm over a medium heat
2. Mix the other ingredients in a mixing bowl until it's the consistency of batter – a thick sauce. Add more flour to thicken and milk to thin as necessary
3. Pour the mixture into the pan so the base is covered and cook for several minutes until it starts to firm up
4. Flip and cook the other side for a similar time
5. Allow to cool and serve

Tip: try serving these with different fruits and veggies rolled inside. Grated cucumber, grated carrot, banana chunks and halved grapes all make great fillings.

Sweet Potato Wedges

Preparation Time: 5 minutes
Cooking Time: 15–20 minutes
Serves 1 grown-up and 1 little person

Ingredients
2 sweet potatoes (cut into wedges)
1 tbsp fresh thyme leaves (chopped) or 1 tsp dried thyme
1 tbsp olive oil

Method
1. Preheat the oven to 200C/180C Fan/Gas 6
2. Toss the wedges in the oil and chopped thyme
3. Roast in the oven for 15–20 minutes or until golden brown

Tip: thyme is a very easy herb to grow in the garden.

Tip: sweet potato contains vitamin A, which will help promote your baby's visual development.

Tip: replace sweet potatoes with baking potatoes for a yummy alternative.

Health: the oils in thyme are a natural antiseptic often found in mouthwash and may help soothe throat infections.

Just to let you know …

- Don't store sweet potato in the fridge – it reduces the flavour
- Sweet potatoes will last usually for 7–10 days when stored in a cool, dark place with plenty of air
- Sweet potatoes are high in fibre so are good for relieving the symptoms of constipation in older children

First Foods: Awesome Avocado

Avocado cut into chunks
Mushy Avocado
Guacamole (recipe on p.161)

Mushy Avocado

Preparation Time: < 5 minutes
Serves 1 little person

Ingredients
1 avocado (ideally very ripe)
Splash of breast/formula milk or water (optional)

Method
1. Cut the avocado in half, remove the stone and scoop out the flesh into a bowl
2. Mash it with a fork to a mushy consistency you're happy with. You can even add some breast milk, formula or water if you want it sloppier
3. Dollop it on the highchair tray and watch your little one go for it with their hands or a spoon

Adult add-on: *skip the added milk and spread on some toast.*

Tip: *use the mushy avocado as a dip alongside the Cucumber Platter so your little one can dunk their cucumber sticks in the dip.*

Tip: *spread on some rice cakes or use as a sandwich filler.*

Guacamole

Preparation Time: 10 minutes
Makes roughly 50 ml of Guacamole

Ingredients
1 ripe avocado (peeled and sliced)
2 cloves of garlic (crushed)
Squeeze of lemon juice
Black pepper to season

Method
1. Blitz all the ingredients in a food processor. Alternatively mash them with a potato masher.

Adult add-on: add some fresh chilli for a spicy kick.

Leftovers: *this makes a lovely sandwich filling.*

Just to let you know …

*   It's best to choose an avocado that is dark green and bumpy
*   A ripe avocado will be firm yet yielding when squeezed
*   Avocados ripen well at home when left in a fruit bowl away from the fridge
*   If storing leftover avocado in the fridge, keep the stone in and wrap in clingfilm to prevent it going brown
*   Avocados last up to a week when stored in the fridge

No food is a 'bad' food

Remember, there is no such thing as a 'bad' food. By marking some foods as bad and others as good you are making the 'bad' foods special and appealing and your child may want them more. Fast-forward ten years when your child is making food choices on their own without you there and they are more likely to go for the forbidden foods than the healthy alternative you have labelled as 'good'. Instead, by making all foods equal and eaten in moderation your child is more likely to eat in a well-rounded way when you're not there.

This doesn't mean that your child can choose to eat as many cakes as they do apples! You can shape expectations by making oranges or natural foods more available than cakes.

Rotate the foods you offer – don't get stuck in a food rut!

Children thrive on routine and predictability because it helps them to make sense of the world and how things work. Familiarity is therefore extremely important for children – it fits with their need to be able to navigate the world in order to survive. It's therefore not surprising that they want the same in the world of food and that they ask for the same thing over and over again. If that particular food happens to be healthy and nutritious then you might not worry too much about it but, even those healthy foods, served repeatedly, can become a problem.

The problem with serving your child the same foods all the time is that, without realizing it, you may be moulding a fussy eater. This can happen in two ways – firstly, by offering them the same foods often and, secondly, by getting into the habit of offering particular foods at particular times. Children cling to routines as much as they do to familiar objects and will quickly get into a food-routine of always having a biscuit after swimming – they will get very upset if this suddenly doesn't happen one day. Creating a routine around which foods your child *will* eat goes against what you're trying to do, which is to encourage your child to eat a wide range of foods (which means you'll have to introduce them to unfamiliar foods) and have a healthy and varied diet. By serving your child the same foods day after day, you're narrowing their palate rather than widening it, and new foods are likely to be greeted with even more suspicion and resistance than they otherwise would be as they get older and these habits and familiarities become more entrenched (see the discussion on p.116 about neophobia for more on why children are suspicious of new foods).

Whether it's mealtimes or snacks, stay away from routine when it comes to the foods you offer. Rotate foods so that your child doesn't start to 'expect' a particular food – this is where you can encounter problems with refusing other foods. So satisfy your child's craving for routine by applying it in other areas of life. This might be a bath

> **Key point:**
>
> **Avoid creating a pudding routine. 'We don't have pudding every day' is a good mantra to prevent the expectation that a yogurt always appears after dinner.**

before bed, consistently eating breakfast together, going for a walk before lunch, reading a book before bed – there are so many ways you can bring routine to your child's life to satisfy their need for reassurance, but it needs to fit in with your family and not start to encroach on you or the foods you eat as a family.

Snacking

Snacking on-demand

Some parents are encouraged to leave bowls of sliced banana and rice cakes around the house so that a crawling baby or toddler can help themselves to a healthy snack. Sometimes parents do this because they're worried that their child isn't eating enough at mealtimes and they want to encourage them to eat without having to persuade them. Other parents might allow free access to a fruit bowl at any time – fruit is healthy after all, right? Well, it's not quite as simple as that. In industrialized countries, changing society and busy lifestyles drive people to more convenient and monotonous food choices and an increased use of snack foods[227]. Many of us will repeatedly cook the same meals and offer the same snacks over and over again, which means narrowing your child's palate and amplifying neophobia (see p.116).

It's important to emphasize here that we are not saying for a moment that snacking itself is bad. The UK Department of Health currently recommends three meals and two nutritious snacks a day and we don't dispute that recommendation. However, it's important to consider *how* your child snacks – this is as vital as how they eat meals. We are addressing the issues with the concepts that:

- snacking means grazing all day with unlimited access to food
- snacking on-demand or allowing a child to graze on food left around the house is a solution for the worry that a child isn't eating enough at mealtimes, or a way of 'encouraging' them to eat

There are several reasons for *not* doing this:

- The first one is that it is a choking hazard to leave your child unsupervised around food, even for a moment – if you pop out to slip a nappy bag in the bin, in that short time, your child could eat something, get into trouble and need your help – you wouldn't be there to assist
- Secondly, you are creating an unstructured snacking habit that you will have to break at some point. Do you want your child grazing on fruit all day, filling up on snacks and not eating proper meals, partly because they're never actually particularly hungry? That approach is teaching your child unhealthy eating habits. It is also important to remember that fruit contains a lot of sugar and that if your child is constantly eating fruit, they may be consuming a lot of sugar every day.

> **Key point:**
>
> **Rotate snacks in the same way you do meals – avoid offering the same snack every day to reduce expectation and expand your child's palate.**

They may also be consuming much more sweet than savoury food, thus reinforcing the likelihood that they will become more familiar with sweet than savoury tastes. This may make them less likely to want to explore savoury flavours

- Thirdly, you want to create a structure around eating, and to make it a social event, for the reasons discussed on p.107. This includes snacking; allowing your child to snack whenever they fancy it is not teaching them about decision-making around food and eating, eating together or operating within the family structure. This is also likely to create a problem should your child attend a nursery setting, for example, where children are expected to eat within a certain timeframe and in a structured way – your child will undoubtedly find this more difficult if they do not have to do it at home. Therefore, snacking also needs to be structured, so that your child's eating framework is similar (and therefore becomes more familiar more quickly), whether they're eating a meal or a snack
- Finally, children who snack on the go do not properly activate their digestive system, as their bodies are concerned with running around or playing. By allowing them to snack this way you

aren't creating the proper context for their body systems to teach them to become aware of hunger and to address it by eating regularly at meal-times. Children who snack on the go are also more likely to aggravate reflux and other digestive issues, because their system is not geared up to digest food while they are being active – for example, movement whilst eating can cause the stomach contents to splash up and burn the oesophagus

Snacks and schedules for mealtimes

There are no hard and fast rules for how many snacks a day you should be offering but some families find it useful to have an eating structure of three meals and two snacks a day. Snacks are ideal for your little one to keep them going. When you watch them bounding around with relentless enthu-siasm and energy, a snack aimed at regulating their blood sugars and sustaining them till mealtimes might be just what they need.

Breastfeeding on-demand is encour-aged for young babies; this often applies to toddlers but in a slightly different context. As a baby, you would probably have allowed your little one to eat as much as they wanted, as often as they needed. Once the toddler years arrive (from roughly twelve months) putting a little more structure in place can be helpful whilst also allowing your child to retain some control – they are after all the one who is feeling hungry. But why do we suddenly need to bring some structure into eating? Well, as your baby matures their frontal lobe begins to develop and a feeling of hunger may not be the reason they want the snack – it could be that they saw a friend

eating a lolly and so want one too! So what do you do?

Balancing work, siblings and all the other things that go into each day in a family can be a challenge. No matter how frantic and hectic family life can be, structure around mealtimes can bring the order and predictability many children crave. Knowing when a meal or snack is going to arrive can help a child to manage their food intake. Young children have very little concept of time so advising that there will be nothing to eat until noon isn't helpful, but associating meal-times with an event – for example, by saying, 'there will be nothing until after we come back from the park' – helps a child put the arrival of food into context. Most children under five will follow the structure of:

Breakfast – Snack – Lunch – Snack – Dinner

This structure gives your child the opportunity to explore a variety of foods in different quan-tities without grazing continuously.

A child who continuously grazes through-out the day never has the opportunity to feel hungry. Children who never have the oppor-tunity to feel hungry can have problems with food relationships later. Many parents hate their child being hungry and immediately respond by offering another breadstick or banana because, after all, as parents one of your primary goals is to meet your child's

> **Key point:**
>
> **Using phrases such as 'your snack will be after swimming' can help a child put the arrival of food into a meaningful context.**

Key point:

From around twelve months of age, frontal lobe development means that your child has the potential to eat for social reasons rather than simply appetite and hunger.

needs. But it is more important to teach your child to manage these feelings of hunger because when they are older they won't be able to graze all day long (at least without eating unnecessarily!).

Snacks: you choose what, your child chooses when

This way, you are creating an eating structure that allows you to ensure your little one has control over their hunger/satiety whilst ensuring that they aren't grazing throughout the day and spoiling their meals. Having this structure has other benefits in that you won't find yourself falling into the trap of using food as an emotional comforter – 'if you stop crying you can have this'. It encourages your little one to learn about action/consequence

– if they happen to gobble both snacks in one go then they will be hungry later and may compensate by eating more at the next meal, but this is all part of learning to make healthy choices around food. Remember that learning what hunger feels like is a developmental leap.

Cereal bars are becoming an increasingly common snack offering for children as well as for adults. Recent research by the consumer group Which? found that, of thirty cereal bars tested, only one was not high in sugar[228]. Why not try making your own cereal bars? Our recipe for Fantastic Flapjacks on p.166 keeps well in a food storage container in the fridge for up to five days and your little one can help get their hands sticky with the mixture.

Key point:

A child who continuously grazes throughout the day never has the opportunity to feel hungry. Children who never have the opportunity to feel hungry can have problems with their food relationships later.

Cereal bars can be a convenient snack but high sugar content in commercial brands means it can be well worth making your own (see p.166 for a recipe).

Shutterstock

Fantastic Flapjacks

(See also p.176 of *Yummy Discoveries: The Baby-Led Weaning Recipe Book* for Fruity Flapjacks)

Preparation Time: 10 minutes
Cooking Time: 20 minutes
Makes around 10–12 snack bars

Ingredients
80 g unsalted butter
1 tbsp honey
100 g jumbo oats
100 g dried fruit (raisins, sultanas, apricots, dates, figs etc.)
50 g mixed nuts and seeds (walnuts, almonds, cashews etc.)

Method
1. Preheat the oven to 180C/160 Fan/Gas 4
2. Melt the butter and honey in the microwave or in a saucepan on a low heat
3. Bash the mixed nuts and seeds in a bag with a rolling pin to break them up or pop them in a food mixer until blitzed into tiny pieces to reduce the risk of choking
4. Either chop the mixed fruit or pop into the food mixer too
5. Mix all the ingredients together
6. Line and grease a baking tin and tip the mixture in, squidging it down
7. Bake on the top shelf of the oven for 20 minutes
8. Remove from the oven, allow to cool and cut into squares. These keep well in an airtight container for up to 5 days

Health: nuts are a great source of protein but are a common allergen so consider this before introducing them to your child (see p.110). Ensure the pieces are small enough to not pose a choking hazard.

Favourite foods

Your child may really enjoy one food and, as their ability to communicate increases, they may begin to ask for it more often. If this is a snack food, you can manage this by deciding *how much* of this food is available and they then choose *when* they eat it. For example, if your little one has a biscuit habit, make it clear that there are two snacks per day and today this biscuit is one of those snacks. Your little one can choose when to eat it. You may notice that this approach with a snack food like a biscuit is slightly different to that of main meals since you are now giving the control of *when* to your child and taking back the *how much*. At mealtimes, you decide *when* and your child decides *how much* (see p.181 for why).

Delayed gratification is not easy at a young age (more on p.176), so don't be surprised if your child chooses to eat their snacks at breakfast-time. That is their decision and they need to experience the natural consequences, which you should explain to

> **+ + + Tip + + +**
>
> **Avoid offering the same foods two days running. Your child will quickly come to expect it. If they love animal crackers then one animal cracker as a snack on Monday is fine but resist offering it again on Tuesday. This will avoid you getting into a food rut where the same foods are expected and eaten daily, which means you can miss out on an opportunity to use those snack-times to expose your child to new foods.**
>
> **+ + + + + + + + +**

Shutterstock

Delayed gratification is not easy for children but it is part of your parental responsibility to teach your child this skill.

them clearly a number of times in different ways before they gobble it up. If they are upset later when they can't have it, comfort and cuddle and explain why things can't change, but don't offer another biscuit or any other snack or juice drink – or do so at your peril! Your child is not going to starve by missing a snack but they will feel hungry and learn the natural consequence of their decision – that is, eating all the snacks at once. Bear in mind that your long-term goal is to teach your child healthy eating habits so they can make healthy choices themselves. You will be so proud when your child, stuffed on crisps and sausage rolls, turns round at a birthday party and 'saves' their cake for later. That is a child 'tuning in' to what their tummy is telling them.

Natural consequences, such as experiencing hunger due to eating a snack early, are an important part of child development and are not to be confused with negative consequences. In the example of a child refusing to wear their coat, a natural consequence would be that the child gets cold. A negative consequence might be the parent putting the child in time-out. Allowing a child to experience natural consequences can help them learn to understand how decisions work. Over time, this will help them to learn to take responsibility for their actions.

Once again, it's important to remind your child each time they choose to eat their snack early of the natural consequences – they easily forget. So each time remind them: 'yes,

Shutterstock

You decide which snacks are available, your child decides when to eat them.

of course you can eat your snack now but remember that means there is nothing to eat until x time'. You may find yourself repeating this phrase a lot but it will be worth it. (Remember: children have little concept of time so avoid using times of day for food; instead, refer to events.)

Children develop at different rates and they are probably not going to be in a position to make decisions involving time (e.g. now or later) until they are at preschool age. However, you know your child better than anyone, so trial and error will help you determine the best time to start offering your child the opportunity to choose when to eat their snack.

Chapter Eleven

Teaching Your Child About Choice and Self-Control

Young children need to learn how to make decisions. Decision-making helps your child to feel confident, develops their independence and helps them to understand the idea of natural consequences. Mealtimes are perfect for encouraging decision-making skills in your child, as there are many opportunities and ways to give them small choices. In the case study with Rachel and Lewis on p.191, Lewis was making a choice: he was choosing to either eat his breakfast at the table or to not have breakfast. Nobody was forcing anybody to do anything.

These same principles can be applied to all aspects of your parenting (within reason, of course – you would not allow your child to make the choice to walk out in the road as the natural consequence might be that they get hurt). It will mean you need to think quickly and recognize the natural consequence yourself beforehand to see whether it is an age-appropriate opportunity, but allowing your child to think for themselves and teaching them to take responsibility for their choices is an amazingly empowering and necessary life skill that creates confidence and independence.

Alex and Theo

I was walking my son to pre-school one morning and I spotted a fellow dad walking his primary school-aged child to school. She wouldn't put her coat on. The statement from Dad went along the lines of 'You are wearing your coat' and the child's reply was along the lines of 'No, I'm not'. Much shouting, upset and tears ensued and eventually Dad physically held his daughter and forced her into the coat – she was crying and screaming. Not a good start to the day for either party. A few weeks later, I found myself in a similar situation. We were at the zoo and it was a snowy day. My son decided he wasn't going to wear his coat. I could probably have manhandled him into it – after all, he is only three – but that tactic isn't going to cut it when he's thirteen and physically bigger than me! Rather than force him into it, I gave him a choice: either wear his coat and run off and play with his friends or not wear his coat and walk holding my hand – his decision. He chose the former and we were both happy with the end result as we both felt that we got our own way. Because he is used to making a choice, at mealtimes and in all other parts of our life, he found this process easy and we both left the situation feeling pleased – he got to run around with his friends and I got him to wear his coat.

Preventing obesity

Your baby is born with the ability to self-regulate their eating. They will eat when they're hungry and stop when they're full. Other factors might impact on this (your baby may want to suck more due to being in pain, for example), but on-demand feeding tunes in to this natural regulator by encouraging you to respond to your baby's cues and feed as and when they ask. During this time, your baby is choosing how much to eat and, if you're breastfeeding, you actually have no way of knowing how much your baby is eating. Many parents justify their decision to spoon-feed their baby purées because it enables them to monitor how much their child is eating, yet by the time your baby was only six weeks old they were able to regulate their own energy intake[229] so why would you want to suddenly take the control away from them at six months old when solids are introduced? More to the point, how is your child likely to react to that?

From the moment your baby was implanted as an embryo, they have let you know when they need food and you have responded. From birth you have interpreted their 'feeding cues' and responded with a milk feed, and they have subsequently stopped when they've had enough. They probably didn't always get it right, overeating and vomiting up milk at times or under-eating and waking up. You may not have realized it, but you helped them to learn by allowing them the opportunity for trial and error and so now you need to consciously repeat the process with solids.

Rather than raising a child to 'finish what's on the plate', you can instead teach your child to respond to feelings of hunger and fullness. This process is about helping your child to learn when to stop eating, which helps to guard against obesity in later life. A jar or pouch of purée is so often seen as a 'meal' but who are you to say 'one more mouthful' or 'finish the jar'? Allow your child to guide you in terms of how much they want to eat. Research has shown that children develop the ability to let you know they have finished by the time they are between four to twelve weeks old so at around six months when solid foods are introduced you should be well-placed to pick up on these messages[230 231].

Harness this window of opportunity and encourage your child to continue to listen to their tummy. By the time your child is three years old those messages of why they eat, when they eat and how much they eat will be influenced by friends, television, food packaging, etc. Don't be another unhelpful influence. Enable your child to stand up to the corporate brainwashing by encouraging them to recognize their own internal signals of hunger and fullness.

Jane and Charlie

I absolutely dread my mother coming to stay. Don't get me wrong, I love her dearly; she helps me no end with the household chores and my son adores her. But I can't leave her alone with my 3-year-old at mealtimes. She just can't seem to help herself and repeatedly says things like 'Eat some more chicken, please'. One time, I came in and she had served herself and my father crispy duck with the pancakes and cucumber and my son for some reason had fish fingers. I watched him reach for a pancake and heard her say 'No — they aren't nutritious, eat some more fish fingers please'! Seriously? I had to intervene — I told my mum to let him take a pancake. I watched my son roll his fish finger up inside a pancake — as he had watched my parents do with the duck. He added some cucumber, spring onion and a dollop of the hoi sin sauce and munched away. I couldn't have been more proud because here was my son eating new foods and learning from his surroundings. As you can guess from my mum's approach to food, my upbringing was very different and possibly has something to do with why both my mum and I have always struggled with our weight.

> **Key point:**
>
> **Avoid categorizing 'adult meals' and 'children's meals'. If you want your child to become familiar with and eat real food, serve real food.**

> **Key point:**
>
> **Allowing your child to self-feed encourages them to self-regulate their energy intake based on their individual needs at that time.**

Spoon-feeding inhibits a child's self-control

Recent research suggests that allowing a child to self-feed helps prevent obesity[232]. It's not the food itself that is influencing this data (since the food wasn't controlled in the study) but the fact that these children are making choices from a young age as to how much to put in their mouths. Your baby starts to learn how to regulate their intake and energy needs from birth and from around six weeks will take adequate calories to support their own energy needs and requirements[233]. With spoon-feeding, you're making these choices for them, and they aren't learning how to regulate their food intake. With this in mind, it is the element of self-feeding that is most important. With spoon-feeding, you're also more likely to get into a battle for control where your child clamps their mouth shut at some point.

Developing control

A little bit of control goes a long way. We all want some control in our lives and children are no different. In fact, making decisions and having control over what happens in their life is very important for your child to develop confidence, independence and an understanding of the consequences of their decisions. Can you imagine what it's like to

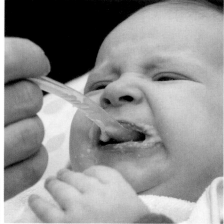

Shutterstock

With spoon-feeding you are removing your baby's control over food.

have your whole world controlled by someone else? Obviously your child doesn't have the same developed sense of independence that you do but, as they grow up, they are designed to develop their own will, personality and sense of agency. When this comes up against continual or all-encompassing parental control, a child who has no freedom to make choices will resist their parent – it's part of their development! As human beings, we need to have independence in order to survive. Therefore, trying things out, making mistakes, making decisions and refusing to comply with what our parents want are all part of our development in this regard.

Mealtimes will eventually occur at least three times a day, so it's easy to see why battles and struggles for control are more likely to occur then than at any other time – it is simply a frequent occurrence and the refusal to eat is a very easy way for your child to exert control. Self-feeding is a very easy way to introduce the concept of control to your child from the very first moment of weaning.

By spoon-feeding, you're controlling the pace and way your child puts food in their mouth. By preventing your child from self-feeding, you are stopping your child from exploring and interacting with food in their own way, at their own pace. In other words, you're removing their control in the domain of food. Your child may respond by clamping their mouth shut and resisting your attempt to feed them as a way of regaining that control. Stop mealtimes from developing into a battleground – give your child a small amount of control by allowing them to make choices and, most importantly, to self-feed, but keep it within the boundaries you have set and the limits you feel comfortable with.

You need to know and listen to yourself to give your child the best food-discovery experience you can. Are you an anxious person?

Do you thrive on order and control? Are you bossy? Are you too relaxed and a little unstructured? Whichever tendencies you have, whether you like them or not, you probably know yourself well enough to recognize them by now. For example, if you've become used to being in control in your life or your work, then you might be more inclined to behave in a controlling way around your child's eating.

Juanita and David

David was a fussy-eating 3-year-old. He would not eat anything that had a sauce, declaring it to be 'dirty' or 'messy'. He refused to eat fish fingers unless they were uniform in size and he had his mum making the fish fingers from scratch and ensuring each fish finger measured the same with a ruler before serving them — if they weren't equal in size he wouldn't eat them. You might not be able to imagine yourself doing something like that but this was reality for this family. On further conversations with the mum it was found she had OCD. She admitted that she cleaned obsessively and that she couldn't bear even one thing to be out of place in her environment. She said that it made her feel anxious and that organizing and controlling everything around her was the only way she managed to control her anxiety (a symptom of OCD).

As we talked with Juanita, she began to realize that David was picking up on her behaviour and, more than that, that he was picking up on her anxiety. She told us about how this was manifesting in other ways that weren't food-related — for example, David would cry hysterically if anyone came into the house and didn't take their shoes off, or if he couldn't take his shoes off when he went into someone else's house. Through a gentle and supportive dialogue, we suggested to Juanita that David seemed to be picking up on her anxiety and that he was also developing a strong preference for things to be exact in his environment. The truth was that, unless Juanita was willing to try to adapt her own behaviour, it was going to be extremely difficult for her to help David to become less anxious or to change his behaviour.

Juanita said that, although she knew she had a problem, she liked being clean and tidy, so she didn't want to get treatment for her OCD. Unfortunately, without that, David wasn't likely to be able to change his behaviour, because her own behaviour would be modelling (and there-

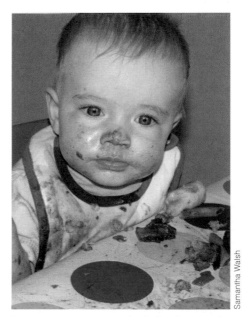

For some parents messy eating is fun; for others it fills them with anxiety. Your feelings matter too.

Samantha Walsh

fore teaching David to do) the opposite of what she was telling him to do. This was one family who we sadly couldn't help at that time – Juanita needed to be ready to make changes herself before we could support her in teaching David.

So take a step back and think about how your habits and tendencies might impact on your child's relationship with food. Make a conscious decision about whether you want those tendencies to shape this process or not. You need to find a balance between doing what you're comfortable with and preventing your unhelpful tendencies from interfering with your child's development. So if you're absolutely *not* comfortable with purées being slopped around and the accompanying mess, then trying to use them is likely to create anxiety and frustration for both you and your baby. However, if you know that you're a bit of a neat freak but you can handle mess if it's all in the name of your child discovering food, then you might decide to put your feelings aside and just deal with it. The most important thing is to be self-aware and to decide how you are going to be before you dive in. You're the model for your child; it's that simple.

Herita and Isabella

Herita came to us because Isabella (aged twenty months) would not try new foods. When we spoke at length to Herita, it emerged that Isabella was born after two miscarriages and IVF treatment, so she was something of a miracle baby for Herita and her husband. Herita said that she was quite an anxious person anyway and that she was always worrying about something terrible happening to Isabella.

As a result, she wouldn't let her walk unaided when they went out. She said that Isabella found it difficult to socialize with other children at nursery and so she had tried nursery for a brief time but then Herita gave up work and kept her at home because she thought Isabella was unhappy. At home, it was just the two of them most of the time, as Isabella was shy around other children and they didn't go out to socialize with other mums and children much. When Isabella did play with other children, Herita found it very difficult to go and sit with the other mums, instead hovering over her daughter as she played and assisting when she felt Isabella needed it.

Herita said that she felt extremely anxious when Isabella was eating, as she was worried about choking, even though she knew that she could feed herself very well. She said that she did tend to jump up and pat her on the back as she was eating, if she even thought she saw a tiny sign of imminent choking. She admitted that she found it nearly impossible to allow Isabella to eat without hovering over her and intervening regularly. More often than not, Isabella ended up crying and mealtimes were a source of stress for both of them.

We talked through the difference between choking and gagging with Herita and she realized that she was not giving Isabella enough space to experiment with food and learn about it, discovering it at her own pace and making mistakes along the way. She understood that her anxiety was likely to be transmitting itself to Isabella, who was therefore likely to be feeling less and less confident about trying things on her own. Ongoing anxiety in the parent and over-controlling parenting can cause the child to feel like they can't do anything on their own and to lose confidence in general, leading to them trying fewer and fewer things.

Herita agreed that she would start to take a step back using foods that worried her less, such as porridge, which Isabella loved. We also suggested that she try serving the same food in different formats so that Isabella could have the safety net of a food she knew, but experience a new texture. Within a few weeks, things were much better and Isabella was beginning to gain confidence with eating. She was happy to try different textures of the same food. Herita decided to get some help with her anxiety and as she began to understand her own background and her reasons for feeling that way so often, she was able to manage it better. Although managing her anxiety continues to be difficult for Herita, she has worked hard at giving Isabella the space to discover new foods at her own pace and Isabella's eating behaviour has improved dramatically.

How do children develop self-control?

Self-control can be thought of as the capacity to manage ourselves to get what we want. In the late 1960s and early 1970s, Walter Mischel conducted a series of experiments called 'The Stanford Marshmallow Experiment', where he tested children's capacity to resist eating a marshmallow in order to receive a better treat (e.g. two marshmallows).

Approximately 30% of 4-year-olds can manage themselves well enough to have self-control at least some of the time. Levels of self-control in toddlers and very young children appear to be related to self-control and social development later on[234]. We need self-control to achieve any of our goals and to conduct social relationships, so it's a very important skill to learn.

Toddlers can't control their emotions well enough to have self-control because their prefrontal cortex, which is needed for self-control, is hardly developed. It won't become fully mature until adulthood, but you can help it to develop with practice!

The following factors become relevant when you're teaching your child how to have self-control.

1. Trust – the more your child trusts you (which comes about through responsive, reliable and sensitive parenting), the easier they find self-control. This is related to the emotion regulation learning process (p.86). Every time your child experiences soothing and their needs being met when they're an infant, their brain strengthens the neural pathways that enable them to calm anxiety and manage their emotions. Later on, the ability to manage emotions is what helps any child to learn self-control or to delay gratification (i.e. to save something for later). This is a relatively mature developmental stage for children to reach and soothing and accepting parenting helps them achieve it.

2. Practice – every time your child makes a choice and gives up one thing for another they'd rather have (note: it has to be something *they* want, rather than something that is imposed on them) they're developing the relevant pathways in their prefrontal cortex. Forcing your child to let go of something they want or never allowing them the opportunity to make these choices doesn't allow them to practise self-control.

Does your child have self-control?

3. Empathic boundaries – boundaries are best established when children can make choices; for example, a child may not want to put their shoes on but they do want to go and see their friend and therefore they make a choice about what to do. Giving the choice that they can either put their shoes on or leave them off and stay at home will help your child to develop self-discipline.

4. Waiting – if your child learns to wait for things, they learn to tolerate waiting and also to tolerate delayed gratification. However, you have to understand where your child is at developmentally, so if they're made to wait longer than they're able to, they get overwhelmed by distress at not having their needs met and they begin to cry/scream. Waiting also has to be structured and practised calmly – shouting at children to wait makes waiting seem like an emergency situation, which again prevents them from learning to handle it and manage their emotions. Waiting makes children feel anxious, so part of the teaching process is to help them to handle their anxious feelings. This is done by empathizing and teaching your child how to distract themselves while feeling anxious (e.g. 'I know you're hungry, it's so hard. Supper is nearly ready, why don't you come and help me lay the table?').

5. Natural self-discipline – for example, playing with other children requires a child to manage their emotions and control their behaviour. Painting a picture requires that they wait until the paint is dry.

The good news is that things aren't set at age four. The plasticity of the brain means it can strengthen during our lifetime, depending on what is required of it. So sensitive, responsive parenting where limits are empathically set and children are encouraged to discover the world is the key for helping your child to become an adult who has good self-control.

Task: Does your child show self-control?

Offer your child a cake/chocolate/sweet and say they can either eat it now or, if they wait until after the park, they can have two. A child with self-control is likely to choose to wait.

If your child is given a lolly and wants to save it for later or walks around holding a satsuma segment all day you should take some delight in the fact that they are demonstrating skills of self-control.

Robert and Emma

Robert, a single dad, came to see us because he was worried about Emma's eating habits. Robert and Alison had divorced a year ago and he had found himself struggling with being a single parent. Robert told us that he felt at a loss when it came to getting Emma to eat healthy food and to eat at mealtimes. He said that he was worried she wasn't eating enough, so he always made sure he had food available and tried to persuade her to eat throughout the day. Robert said he wasn't that confident a cook, so he often found himself giving Emma whatever was easiest for meals, like mini pizza or sausage rolls. He did try to give her something fresh at each meal, such as tomatoes, but he found that she never ate them and that trying to persuade her to resulted in Emma crying. He also said that Emma had begun to get very distressed (and often became hysterical) if she asked for something and didn't get it immediately, so he always gave in and often gave her food to calm her down — he just didn't want her to be unhappy, particularly as Emma didn't live with him full-time. He

wanted their time together to be fun. She had begun to ask him for biscuits and banana throughout the day and, because he didn't want to deprive her, he always asked her if she wanted more and allowed her unlimited snacks. He said that he snacked a lot himself in front of the TV and also allowed Emma to eat in front of the TV because it was easier. On occasions when he had tried to break this habit, he found himself having trouble facing the tantrums when he tried to get her to sit at the table.

Together with Robert, we identified several problems that he wanted to work on with Emma. One important issue seemed to be that Emma wasn't learning self-regulation (or rather, her natural capacity for self-regulation that had been developing during breastfeeding was being trained out of her). Robert was unwittingly overriding Emma's ability to continue developing these skills in various ways. For example, his worry that Emma wasn't eating enough was leading him to teach her, unwittingly, that eating wasn't about feeling hungry or satisfied. The unlimited availability of food and the unstructured 'grazing' that Emma was doing throughout the day, combined with her developing preference for the fat- and carb-laden foods she was eating at mealtimes, meant that she was learning to eat because food was available and always being offered, or simply because she liked something. Meal- or snack-times weren't any different from the rest of the day for Emma, because she was eating throughout the day and meals were had wherever she was, while being distracted by the TV. She was also seeing and learning from Robert's

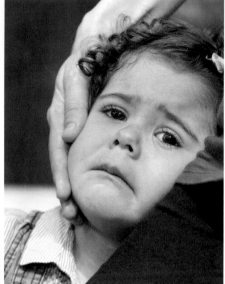

Shutterstock

When older children cry, respond with comfort, cuddles and reassurance instead of food.

snacking habits, as well as learning that eating was the way to calm down.

Robert spoke to Alison and they decided to both implement our recommended strategies in their homes. We suggested that Robert start dealing with the issues step-by-step. First, we explained to him about portion sizes and about how much food Emma needed for her age, as well as giving him easy recipes to help him prepare healthier foods that they could both eat. Robert was shocked at how much he had been expecting Emma to eat, as he realized he had been providing (and wasting) far more food than she needed.

The next thing we did was to help Robert to introduce some boundaries around mealtimes. We explained to him that getting upset wasn't a bad thing but was simply a normal way for Emma to express herself when she wasn't happy

with something, as children can't regulate their emotions on their own. It didn't mean that she wasn't 'happy' during their time together. We also explained that Emma needed to be able to pay attention to her eating during mealtimes, rather than being distracted by the TV. We coached him in comforting Emma but keeping the boundaries firm. Emma didn't take long to catch on and within a week or two of reinforcing boundaries and comforting, Emma and Robert sat together at the table for meals. By learning this strategy, Robert also stopped feeling like food was the way to calm Emma down, so he stopped offering food when she was upset.

Robert also introduced structure around how many snacks Emma ate and learned how to give Emma much smaller portions at mealtimes. We showed him how to give Emma A-B choices in everyday life and when it came to food. Robert started to build a framework that helped Emma to learn about making choices, and to make food-related choices based on hunger. He modelled this (e.g. by saying something like: 'What would Daddy like to eat? An apple or an orange? He'll have an apple'). He also gave Emma a small portion and allowed her to ask for more when she wanted it, asking her if she was still hungry first when she did. We recommended asking her if she was sure several times before acting. By doing this, Robert was encouraging Emma to make food-related choices that required her to decide whether she was hungry or satisfied.

We also suggested that he began to practise 'waiting' for things with Emma and that he could make it a game where they waited for things together. Robert modelled the behaviour and verbalized it in whichever context they happened to be in. At first, he did not suggest waiting when it was something Emma was asking for, but instead when it was something he was requesting, e.g. 'We're going to put our coats on but we're going to wait a bit first, okay? Why don't we put our gloves on in the meantime?' He was eventually able to make waiting into a game, even when Emma wanted something. He then helped Emma to learn to wait longer (and develop the ability to control her behaviour and delay gratification) by saying things like: 'Let's take our coats off first and then we'll have a snack, okay?'

We also worked with Robert on the other issues, such as introducing new foods. One of the most important reasons that these strategies worked so well was that Robert and Alison worked together on them, so that Emma became familiar with doing things in the same way, whether she was with Mummy or Daddy. For any strategy to work properly, it needs to be consistently applied, above all else. As humans, we are all naturally inclined to develop in a way that allows us to regulate our behaviour (we need to do this to fit in socially) and to self-regulate our eating, so it doesn't take long for children to learn how to do this again — within a couple of months, Emma's behaviour had drastically improved, as had her eating.

Re-regulating a toddler's appetite

If you believe your child's capacity for self-regulation has been compromised, all is not lost. The body is an adaptive structure with

> **Key point:**
>
> **How you parent in everyday situations impacts on your child's eating behaviours.**

huge potential to change. Basic parenting approaches can not only re-regulate the appetite but also ensure that a child's capacity for self-regulation continues to develop as they get older. You may not have considered until now that how you parent your child in everyday activities can have such an impact on their eating, but if you can help your child to develop self-regulation skills in all areas, it will help them to transfer these skills into the eating domain.

Two aspects of self-regulation that are particularly relevant to controlling food intake are[235]:

- Sensitivity to reward
- Inhibitory control[236 237 238]

So it stands to reason that working on these two areas can help reignite the skills of self-regulation within your child.

Sensitivity to reward
Sensitivity to reward reflects both a person's sensory pleasure associated with rewards and their motivation to obtain rewards. According to the hedonistic principle (the idea that people engage in activities that make them feel emotionally positive because it gives them a sense of pleasure), it is suggested that children learn how to behave so that they can maximize pleasure and minimize pain[239].

If we go back to attachment theory for a moment, which suggests that children need to form nurturing and enduring relationships with their caregivers in order to survive, it means that children need to learn how what they do affects their parents' reactions to them – those reactions inform the child of how that relationship is doing. Given that this relationship is the most important one of all for a child, their sensitivity to reward (i.e. the pleasure they receive from a reward that affirms that relationship) and their motivation to obtain it are understandably high.

When it comes to how this applies to you in your role as a parent, it means that your child will want to maximize the pleasure they receive when you approve of them, praise them, cuddle them, bond with them or engage with them, for example, and mini-mize the pain they feel when they experience disapproval (e.g. being scolded or disen-gaged with). They begin to learn that certain behaviours result in positive and pleasurable experiences for them while others result in negative ones.

As an aside, in relationships where chil-dren do not experience their parents as loving, accepting and bonded with them, they can begin to work out how to behave based on avoidance of pain rather than enjoyment of pleasure. The child then tries hard to avoid disapproval because, in the same way that the pleasure they would experience from affirmation would be partic-ularly powerful, so is the pain they experience from a negative outcome – in short, as many people can tell you, rejection by your parents hurts like nothing else. If you have parents whom you experience as critical and distant, you might grow up being completely focused on doing things perfectly, while never feeling like anything you do (or the way you are) is good enough.

As a parent, your behaviour is therefore paramount in how it shapes your child's developing capacity for self-regulation. When you encourage them to explore or to do things themselves and praise and validate them when they achieve those things, your child experiences a real, felt sense of pleasure. In adult terms, if your partner told you that you were the most amazing person they'd ever met and they were lucky to have you, how would you feel? Pretty good, eh? And it's not intellectual, is it? It's a feeling that you can't control that makes you want to smile and gives you a warm feeling. That's visceral pleasure and it's unlike any other feeling – it affirms and validates us at our core. However, it is important to note that praise doesn't equal affection. Therefore, if your child does not do as you wish, you can show disapproval and act accordingly but it is never advisable to withdraw love. Your child should never feel that something they do can make you cold and distant towards them – this will create insecurity. Make sure you parent in a way that says: I always love you, but I praise/disapprove of your actions appropriately, in a way that is consistent so that you understand.

The more you set your child up to achieve the things you would like them to (i.e. you give them goals in the right way and facilitate their choices), the higher their chance of receiving validation for making the choice. You can increase your child's experiences of being rewarded simply by making sure that:

a) you are happy with whichever options you give them
b) you give them small challenges that they can achieve
c) you phrase things positively when you're asking them to do things and engage them in the activity. For example, rather than saying: 'No, don't do X!', turn it around into what you *do* want them to

Key point:

Teach your child how to make positive choices and experience satisfaction by giving them your approval and acceptance, but never withdraw love when they get it wrong.

do. Make tasks into a game: 'Where are Charlie's shoes?? They're here, aren't they? Can you give me your foot so I can put your shoe on? Well done!'

Parenting in this way teaches your child to make positive choices and experience satisfaction through using the rewards that matter most in the world to them – your love, approval and acceptance. Every time you give your child pleasure in this way, you're increasing their sensitivity to reward, because you're teaching them over and over again that certain behaviour gives them a really good feeling. This is beneficial when you're trying to help them to learn inhibitory control, which isn't easy. If they have really positive experiences when they show inhibitory control, it makes it that much more motivating for them to try and practise building those skills.

Inhibitory control

Inhibitory control is one of the processes controlled by your child's cognitive system. It contributes to your child's ability to control unhelpful impulses and behaviour and choose better ones. It is regulated by the prefrontal cortex, a part of your baby's brain that doesn't develop until much later, which is why when your child wants something they want it NOW!

If your child develops good inhibitory control, they will be able to demonstrate self-control. The more self-control your child shows, the better off they will be in terms of being able to manage their behaviour and make choices that help them to achieve their goals. Much of teaching your child to have self-control comes down to giving your child choice: teaching them about decision-making by explaining how it works and allowing them to experience it.

The basis of our advice to allow your child to choose when to eat their snacks is that it will teach them delayed gratification, which contributes to the development of inhibitory control. They can choose to eat the snacks all in one go and then go hungry later or they can space them out. They are going to get it wrong the first time, but that is okay – they are learning and until the frontal lobe has developed substantially, they will not gain this control.

The basis of our advice to occasionally serve pudding alongside a main meal at dinner-time is that it can be another way of learning inhibitory control. A child who chooses to eat the pudding alongside or after the savoury, rather than gobbling it up in one go, forgoing the savoury, is demonstrating self-control.

Offer solutions to problems

It's actually quite difficult for young children to process negative and abstract concepts, so

Key point:

Key point: much of your child's development of self-control comes from allowing them to make choices.

using language that tells your child what you *do* want them to do, rather than what you *don't* want them to do, can be beneficial. For example, if you find yourself saying: 'Don't throw food on the floor', your child will hear 'food' and 'floor' and don't be surprised if what follows is another food on the floor incident! By using negative statements, you're almost setting your child up to do the opposite of what you want them to do, which leads to disapproval.

Instead, by telling them what you *do* want them to do, you can set them up to do well, which will give you an opportunity to praise them and show approval, while they feel the pleasure of being told they've done well. Children get extra bonding experiences and gain confidence when you hug and kiss them and tell them they're good or clever. For example, you may choose to say: 'Food stays on the plate.'

This can apply to all aspects of your parenting. If your child hits or pushes, instead of saying 'no pushing' replace this with 'touch gently' or something positive. Children respond well to direct instruction and direction, and they crave your approval.

Use A–B choices to teach your child about making decisions

Young children find it overwhelming to make a decision without boundaries or structure, and it can actually distress them and make

them anxious if they are given too many choices or open-ended choices (i.e. choose whatever you want). This is because they aren't yet able to hold lots of different and abstract ideas in their heads and make a choice. Children in their early years, on average, can only hold two pieces of information in their short-term memories at once, and even the average adult can only hold five in mind, so giving your child a list of things they are able to eat is confusing and unfair. It is likely to be overwhelming and children faced with this situation are more likely to repeat the last thing you said instead of making an actual choice.

Julia and Milo

When we observed Julia and Milo, Julia gave Milo choice and offered him a snack of raisins, breadsticks, an apple or a banana. On this occasion, Milo chose a banana. Later that day he saw his brother eating raisins and said he wanted those. Julia stuck to her guns, reminding Milo that he had made a choice. Milo cried.

In one respect, Julia did the right thing by giving Milo choice. However, two errors were made: Milo was highly likely to have chosen an apple or a banana as his snack because the list of four items that Julia had given him was too long for his cognitive stage to accommodate. By the time Milo made the decision, he had only retained the items apple or banana — it is likely the raisins and breadsticks had gone out of his mind and so he wasn't able to make an informed decision.

The second mistake was the time that elapsed between choosing the snack and eating it. Milo was likely to have forgotten the snack he chose in the morning by the time it was given to him because children of this age have little concept of time. The next day, Julia took two snacks in her bag (raisins and a banana in this case) and when it came to snack-time she showed both to Milo, asked which he would like and he made the decision then and there. No fuss. No tears. He made a choice within the realms of his cognitive capability. He ate the snack and was happy.

Sometimes, having too much choice is overwhelming for all of us, even as adults. For example, if you're researching buying a new gadget, are the hundreds of available options a bit much? Do you sometimes wish that someone would just give you two to choose from so you could pick one? This is often how our thought process works, as

Give your child a choice from two options to help them have control within the limits you set.

eventually we reduce that enormous list of options down to a choice of a few and then make the decision between the front-runners.

Give your child's choices some structure through the use of A–B choices – children can manage these from a young age. For example, if you ask a child to draw a picture of anything at all, they may stumble and struggle, but ask them to draw a picture of a cat or a dog and they will be happier to choose. This principle is valid in every area of your child's world, not just with food. Your job is to teach your child to learn how to make choices, and that starts with choosing from just two things (the A–B choice).

> **Key point:**
>
> **You decide what the A–B choices are and your child decides which of those to choose. This fair approach gives everyone a sense of control over the situation.**

You make the big decisions and your child makes the small ones

Give your child a small amount of control at mealtimes, and model this 'choice-making' for them, even before they can talk. For example, you make the 'big' decision that you're having lasagne and then let them decide which vegetable they would like ('With your lasagne, would you like peas or sweetcorn?'). They make the 'small' decision ('Peas please' – when they can talk – or 'I think we'll have peas today' – reply for them if they can't talk yet). This small opportunity to make a decision is giving your child some control

Avoid serving a plate of a single food as this removes choice.

over what will appear on their plate and is helping them to develop their sense of self, confidence and independence. Go through this kind of conversation whenever there is a choice to be made and your little one will soon come to understand that this is the way that all decisions are made.

This model applies even before your child is introduced to solids, but you probably haven't considered it. Ideally, as a newborn your child was encouraged to feed on-demand, which follows this model of a baby's psychological development. You decided the big things (what they were going to eat – breast milk, expressed breast milk in a bottle, formula etc.) and your baby decided when they ate and how much they took. So this decisional hierarchy is not new to your child – they have been doing it from the moment you first met and it will probably continue well into adolescence. Imagine yourself making these decisions in fifteen years' time: your child decides which disco they will go to, you

decide what time they should come home, your child brings a boyfriend/girlfriend home, you decide whether they can stay over. Right now, through food, you are implementing a parenting framework that will support you and give you structure well beyond weaning.

Always offer more than one food at each meal

Another way of giving your child choice as they eat is to have a variety of foods available on the plate. Being given a single bowl of porridge or a solitary omelette may not be appealing so, instead, have porridge and fruit, or omelette, peas and potato. You are providing choice. You could even serve the omelette but have half of it intact and the rest of it in pieces; again your child can choose which to eat (don't forget that the omelette presented in two different ways appears as two different foods to your child). The key here is simply that there is a choice

> **Key point:**
>
> **Creating a hierarchy of choice ensures that all family members have input into the food that's available at mealtimes.**

of foods to eat because having a choice is empowering.

How you choose the foods on the plate will have been decided through the 'hierarchy' system, so you, as the parent, may have decided that omelette is on the plate and your child has decided between peas and sweetcorn. If there is a sibling, they may have decided between potatoes and rice so you now have a plate of omelette, peas and potatoes that everyone is eating. Everyone feels empowered because they had a say and everyone has at least one food they selected. This is far more likely to lead to a happy mealtime than serving up a single bowl of cottage pie, porridge or even baby rice, for example, with nothing else to choose from. Put yourself in your child's situation – sometimes you just don't fancy something, so why shouldn't your child feel the same?

This hierarchy of choice might be applied at breakfast, for example, where you as the parent decide that cereal is for breakfast. Your children may then decide which cereal to choose from the selection you have given them. This choice-making – within boundaries you have set – avoids you

> **+ + + Tip + + +**
>
> **Your child may enjoy choosing the filling for an omelette.**
>
> **+ + + + + + + + +**

finding yourself asking 'What would you like for breakfast?' and hearing a request for scrambled eggs on a day when there are no eggs in the house. This brings us back to our foundational principle – that you and your child both matter in this process.

Just because your child chose the food does not mean they have to eat it. Your child decides which foods and how much they should eat.

Giving your child control in other parts of their life is important

It may sound like a contradiction but, in fact, the *more* control children have in other areas of their lives, the *less* likely they are to feel the need to exert control at mealtimes. When children don't have the opportunity to exert control and develop independence in other areas, food is the one area where it's easy for them to do so – you can't force food into their mouths and down their throats. Look for every opportunity you can throughout your child's day to give them A–B decisions. Examples might be 'Would you like to get in the left side or the right side of the car?', 'Would you like to drink from your red cup or your blue cup?' or 'Shall we brush your teeth or wash your face first?'

Creating these small opportunities for your child to have control over what happens throughout their day will not only ensure your little one is used to making A–B choices but it will also have a positive effect on your relationship with them. By sharing control with them, you're creating a relationship where battles become less likely, as they understand how things work but feel able to have a say, too. Having control is also important for your child when they are learning to make decisions, as it will develop their confidence and a secure sense of self. If you teach your child that only two choices exist, you will also

Shutterstock

Teach your child to save room for pudding, not make room.

find it easier to parent them through tantrums, because you are giving them choices but they aren't overwhelming ones.

Rachel and Charlie

Rachel and Charlie had just headed to the zoo to meet their friends. On arrival, Charlie called his mummy a 'poo-poo mummy' (a rather popular phrase amongst the 3-year-old boys at that moment). Rachel spoke with Charlie and explained that she didn't like to be called that and if he called her that again they would be leaving the zoo. Within a few minutes Charlie called Rachel 'poo-poo mummy' again and Rachel, sticking to her word, said goodbye to their friends and left the zoo. All of her friends were gobsmacked that she actually left after only a few minutes, but Charlie made a choice and he chose to call her the name and there-fore he received the consequence of his action.

Through this process, your child learns that decisions have consequences and that they need to take responsibility for their decisions. Everyone's a winner. You can teach babies about decision-making in this way before they can speak. Every time there is a decision to be made, verbalize it: for example, shall we wear the blue trousers or the red trousers today? Let's wear the blue trousers. Your baby will then get used to you giving them two choices and they will begin to choose, as soon as they are able.

Catherine and Barnaby

Catherine asked Barnaby each morning what he wanted to wear and one day Barnaby spotted his swimming shorts and said he wanted to wear those to nursery. Catherine didn't want him to, she wanted him in his trousers — it was, after all, the middle of winter with snow on the ground. After almost twenty minutes of screaming and tantrumming they were very late and Catherine gave in and let Barnaby wear his swimming shorts. From Barnaby's perspective he wasn't deliberately trying to be naughty or wind his mummy up, he had been asked a question and he had replied. He did not know that swimming shorts weren't allowed and he made a choice, as she had asked him to. Taking that choice away by saying that shorts weren't allowed was understandably distressing. Instead of asking 'What would you like to wear?' Catherine could have avoided this situation by making Barnaby aware of the boundaries with her questioning. Asking 'Would you like to wear the red trousers or blue trousers?' would enable everyone to get satisfaction – Catherine ensures Barnaby wears trousers and Barnaby gets to choose which ones.

Save room, don't make room!

Puddings are commonly used as a bribe for children to finish what's on their plate. Having that ice cream if you eat one more spoonful is a common sentence in most households. Unfortunately, that is a great way to create an over-eater and a fussy eater.

By encouraging your child to eat 'one more mouthful' you are claiming to know how full they are feeling. When the stomach is full, the stretch receptors in the stomach lining activate the nerves, which tell the brain 'I'm full'. By telling your child to eat more, you are teaching your child to over-ride their natural brain signals – an action that won't need to be repeated too many times before it is hard-wired. That's not the only reason not to encourage your child to eat – research shows that encouraging children to eat a certain food can influence their forming a dislike of that food[240]. Haven't you ever wondered why so many adults you might encounter 'don't like sprouts' or 'don't like cabbage' – those are precisely the foods their parents tried to pressurize them to eat throughout childhood! This sort of strategy is likely to breed resistance to

Puddings don't need to be naughty treats. Yoghurts, fruit and other foods served after the main meal all count as pudding and should be treated as such. However, there is no need to serve these kinds of food items every day.

Shutterstock

David Bertin

This child is choosing to eat his sugarsnap peas while ignoring his raspberry fairy cake.

further exposure, often resulting in a rein-forced and legitimate 'dislike'. It can be a vicious cycle.

Of course, as we mentioned elsewhere, some people are genetically predisposed to dislike bitter tastes, but this is not a black and white issue. A genetic predisposition may mean that left to your own devices you'd steer clear of certain flavours, but socialization and repeated exposure may well play a part in allowing tastes to change.

Another important point to make on this issue: there is no need for pudding to be served every day – do you eat pudding with every main meal or every day? If you do get into the habit of serving pudding all the time, your child will quickly come to expect dessert – if you then can't deliver one day, watch out! Variety is key to your child developing a healthy relationship with food and so if you only eat puddings occasionally then it's not a problem if your child does too.

Springing pudding on a child at the end of dinner is also unfair. They will have eaten their dinner to fill themselves up and then if they suddenly find a bowl of jelly waiting for them, they will override their fullness signals and overeat. Let your child know at the start of the meal that there is going to be a pudding, so they will undereat to save room for it. That way, you're helping your child to regulate their food intake by understanding and making judgments based on the signals their tummy is sending (or will send) to their brain.

Key point:

Avoid serving pudding every day. Fruit and yoghurt count as puddings.

Chapter Twelve

Feeding the Schema

There are plenty of theories on schemas, dating back to 1896 when Jean Piaget started to recognize organized behavioural patterns in children under five years old. He stated that schemas are the building blocks of knowledge[241]. Over the years, many pioneers in childcare, including Maria Montessori and Rudolf Steiner, recognized the importance of schema-type behaviour in a child's development.

What are schemas?

Have you ever noticed your child repeatedly dropping their food on the floor or dropping toys from their buggy? This isn't your baby trying your patience but an example of them exhibiting a schema. Schemas are patterns of repeatable behaviour that you may notice in your child's play. By exploring and practising their schemas, your child becomes more knowledgeable about the world around them. Schemas are what motivate your child to learn and are a direct reflection of their interests at that time. They can lead to

your child engaging in and exploring concepts associated with whichever schema is relevant at that time.

How are schemas useful?

An understanding of schemas is useful for helping to understand your child's motivation for doing something, and that includes eating. Spotting the schema allows you to extend their learning by matching learning opportunities to their individual interests. For example, if you have a little one who's interested in moving objects from one place to another, you might say they are exhibiting the Transporting Schema (see p.203). If you're playing in the sand, you might notice your child is drawn to moving sand in buckets and trucks rather than digging or burying objects in the sand.

Accomodating schemas is part of our original weaning approach, based on our professional experience – but it makes sense from a child development point of view. Take the schema and apply it to engage your child with eating. Food is

---

Key point:

Repeatedly dropping toys or food on the floor isn't your child being naughty. They are exhibiting a schema – the foundations of child development.

Key point:

One of the earliest ways that your child will learn about their environment is through their mouth, and food and eating are an extension of that.

Putting objects in the mouth is another way of a child exploring and understanding them. It could be food, a toy or a plate – it's their way of understanding it.

merely an extension of toys in terms of how a child learns. Remember: children learn most when learning is fun.

One of the earliest ways your child will learn about their environment is through their mouth, and food and eating are an extension of that.

The way a child interacts with a toy is to:

- See a toy that sparks their interest
- Reach for the toy
- Put the toy in the mouth to explore it

The way a child interacts with food is to:

- See some food that sparks their interest
- Reach for the food
- Put the food in the mouth to explore it

So why not apply this to the process of eating – an activity we will eventually do at least three times a day?

As you will hopefully appreciate by now, it makes sense to start off by offering bright colourful foods that will spark your child's interest rather than boring old beige baby rice. Serving up bright, colourful foods and giving your child the opportunity to choose them is an extension of learning and will encourage your child to get off to the best start in life developmentally.

It is easy to see how some children may go through a phase of becoming a fussy

> **Key point:**
>
> **Remember: children (like adults) learn most when learning is fun!**

Food throwing is often a sign of the trajectory schema.

The movement of bubbles reflects the trajectory schema.

eater when they would rather be down from the table playing than sitting at the table eating. Continuing with food being an extension of play and creating meals targeting your child's schema can help prevent boredom. We don't mean putting foods in patterns to resemble cars but rather serving up home-cooked food that complements your child's stage of development.

There are many different schemas that have been identified over the years. In this chapter, we explore those most commonly seen in children under the age of one.

Frequently exhibited schemas (including those that older children experience) are:

- Trajectory
- Rotation
- Enclosing
- Enveloping and containment
- Transporting
- Connecting and disconnecting
- Positioning
- Orientation
- Transforming

The trajectory schema

Many parents presume that a little one sweeping food onto the floor is a sign that they've finished their meal or maybe they are being a little pickle. This may not be the case. Another way to look at this is that the child could be behaving in a way that reflects their schema. Your little one could be showing signs of being in the trajectory schema.

Spotting the trajectory schema
One of the first recognizable schemas in a baby is the trajectory schema. The horizontal

Shutterstock

Interest in water falling can be a way of exploring the trajectory schema.

trajectory is expressed in the patterns of movement your baby shows in moving their arms and legs when kicking under a baby gym or crawling. The vertical trajectory is expressed in picking things up, posting things and, of course, the dreaded dropping of things. Many parents interpret the repeated removal of a hat as a sign their baby doesn't like something on their head, but this could be another representation of this schema – the hat moving up and down on their head is another expression of movement.

These first explorations of height, distance and length are not intended to annoy; it is a developmental phase. Swiping things off the highchair, dropping things from the pushchair and wanting them to be retrieved are all identifiable patterns of behaviour and, rather than fight it, you might embrace this developmental phase and accommodate it as much as you can.

Many children are ready to explore solid food from around six months and it is around this age that children are able not only to gaze at an object but to track it with their eyes and even their head – an example of movement and an expression of the trajectory schema. It has been shown that, 'From six months, when toys fall from the infant's hand, he or she will watch the fall to the point of arrival, providing all the action is within the visual field'[242]. To a child, the food is no different to a toy so is it any wonder that, with this newfound ability, they will sit in the highchair, elevated high above the ground and watch the food fall to the floor. To a child it's fascinating and they are learning, but to a parent it can be frustrating.

Accommodating the trajectory schema through play

Your little one might enjoy throwing things, so accommodate this by allowing them to throw safe things such as soft balls or bean-bags. Pointing out birds or aeroplanes in the sky can be interesting since they are moving in straight lines. Many babies are fascinated by floating bubbles and falling feathers due to their movement, again supporting the interest in this trajectory schema. Opening and closing drawers and cupboards, turning switches on and off and enjoying a ride in the pushchair can all be ways of exploring horizontal and vertical movements.

Feeding the trajectory schema

Understanding why your little one is dropping food on the floor can help you do something about it. One option is to remove the ability to drop something, so having a picnic can be a fun idea. Of course, this isn't always practical (although it's worth trying a kitchen-floor picnic on rainy days!) so another option is to try offering foods that support the schema. Check out our recipe ideas on p.194.

Dribbling foods can also be fun – taking a spoonful of something gloopy, such as porridge, and letting it drip from the spoon to the bowl can be stimulating. You could, of course, let your baby use their hands and fingers to do this too. Thick soups and yoghurts are great for this stage as they

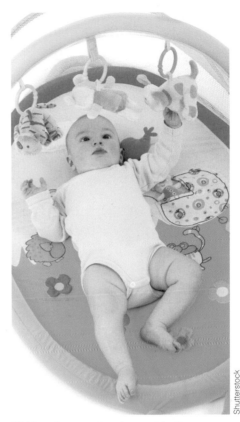

Shutterstock

Kicking of arms and legs is one of the first expressions of the trajectory schema.

enable the food to fall from the spoon to the bowl/table.

Drinking through straws can also satisfy this schema, again because the liquid is being transported from one place to another.

Recipes for trajectory schema

Plain Porridge

Preparation Time: < 1 minute
Cooking Time: < 5 minutes
Serves 1 little person

Ingredients
Handful of oats
Splash of water and milk

Method
1. Mix the oats, water and milk in a microwave-proof bowl and pop it in the microwave for 1 minute
2. Remove the porridge and stir, adding more milk or water if not drippy enough
3. Return to the microwave for another minute
4. Allow to cool for a few minutes and serve

Tip: Use more or less milk to change the texture for a new eating experience.

Posh Porridge

Preparation Time: Overnight
Cooking Time: 10 minutes
Serves 1 little person

Ingredients
Handful of oats
Splash of water and milk
Handful of raisins/prunes/apricots
Pinch of cinnamon and nutmeg

Method
1. The night before, soak the oats, water, milk, dried fruit, cinnamon and nutmeg in a microwave-proof bowl covered and kept in the fridge
2. The next morning, cook in the microwave for 5 minutes. Remove and stir at 1 minute intervals, adding more liquid as necessary
3. Allow to cool and enjoy!

Another great trajectory schema option is veggie sticks with our Cucumber & Mint Dip (see p.155) or hummus.

The up and down movements of dipping supports the trajectory schema. Watching the dip drip off the sticks supports an understanding of vertical movement.

Playing peek-a-boo is a way of expressing the enveloping and containment schema.

Dressing up can be an expression of the enveloping and containment schema since it is seen as 'wrapping' oneself.

Enveloping and containment schema

The enveloping and containment schema is all about 'insideness' and can show itself at any age. Children following this schema are starting the journey to understand space, size, volume and capacity – components key to mathematic and scientific skill development.

During their play, your young discoverer will estimate whether this can fit inside that and guess whether something is big enough to cover something else.

Spotting the enveloping and containment schema

If your little one loves hiding from you, dressing up and wrapping things, they may be exhibiting the enveloping schema. It can be heartbreaking for a parent to see a beautiful colourful picture suddenly covered by a solid layer of paint but, again, this could be your little one hiding the colourful paint inside the big splodge. Hide-and-seek or peek-a-boo could be a favourite game along with posting letters and making dens.

Accommodating the enveloping and containment schema in play

Dried pasta play:

- Fill a bowl with dried pasta and hide objects inside that your child has to find
- Fill socks, envelopes, old slippers, icing bags or anything else you have around with the pasta

Children find all sorts of ways to express their schema.

Water play:

- Blow bubbles
- Fill up bottles and funnels with water

Feeding the enveloping and containment schema

Sausage Pasta

Preparation Time: 20 minutes (to cook the sausages)
Cooking Time: 10 minutes
Serves 1 little person

Ingredients
1 sausage (see recipe on p.197 for chicken and apple sausages)
Handful of pasta

Method
1. Cook the pasta and sausages according to their packaging or your recipe
2. Cut the sausages into chunks and stir through the pasta – your little one will enjoy trying to find the sausage in the pasta
3. Based on your child's age you might use hands to find the sausage initially but as they get older you can encourage them to use a fork or spoon to fish the sausage out to encourage exploration of different cutlery

There's no need to limit yourself to just sausage and pasta. You can mix this up by serving rice and peas or any other food – the premise that the food is hidden is the same.

Chicken and Apple Sausages

(Taken from *Yummy Discoveries: The Baby-Led Weaning Recipe Book*)

Preparation Time: 10 minutes
Cooking Time: 20 minutes
Serves 1 grown-up and 1 little person

Ingredients
2 chicken breasts/skinless and boneless chicken thigh fillets/turkey steaks
2 carrots
2 apples
2 slices of oldish bread
1 egg
1 tsp unsalted butter

Method
1. Blitz the bread in a food processor to make breadcrumbs. Alternatively, pop in a freezer bag, cover with a tea towel and beat with a rolling pin until you have the required texture. Tip into a separate bowl
2. Whisk the egg in a bowl and set aside
3. Blitz the chicken, carrots and apples in a food processor to make a gooey sludge
4. Shape the chicken mixture into sausages or nuggets
5. Dip the chicken pieces in the egg, then the breadcrumbs. If freezing, do so at this point
6. Melt the butter in a frying pan on a medium heat
7. Shallow fry the coated chicken in the pan until golden
8. These can also be oven baked on a greased baking tray at 200C/180C Fan/Gas 6 for 20 minutes

Mixed Noodle Salad

Preparation Time: 10 minutes
Cooking Time: 10 minutes
Serves 1 grown-up and 1 little person

Ingredients
Handful of shredded lettuce
Handful of cucumber chunks
Handful of grated cucumber
Handful of apple chunks (optional – a common choking hazard in babies under twelve months – see p.113)
Handful of grated apple
Handful of raisins/apricots
100 g noodles

Method
1. Cook the noodles according to the packet instructions
2. Mix the food together and let your little one enjoy exploring and searching for the different foods they want to eat – such as finding an apricot or raisin

Tip: picking the raisins up with the pincer grip (see p.219) helps improve your child's motor skills. Identifying foods can help improve the ability to categorize things (differentiating between a vegetable, a fruit ... etc.).

Fruit–filled Pancakes

Preparation Time: 5 minutes
Cooking Time: 15 minutes
Serves 1 grown-up and 1 little person

Ingredients

300 ml (½ pint) full-fat milk
2 eggs
100 g plain flour
1 tsp unsalted butter
Filling of your choice, such as:
blueberries/strawberries/blackberries/rasp-
berries/grapes/banana

Method

1. Measure the milk into a measuring jug, add the egg and whisk with a fork
2. Put the flour in a bowl and make a well in the centre
3. Add the milk slowly and whisk briskly until the mixture has a batter-like consistency, then chill in the fridge until needed
4. Heat the butter in a frying pan and ensure the whole of the base is coated
5. Pour a large spoonful of batter into the pan and tilt the pan so the batter is swirled around the base
6. When the underside is cooked, flip over and cook the other side
7. Once cooked, tip onto a plate, add your filling and roll

Tip: serve the fruit on one plate and the pancakes on another and let your little one try to roll them up. Hiding the food inside is perfect for the enveloping schema.

Shutterstock

Fruit-filled pancakes are ideal during the enveloping and containment schema.

Mini Pasties

(Taken from *Yummy Discoveries: The Baby-Led Weaning Recipe Book*)

Preparation Time: 10 minutes
Cooking Time: 20 minutes
Makes 4–6 pasties

Ingredients
500 g beef stewing steak
½ packet of puff pastry or shortcrust pastry
1 egg

Method
1. Preheat the oven to 200C/180C Fan/Gas 6
2. Fry the beef until cooked through
3. Roll out the pastry and cut into circles of whatever size you would like your pasties. A large mug is a good template for finger-food-sized pasties
4. Spoon several pieces of beef in the middle of the pastry circle, leaving a 1 cm gap around the edge. Be careful not to overfill otherwise the pasties may burst when cooking
5. Beat the egg and use a pastry brush to brush over the 1 cm space
6. Fold the pastry edges together so they meet and use your fingers or a fork to seal shut
7. Brush the outside of the pasties with the egg and pop in the oven for 20 minutes or until the outside is golden

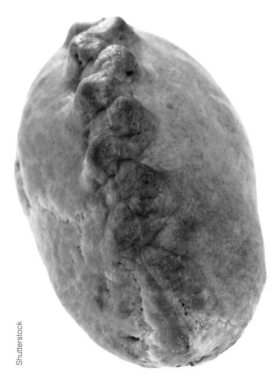

Shutterstock

Mini pasties are another fun option for exploring the enveloping and containment schema.

Salmon & Couscous Parcels

Preparation Time: 10 minutes
Cooking Time: 20 minutes
Makes 2 parcels

Ingredients
100 g couscous
Zest of ½ lemon
1 tsp garlic
200 ml hot vegetable stock
½ onion (chopped)
Glug of olive oil
4 sundried tomatoes or cherry tomatoes (chopped)
Handful of chopped rosemary and thyme
Ground black pepper
3–4 spring onions (thinly sliced)
2 salmon fillets

Method
1. Heat the olive oil over a medium heat and add the onions until soft
2. Add the garlic and cook for 30 seconds before adding the stock
3. Add the couscous, remove from the hob and set aside, covered with clingfilm for around 10 minutes
4. Remove the clingfilm and fluff up with a fork
5. Add half the chopped herbs and spring onions
6. Pre-heat the oven to 200C/180C Fan/Gas 6
7. Cut 2 squares of non-stick baking paper and spoon the couscous into the centre of each
8. Place the salmon on top and sprinkle with the remaining herbs and black pepper
9. Fold the paper over and twist to seal into a parcel
10. Place the parcels on a baking sheet and bake in the oven for 20 minutes or until the salmon fillets are cooked through
11. Allow to cool and serve in the bag

Fajitas are yet another interesting enveloping and containment meal option.

Fajitas

Preparation Time: 10 minutes
Cooking Time: 30 minutes
Serves 2 grown-ups and 2 little people

Ingredients
500 g skinless and boneless chicken thigh
fillets or chicken breasts (cut into chunks)
1 tsp mild chilli powder
1 onion (sliced)
1 red pepper (sliced)
1 tin of chopped tomatoes
Glug of olive oil

*Tip: instead of using chicken, try prawns or
strips of steak, or even a combination of
them all. Replacing the meat with a tin of
kidney beans will make this a vegetarian
meal, and adding beans to the meat will
make the mixture go further.*

TO SERVE: wraps with green salad,
Guacamole (p.161), salsa and grated
cheese

Method
1. Heat the oil in a large pan over a high
   heat
2. Add the chicken (it should sizzle) and
   cook until browned all over
3. Add the chilli powder, stir until the
   chicken is coated and cook for a couple
   more minutes
4. Scoop out the chicken with a slotted
   spoon and set aside
5. In the same pan, fry the onion and red
   pepper and cook until soft
6. Add the tomatoes and chicken, cover (if
   you can) and simmer for 15 minutes.
   Add some plain flour to thicken if necessary and check the seasoning, adding
   more chilli powder if necessary

Hiding fingers with raspberries is an example of the enveloping schema.

Shutterstock

Sandwiches

Preparation Time: 5 minutes
Serves 1 little person

Ingredients
1 slice of bread
Unsalted butter (optional)
Filling of your choice, such as: full-fat soft cheese with any of the following: avocado, grated cucumber, chopped tomato, tinned tuna, tinned salmon, Guacamole (p.161); grated cheddar cheese with grated cucumber or tomato; hummus; hard-boiled egg; scrambled egg

Method
1. Cut the sandwich into fingers or triangles for your baby to chew on

Development: *avocado is the ultimate baby food. It contains the highest protein and oil content of any fruit and may have up to 30% fat so is perfect for fattening up your growing baby.*

Health: *wholemeal bread is high in fibre and may help relieve the symptoms of constipation.*

Tip: *if you don't use the whole avocado, leave the stone in the fruit and it will prevent it from turning brown. See p.161 for more on avocados.*

Shutterstock

Moving things from one place to another is a child expressing the transporting schema.

Transporting schema

The transporting schema is all about transferring things from one place to another and helps develop an understanding of quantities and numbers. When children gather objects or make piles of things, this can be an opportunity to estimate quantity and predict the size or the weight. They are experiencing early equivalences of distance, length and speed.

Spotting the transporting schema

Your child will be interested in transporting things – and this could be absolutely anything. If there is a walker with blocks, they may enjoy transporting the blocks from one end of the room to the other. They may enjoy pushing a friend around in a pram and loading up a shopping trolley. Anything with wheels is usually appealing to a child in this schema – whether it be a shopping trolley, car or lorry; if it transports something then it is usually a winner.

Accommodating the transportation schema in play

One of the points of recognizing a schema is to use it to develop other areas of learning. Here are a couple of ways you can give this a go:

- Using a selection of coloured balls, transport them from one box to another and point out the different colours. Maybe ask whether your child can

Wheeling a walker and transporting objects is an example of the transportation schema.

Playing with cars is a good example of transportation schema play.

transport just the blue ones or red ones to help colour recognition and also request certain volumes, for example: 'Please can you bring me three blue balls?'

- Toy animals can be counted as they are transported from the farm to the field, or trains can be counted as they're being transported to the engine shed

Feeding the transportation schema

Give your child the opportunity to self-serve as much as possible. Have small bowls of food on the table, allowing your little one to either use a spoon to put some food on their plate or even their hands. If they are old enough, they might even like to help serve the family and lay the table (transporting cutlery).

Tortilla Tapas

Preparation Time: 25 minutes
Cooking Time: 30 minutes
Makes 8–12 tortilla snack squares

Traditional tapas are made over a hob in a frying pan but, for busy parents, this isn't always practical. Popping your tapas in the oven is a much easier way of managing this without the risk of it burning when you're changing a dirty nappy!

Ingredients
Glug of olive oil
1 onion (thinly sliced)
3 small potatoes (peeled and thinly sliced) – use waxy potatoes such as charlotte or jersey royals else they fall apart in the pan
2 garlic cloves (crushed)
½ tsp paprika
Handful of fresh chopped parsley (optional – this is just for colour)
2 red, yellow or orange peppers (deseeded and thinly sliced)
6 eggs (beaten)
½ tsp fresh chilli

Method
1. Heat the olive oil in a pan and add the onion and potatoes, frying for around 15 minutes until the onions and potatoes are soft
2. Preheat the oven to 200C/180 Fan/Gas 6 and pop the baking tin in at the same time to preheat
3. Add the garlic and peppers to the pan and cook for another 5 minutes
4. Remove from the heat and stir in the eggs, chilli, paprika and parsley (if using)
5. Remove the baking tin from the oven and brush with oil
6. Tip the egg mixture into the pan
7. Pop in the oven for 20–25 minutes – press the top and if it's still squidgy pop back in for a little longer
8. Remove and leave to cool for 5–10 minutes before tipping it upside-down onto a board
9. Cut into squares and serve

Tip: I love putting a couple of squares of this in my son's lunchbox. It makes a great picnic food or snack.

Tip: pop these in the middle of the table and allow your child to help themselves (transporting the food).

Tip: consider serving the tortilla in a circle – the shape is associated with transportation (as in wheels).

The whole family can enjoy tortilla tapas and leftovers are great for lunchboxes.

Fake Paella

Preparation Time: 15 minutes
Cooking Time: 15 minutes
Serves 2 adults and 1 little one

Real paella takes quite a long time to make, and sometimes there just isn't the time. Using leftover already cooked rice, make this fake paella.

Ingredients
300 g leftover pre-cooked rice
3-inch chunk of chorizo (sliced) or a handful of cooked diced chicken pieces
1 onion (sliced)
1 garlic clove (chopped)
½ tsp turmeric
½ tsp chilli
Tin of chopped tomatoes
100 g cooked prawns (frozen or fresh) or mixed frozen seafood (see p.110 if unsure about this)
Handful of mushrooms (chopped) – optional
2 handfuls frozen peas/green beans
Squeeze of lemon juice

Health: prawns can be served from six months of age.

Method
1. Pop the chorizo in a dry frying pan and heat for 5 minutes until it's sizzling – the oil from the chorizo will come out in the pan
2. Add the onion, garlic and chilli and cook for 5 minutes until the onions soften
3. Add the rice, turmeric, prawns, peas and stock
4. Add the chopped tomatoes and mushrooms (if using)
5. Stir through for around 10–15 minutes (add some water if necessary) and serve with a squeeze of lemon juice
6. Serve in a big pot and allow your little one to self-serve a portion

Tip: if I don't have any leftover rice, I like to pop the steamer on in the morning and get the rice cooked before whipping up the paella in the evening.

Tip: chorizo is quite salty so consider substituting it with some chicken and apple sausages (p.197) or cooked chicken. If you use these options, you will need to use olive oil in step one.

Tip: I often pop a spoonful of leftover Fake Paella in my son's lunchbox. It's delicious cold.

Shutterstock

Try our quick and easy Fake Paella recipe for a little taste of Spain at home.

Holding hands is a way of connecting two people.

A child exhibiting the connection schema through play.

Connecting (and disconnecting) Schema

Joining and connecting things together is great fun for children exhibiting this schema. Connecting pieces of train track together, tying or hooking things onto others – you will be amazed at how versatile a piece of string can be, tied round cars and trains. You may recall your own childhood of junk modelling where you would stick yoghurt pots to washing-up liquid bottles – all examples of the connecting schema. The connecting schema can also be seen as one of the foundations for interacting with other people – holding hands with Mummy or a friend is a connection between two bodies.

Accommodating the connecting and disconnecting schema in play

The connecting and disconnecting schema is a great one for using your imagination, as nearly anything around the home can be connected. Just grab a ball of wool and connect cars or dolls to each other. Making paper-chains and threading activities can all help stimulate this schema too. Pop into the garden and hang string from the trees or draw maze-like patterns where your child needs to find their way from one place to another.

Feeding the connecting and disconnecting schema

There are so many ways to open up this schema through food. A current trend in cooking is 'deconstructed' food where a basic dish such as a banana split is served in pieces – a similar concept can apply to your cooking.

Your little one may enjoy deconstructing a sandwich you have prepared, taking out the filling and eating each component separately. Or you can use the tines of a fork to

Kebabs are a great example of connecting food.

pierce a series of blueberries. How many can you connect with the fork? If your little one is old enough to be supervised with a skewer, piercing fruit and threading it onto the skewer can be an interesting activity – you can even disconnect by sliding the food off again.

Taking apart a sandwich and exploring it further can be a child's way of exploring the disconnecting schema.

Kebabs are a great example of connecting food.

Fruit Kebabs

Preparation Time: 10 minutes

Ingredients
Selection of fruit such as grapes, strawberries, pineapple, melon, kiwi,
Bamboo skewers

+ + + **Tip** + + +

Allow your child to self-serve from different bowls. This way they can construct various different kinds of fruit kebabs.

+ + + + + + + + +

Method
1. Slice the fruit into large chunks, pop into little bowls and set on the table
2. Sit with your child and thread the fruit onto the skewers
3. Enjoy!

Note: the skewers can be sharp so close monitoring and care needs to be taken with this activity. Monitor the shape of the fruit you serve too, to reduce the risk of choking; for example, we suggest halving grapes.

Dipping toast soldiers into a boiled egg is a yummy learning experience for little ones.

Dippy Eggs (for children over twelve months)

Preparation Time: 5 minutes
Cooking Time: 20 minutes
Serves 1 little person

Ingredients
1 egg
1 slice of bread

Method
1. Bring a small pan of water to the boil and add the egg, cooking for 3–4 minutes
2. Meanwhile, toast the bread and cut into chunky rectangles
3. Drain the egg and allow to cool by popping in a bowl of cold water and putting in the fridge for around 10 minutes
4. Serve to your little one and show them how to tap the top, peel the shell and dip their toast into the egg

> ### Key point:
>
> **Eggs may be offered from six months but the yolk should be solid until twelve months. Children could also dip toast in fruit purée or another kind of 'dip', if they aren't old enough to eat soft yolks yet.**

Chapter Thirteen

Helping Hand Development

Introducing cutlery

Did you know that rushing your child into using cutlery can actually hold them back developmentally?

Big to small and close to far

The principles of child motor development are 'big to small' and 'close to far'. This means the bigger, chunkier muscles of the trunk and arms will develop before the smaller muscles of the hands, and the muscles closer to the trunk (e.g. the shoulders) will develop before the muscles further away (e.g. the hands).

Your child may choose cutlery and hold it in all sorts of strange ways – and that's okay.

When a child is encouraged to use a 'proper' grasp of cutlery before the shoulder and arm muscles are ready to support it, fine motor problems may emerge, such as holding the cutlery in peculiar ways, avoidance of using cutlery or even tantrums and refusal to sit down to eat. So don't be in a rush to make your little one hold their cutlery properly. Let them learn naturally and, probably, by around the age of four years they will have naturally suppressed reflexes and learned new skills, and will be holding their spoon or fork in a more 'adult' way.

However, this doesn't mean you shouldn't encourage them to use cutlery or allow them to explore it from the moment you introduce food. Make cutlery available to your little one from the moment they start to wean by using items like rubber-tipped spoons. They can then become familiar with handling it and, since you are using cutlery to eat *your* food, they will have the opportunity to copy you, which is something they so badly want to do. Opt for cutlery with big, thick, chunky handles since the primitive fist grip will be around for a while and the chunky design will make it easier for them to hold in a fist grip.

When you start weaning, forks are often a problem for children. At the time of writing, forks for children need to adhere to certain safety standards and sadly this means they can't be sharp, which pretty much means your child will have difficulty piercing food with one. Knives also have a problem; there are even some on the market that have serrated edges drawn on to give the impression that they will cut – but they will do nothing. So avoid knives until your child has the hand control and power to use them and instead opt for spoons in the meantime.

My child used to hold a spoon – now they have stopped!

Each child develops at their own pace but there are some things you can do to help integrate the reflexes that might inhibit cutlery use and allow fine motor control to develop. Children go through phases of using cutlery – some parents report that their child grabbed a spoon from the moment they were weaned, only to shun the spoon at around a year to eighteen months and opt for hand-feeding. This is normal. The way cutlery is held in a 10-month-old is a lot different to the 'adult hold' and, as your child develops, they will change their mind. For example, a child who likes to hold a spoon when weaning initially might rely on their palmar grasp reflex to hold it, but once that reflex is suppressed they need to rely on conscious muscle control to grasp the spoon, which makes it a little more challenging – they may stop trying altogether but this is normal.

Forks are often quite tricky to master since the strength needed to pierce a food and put it on the fork is initially hard to judge. It doesn't help that many children's forks are far too blunt to actually stab a food effectively and the patience needed to master this often leads to a child giving up – it is much quicker

Shutterstock

Many items of cutlery aimed at children are not fit for purpose. Knives don't cut and forks don't pierce, which can lead to frustration when a child tries to copy you using your sharp cutlery.

to eat with the hands. Spoons are easier when used in the primitive way where the palm of the hand faces downwards and the bowl of the spoon faces the ceiling the whole time. The action of being able to turn a spoon in the 'supination' movement to scoop food up in the way an adult would is an advanced movement, so don't expect it too soon. You

---

Key point:

Cutlery available at mealtimes but allow your child to choose whether or not to use it.

will be surprised at how much you are already doing through play to get your child ready for cutlery. Focusing on the motor development of the hand and hand-eye co-ordination will help. Simple games such as sitting on the floor and handing your child a toy from different directions will help improve the perception of direction and space as well as hand-eye co-ordination.

Awareness of the hands and fingers through manipulating different objects and textures is useful – things like messy play where children can finger spaghetti and squelch corn-flour are wonderful for this. Mastering cutlery involves judging the different weights and sizes of foods and considering how to contract the muscles appropriately in the arm to bring the loaded fork to the mouth, so manipulating toys of different weights, sizes and consistencies prepares for this. Specifically, the following actions are useful:

- Practising holding and releasing (conscious control is needed to pick up cutlery)
- Crawling on the floor (to build the strength in the upper body and build a cross-pattern where one arm can move up to the mouth whilst the other stays down)
- Playing give-and-take with different sized objects (needed to be able to judge weight)
- Building towers (precise release of blocks is needed here)
- Dangling from the climbing frame in the park (this can help build upper body strength)

One of the most important things required for managing cutlery is body awareness – playing with the fingers and painting the hands, for example, all stimulate the feedback to the brain and increase aware-ness of the fingers – building the sensory homunculus in the brain.

Hand development

As when learning to walk, children go through sequential phases of sitting, crawling and standing. The same applies to the devel-opment of the hand.

Stage 1
Initially, you may find your little one holding their cutlery in a fist (grasp) with their elbow high up in the air or an underhand fist grip

Building towers helps build awareness of the hands and fingers.

Shutterstock

Fist grip with high elbows is a common way to first grasp cutlery.

An underhand fist grip is a common way for children to hold cutlery initially.

with their elbow down low. This is the remnants of the grasp reflex – you might remember how you would offer your newborn your finger and they would respond by clenching their fist tightly around it.

Stage 2

Before your child can move on any further, the grasp reflex needs to be fully inhibited, which means they should be able to let go of an object quickly, easily and voluntarily. Building towers with blocks is a great way of doing this since your little one needs to precisely release an object to stack it. Don't be surprised if during this time lots of food is being dropped from the highchair – this is your child developing.

Stage 3

Your child will start to straighten their index finger to gain control over the cutlery – this is a key transition stage and is a sign that your

Building towers helps your child judge when to release objects.

This child is starting to extend his index finger when using cutlery to gain more control

child is developing independent finger control. No longer are the fingers treated as a single entity but are ten individual digits in their own right. Your little one, by this time, will have probably had hundreds of different foods on their hands. They will have separated spaghetti strands and licked slimy sauces off their fingers. These different textures and sensations on the hands and fingers help disassociate them from each other, allowing your child to recognize that they are each individual, and so through self-feeding and food exploration, your child should be well on their way to mastering finger dexterity.

Stage 4

At around three or four years of age, a 'brush grasp' might be used, so the cutlery is held in the fingers rather than in the fist and the elbow is usually still up high. You will probably see this same grip being used when your child is painting.

The brush grasp is often used both in painting and when using cutlery.

Shutterstock

Notice how the elbows are lower, the index finger is extending and the control over cutlery is developing.

Stage 5

As your little one spends time watching people eat with cutlery, they learn that bringing the elbow down and resting the forearm on the table gives better control – another good reason to eat together. With so many of us eating with just a fork nowadays, children don't know what to do with a knife when they get to school (and don't get us started on those knorks (a combined knife and fork), which are quite ludicrous!). Using a knife to eat with is a life skill and is another step towards your child's independence, and so age-appropriate, supervised use of a knife when eating is a key part of learning.

Stage 6

Up to now, the cutlery control has all come from the shoulder and wrist (big muscles and those closest to the body) but, providing finger control has been allowed to develop (hopefully by you allowing your child to self-feed from the weaning stage, through picking up different shaped/weighted food with their hands), your little one will now have the fine muscle control in their fingers and hands to manipulate the cutlery. In most children this won't be until they are around four-and-a-half years old, but every child is different.

Perfect preparation for pencils

Allowing your child to self-feed involves allowing your child to choose between using their hands or cutlery to eat their food. You may find people criticizing you for making such a mess – after all, the purée-spoon-fed babies are eating from spoons, which is the goal, right? Wrong. In fact, you are giving your child so many opportunities to work on their motor control by encouraging them to use cutlery properly that this will set them up nicely for pencil control later on.

We've said it before: food is an extension of toys. Your child sees a toy, is interested and puts it in their mouth, and the same process occurs when eating. Toys are used as educational and developmental tools, and food and mealtimes are no different. The hand development required to use cutlery is the same as that required for writing so gaining good hand control will help refine motor control. Here's how …

> **Key point:**
>
> **The hand development required to use cutlery is the same as that required for writing.**

These pictures show how our hands often start in fist grips but, as we mature and develop, the end result is our fingers functioning individually, with the index finger extended and better control over the cutlery.

Inhibition of the grasp reflex

Your child is initially likely to be using their hands each time they self-feed. In order to get the food to their mouth, they need to let go of it, which is the beginning of grasp reflex suppression. Remember how your young baby would grab onto your hair and not let go? Those days are being left behind as your little one learns to let go of things voluntarily. Be prepared for phases of dropping food from the highchair as they go through this – it is a developmental phase and not naughty behaviour (see the information on the trajectory schema on p.191–4).

Fisted grasp refinement

First weaning foods are often big sticks of roasted veggies or broccoli spears. Serving up a selection of foods of various weights and textures, which need different degrees of muscle recruitment to pick them up, help improve the control over the muscles of the arms. Learning how tight to hold the fist so the sweet potato chunk doesn't squidge everywhere, or how much shoulder muscle recruitment is needed to hold the empty cup versus the full one, are all essential lessons. Even now, you may find yourself picking something up expecting it to be heavier than it is and flinging it high in the air!

Multi-grasp release

Initially, your baby will grasp with one hand and the other will automatically do the same. This will change over time and they will, given the opportunity, grasp an object with one hand whilst picking up another with the other hand. Offer your child a choice of foods on a plate and they will pick up one thing they like with one hand and put it in their mouth whilst

Sticking the tongue out whilst using the hands to perform actions such as drawing or painting can be a sign that the Babkin response reflex is still present.

they reach for another with the other hand. You may see this in a child who enjoys strawberries. They may have several slices on a plate and be reaching for the next whilst the first is being shovelled into their mouth. Only once this skill is mastered can your child move on to the next stage of refining finger movement.

Suppression of the Babkin response
Initially, as your newborn suckles, their fists will clench (the Babkin response) and this is because in the early days the hands and mouth are your baby's main ways of expressing their feelings. Over time, this neurological link needs to be integrated else you may find your child sticking their tongue out when they write (showing that the connection between their hands and mouth is still there) and other developmental skills won't be able to come forward.

Speech development delays are common while this reflex remains because the mouth can't be controlled independently of the hands. Your child will need to use their hands and mouth independently when self-feeding in order to pick up other foods as they eat, thus the self-feeding process helps this response to become suppressed.

Development of the pincer grip
Picking up foods of different shapes and sizes will encourage hand dexterity and development of different grasps. Picking up peas, sweetcorn and blueberries will probably initially be done as a fisted pick-up with all the fingers in use, but over time the pincer grip where the finger and thumb are used alone will come through – a massive developmental leap for the fingers. The muscles of the fingers are now being put in a different position and will start to

Your child has been learning through copying for many months, long before solid food has been introduced

strengthen – perfect preparation for gripping pencils.

Copying

With everyone in the family eating the same foods and enjoying mealtimes together, your child will learn that using cutlery is how one eats to fit in (see p.67) and will want to try different arm positions. This strengthening of the hand and arm and early manipulation of the fingers are all warming up the motor control of the hand ready for writing.

Hand dominance

At any time from two years old your little one will develop a dominant hand. For some children this doesn't happen until they are three or four so there need be no concern if they aren't showing early signs of sided dominance. Some parents mistakenly think that being ambidextrous is the goal but it is

A child picking up a leaf using the pincer grip.

much better for your child to develop strength and dexterity in one hand so it flourishes in fine motor skills, while the other hand can work on being a supporting hand. Think about it – it is far better to have two specialized hands that do their jobs well rather than a pair of mediocre hands trying to be everything to everyone. Allowing your baby to self-feed gives them a head start, since self-feeding develops their sense of bilateral co-ordination. For example, holding the pod steady while they pick out the peas, holding the plate while they help themselves to another serving, holding the orange while they peel the skin are all ways your little one is starting to rehearse their sided dominance. Their hands are rehearsing their jobs already!

Hand control and spatial awareness

Hand control and spatial awareness are intrinsically linked, so being able to grasp objects coming from different directions in the hands will help with the hand development.

Having foods on a plate or spread across a highchair table improves spatial awareness since children will need to reach for the food, pick it up and put it in the mouth. That's a lot of things going on and your 6-month-old is rehearsing many skills through self-feeding.

Hand awareness

Hand awareness is another key part of hand development. Allowing your child to explore different shapes, textures and objects with their hands will encourage this. Children often have lots of toys but repeatedly use the same six or seven. This is not enough and so self-feeding with hands from the moment a child is weaned is ideal since, each time a child eats, a variety of foods are made available – all with different colours, textures, sizes and shapes.

As an aside, making new foods available to your child may encourage speech since they will be encouraged to describe or name the foods they particularly enjoy in order to request them.

Chapter Fourteen

Troubleshooting

What if my child really doesn't eat?

There are some children who do not eat enough food to sustain their body requirements. In these cases, your child will begin to lose weight and it's important to have the GP make an assessment for any underlying pathology that might be causing weight loss or loss of appetite.

If your child is physically healthy, then it's time to think about what their refusal to eat might be about. It's important to remember that refusing food is a normal part of learning to eat, and that sometimes children are more or less hungry. You may or may not have been surprised by the actual portion sizes (see p.131) that children need versus what we as adults may perceive they need. In fact, when parents contact us saying their child really doesn't eat – the majority of the time we discover that they do eat – they just don't eat as much as their parents perceive they should eat or else they have a very restricted diet and don't eat a variety of foods. Remember:

- If your child is between six months and five years and having a vitamin supplement or sufficient volume of infant formula, you can rest assured that they are receiving all the vitamins they need. You can then focus on ensuring you are exposing them to a wide variety of foods without worrying about whether they're getting all of their vitamins (see p.144)

- Children balance their calorie intake out over a number of days (p.131) and so may eat less one day and more the next

Another thing to consider is whether you are with your child all day every day. Are you absolutely sure of the snacks they have eaten at Grandma's or how much of their friend's lunchbox they polished off at school? A further possibility if your child isn't eating is that there may be a psychological reason for their refusal to eat – has there been a change in the household such as a divorce, a return to work or a bereavement?

As we said earlier (see p.161–2), children need routine and familiarity, which serves an evolutionary purpose because, in order to survive, they need to understand how society functions and fit into it through their relationships with caregivers. It's a fundamental need for them and when infants and toddlers experience a major change in their daily routine, it's extremely distressing. The distress that a baby or young child feels manifests in their behaviour, because this is the only way they can express it. They also haven't developed emotionally to the point where they can be self-aware or manage their emotions in the way an adult might. Eating problems are one of the ways that distress can show itself, but it can be shown in a myriad of other ways, such as regression, aggression, sleeping problems, lethargy, tantrums and night terrors.

As children get a little older (for example, between three to five years of age), ongoing emotional distress can cause developmental delay (or the loss of previously accomplished skills/habits) in eating, as well as problems with sleeping, motor skills, language, toilet training, social skills and emotional independence.

There are some physical or psychological conditions that can lead to eating aversion, such as autism or cystic fibrosis and, in these cases, parents will need intervention tailored to accommodate their child's condition. But if there is no underlying pathology or psychological reason for your child not to be eating and you have been to the GP to confirm this, then your child will not starve. If you can work out what their behaviour is about and can adjust your parenting to address it, then you'll facilitate them to make positive choices around food.

Remember, there is nothing wrong with allowing a child to experience the natural consequences of their actions and recognize that choosing to not eat results in feelings of hunger, while eating food takes those feelings away. Indeed, you *need* to give your child the opportunity to learn this and it's worth remembering that sneaky snacks, drinks of squash and smoothies are likely to make this harder for them, rather than easier. The advice we have read in a number of parenting books to have a 'snack box' of healthy treats accessible to your child at all times is not going to solve the issue – you're just delaying tackling the underlying problem.

Why won't my child try new things?

There are certain ages where children develop a fear of eating new foods (see p.118). During this time, your child will go from

Refusing to try new food is normal, but don't be put off – keep offering it.

happily eating anything you put in front of them to narrowing their repertoire of foods down to the same old favourites. If you are in this stage, don't force it, don't get frustrated, just accept that this is a natural evolutionary behaviour and a part of child development. They *will* come out the other side, as long as you continue to do the following:

- Eat the same foods as your child and eat with them (see p.106–7)
- Continue to offer new foods to your child while ensuring there is always something they will eat on the plate (see p.171–5)
- Give your child permission to spit! (see p.122)
- Offer the food over and over again. Not every day, but regularly, to ensure that they become familiar with seeing it, smelling it and watching you eat it (see p.125–6)
- Don't trick your child. If you have served rabbit while telling them it is chicken,

you are risking the trust your child places in you, which is dangerous ground to be on. Your child sees you, their parent, as their rock and foundation – if you damage that foundation you are negatively affecting your relationship, which is not what they need for optimal development (for more on this see p.63). Also remember that hiding food means you're not exposing your child to that food in a way they can recognize. Visual familiarity is a key step in a child accepting a food (see p.121–3)

- Try using a safety net with 'liked foods'. For example, if your child 'likes' yoghurt but not strawberries, you might try serving strawberries in yoghurt to encourage familiarity. This is not the same as hiding foods – announce to your child what you are serving and ensure that the 'disliked' food retains its form (rather than mushing it up until it is indistinguishable)
- 'We try everything in our family before we decide if we like it' is a good motto to have (see p.126 for more on this)

Is it bad to eat in between meals?

If your child snacks all day long, you can't expect them to be hungry when it comes to sitting down to enjoy a meal. But snacks are an important part of a child's day and they are necessary for energy so two snacks a day and three meals works well for many families. The important thing when it comes to making sure your child isn't filling up on snacks and then being expected to eat dinner thirty minutes later is to think about snack size and timing. The framework you create around this should fit in with your individual routine. See p.162 for more information on snacks.

Why does my child eat at nursery but not at home?

Many parents are surprised when they pick their child up from nursery or the childminder to discover that they picked up all their toys when asked or they were taken out for the day and the report back is 'they behaved like an angel', yet your experience as their parent is entirely different. This doesn't mean that they have you wrapped around their little finger or that they're manipulating you, but merely that they feel secure with you and are testing the boundaries. Think about your own behaviour; for example, how you might treat your boss at work versus how you treat your family or partner. You are probably more relaxed and able to show yourself to your partner and you probably tolerate a lot more rubbish from your boss, because you have to guard yourself at work and the relationship isn't safe and secure like your personal relationships (hopefully) are. It's the same much of the time with in-laws, in that when an adult returns home to their own parents, they often 'act-up', yet with in-laws they wouldn't dream of behaving that way. So when your child behaves differently when they're away from you, it is likely to be because they don't feel as safe elsewhere to express themselves. That means that your bond is far stronger, as is their love for you. The most important thing is not to take it personally.

When it comes to eating, however, there is often more to it – the carers at nursery or a childminder are not emotionally affected by whether your child eats anything because they do not have your vested interest in your child. Without that pressure to eat (or the sense that control that is unavailable elsewhere can be exerted through refusal to eat – see p.185), children are more likely just to get on with it because it isn't a loaded issue.

Your child might eat more cheerfully outside the home but don't take this personally!

Another reason is being around peers – children want to feel part of a group. The reason that certain friends appear to be 'leading your little one astray' is that all children want to fit in. If your child is surrounded by peers eating, they will want to fit in and eat too. This is totally natural.

Some schools and nurseries reward children for eating their food and if your child comes home with a 'well done' sticker for eating their lunch we strongly recommend that you have a word with them (and take a copy of this book in for them to read) so that they can be better informed about the potentially negative effects of rewarding behaviour that should just be normal.

Eating is not a 'good' behaviour and should not be rewarded as such. If it is, this teaches children to make eating decisions based on praise (which also adds an unhelpful emotional association with eating) rather than listening to their bodies and eating in response to hunger. (This is not the same as praising a child for trying a new food, which is something to be encouraged.)

How many calories does my child need?

There aren't many parents who can give you the number of daily kilo-calories a child needs. In fact, most paediatricians and health professionals will probably need to pick up a medical book to find the answer and often this is only necessary when using a feeding tube in a medical setting. The amount of

Avoid praising your child for eating all their dinner.

calories a child needs will vary from day to day, just like it does with any human being so an exact number is not going to be helpful.

Even among professionals, there is debate about the number of calories a child needs. For example, in 1985, WHO recommended that all children, regardless of gender, aged between twelve months and twenty-three months should consume 1170 kcal per day yet in 2000 a study recommended 894 kcal per day[243]. In the course of fifteen years, the recommended number of calories had been reduced by almost 30%. This goes to show how quickly guidelines can change and is another reason to think independently as a parent about how you introduce food to your child. Even with calorie guidelines, you cannot know how many calories your child is taking in unless you weigh and measure everything, including fluids and bits of food left on the plate. For a rough guide to calorie requirements by age, take a look at our serving guidelines on p.131, but day-to-day we recommend that you forget how much your child is eating and focus your attention on giving them the best opportunity to learn how to eat.

Is there any harm doing a bit of spoon-feeding alongside self-feeding?

If you've read to this point then you will have encountered the evidence around spoon-feeding leading to overeating as well as the other studies and statements we have cited. However, some parents, despite knowing these facts, will still wish to 'do a bit of both' and our response to this statement is often 'why?'

That's not flippancy. It's important to really reflect on why you want to do a bit of both. Is it the need to know they are eating some-thing? Is it the need to fit in with your friends? Is it your discomfort around the mess? Is it because you feel you don't have time for self-feeding? It's okay if it is – we aren't here to change your mind or persuade you – but understanding your motivation for doing something can help you establish whether it really is best for you and your baby. Self-feeding may be messier and more time-consuming, for example, but you could also see it as investing in helping your child to develop as healthy a relationship with food as you can, based on facilitating their own exploration of it.

Whichever approach you choose, we think it makes sense to choose an approach and stick with it, for the sake of establishing familiarity, continuity and predictability, which makes children feel safe. We have worked with parents who have taken the 'bit of both' approach so let's draw your attention to some of the more common issues that pop up so you can make a fully informed decision:

- Your child may get frustrated if they expect to self-feed and then you don't let them do it one day. They won't have any concept of time or needing to hurry, so it may well turn into a battle rather than being the quick fix you'd hoped for
- Every time you spoon-feed, you're creating an opportunity for your child to clamp their mouth shut, which is the first step to food becoming a control battle
- Self-feeding is a lot less convenient for you as the parent, but if you're doing it, you're doing it for your child's benefit. However, it's pretty easy to slip into doing whatever's easiest, so once you get into the habit of spoon-feeding, it may be difficult to revert to the longer, messier business of allowing them to self-feed. You may find yourself spoon-

feeding most of the time when that really wasn't your intention to start with

- If you're spoon-feeding, you're intrinsically deciding how much your child should eat and administering that amount of food
- With spoon-feeding you're dictating the pace at which your child eats rather than letting them engage with the experience at their own pace
- Eating only ends with a refusal if you spoon-feed. With self-feeding, your child will stop eating on their own because they've had enough

Every time you spoon-feed, then, the processes involved make it a completely different eating experience for your child, which undermines what you're trying to teach them when you allow them to self-feed (e.g. to listen to their physical cues regarding hunger/satiety, to make independent choices around food, to regulate their own food intake, to explore food at their own pace).

Is self-feeding going to involve a lot of mess and waste?

The short answer is that, yes, allowing your child to self-feed is going to be a lot messier than spoon-feeding (and some food will undoubtedly be wasted, although not as much as you might think – we'll pick up on this shortly!). However, when you're deciding which to go for and why, this is when you need to pause and make a considered decision based on your parenting values and priorities. Every decision feels best when you know it's based on your values, rather than on what you think you're 'supposed' to do. So take a moment to think – what are your priorities when it comes to this process? What do you value?

For example:

- Is it about facilitating your child's learning and development? Is that your first priority as a parent?
- Do you see weaning as another chance to help your child to discover something (in this case food) at their own pace? Is it important to you to facilitate all their learning in a way that maximizes their experiences of discovering things themselves?

If you're weaning from a perspective where you're prioritizing the learning and development process, then self-feeding is going to allow you to do that. Mess (and some waste) could be viewed as a side-effect of the fact that your child is learning through eating. It is just like when you get the paint pots out – there is going to be mess and some waste. (Toys and food are the same!)

Self-feeding also facilitates a child to learn at their own pace and in their own way. However, it's important that you're honest with yourself about how *you* feel. While prioritizing your child's needs is one of your main aims as a parent, you do have needs too, and trying to ignore them because you feel guilty will only make it less likely that you'll reach your goal in a relaxed and positive way with your child. So with that in mind think about things like:

- How will you feel about prioritizing these things? Will it come at the expense of your sanity and will it make mealtimes an unhappy experience for you both?

If you absolutely can't stand the idea of mess or waste, then, unless you can manage those feelings well, you're likely to be stressed, irritated or less patient at mealtimes, which will be counterproductive for everyone. It'll change the way you parent around food and you'll both have a much worse time of it if, for example, you end up pressuring your child to eat everything in front of them, or you get irritable with them when they throw food on the floor. It's important that you give yourself permission to have feelings and opinions about this, just as much as about everything else, because none of us are perfect, much less perfect parents. You're just doing the best you can, and the best you can do for your child is to be honest with yourself about your needs and factor them into the process.

• Will you be anxious that your child won't get enough food?

Weaning is absolutely about helping your child discover the world of food and learn how to eat; it's not about getting food into them. As we've said countless times before, if you start weaning at around six months, for example, your child doesn't need to transition immediately to food for the sake of nutrition – milk is giving them all they need from that perspective, so it's all about discovery.

• Will you be stressing about waste?

It's worth mentioning that eating the same foods as your child encourages your child to copy you. Because you are using 'real foods' rather than 'baby-specific' foods, leftovers are much more likely to be reusable. You are more likely to find a culinary use for untouched cherry tomatoes (chuck them in your own salad) than you are for untouched apple and parsnip purée!

It's also worth making a good amount of food and freezing/storing it in small portions so that you can use it all and don't end up wasting what your child doesn't eat. If you look at the portion sizes you should be serving them (see p.131) then you may well find that there's no need to waste much food, as they aren't supposed to be eating that much (another reason why cooking a decent amount and freezing in batches works well). In addition to reducing mess, this also saves you time.

• Will you be able to stand the mess?

Some mess is inevitable with this approach; self-feeding is not a tidy process. But mess can be a good thing, according to one recent study[244], which suggested that playing with food during mealtimes in a highchair is a learning experience that helps children to name and categorize those foods more quickly.

Nevertheless, we also know that mess isn't always welcome, so there are some simple tips you can follow to make things a little easier.

Shutterstock

Learning by creating mess!

- Check out our getting started guidelines on p.106 for tips on how to keep things as clean as possible
- Keep an eye on portion sizes (see p.131), as you may be serving too much at any one sitting; also, don't give your child a whole bowl of whichever food you're serving. Give them a few small pieces of food to deal with and then offer more. Firstly, this will help them not to feel overwhelmed by the amount of food in front of them and, secondly, it creates less of an opportunity for the rest of it to go everywhere while their attention is on trying to pick up one particular thing. Think of it almost as giving them several small servings of food in succession.
- *Yummy Discoveries: The Baby-Led Weaning Recipe Book* was written to address the issue of waste in baby-led weaning, with recipes created specifically to be great for your child that can quickly be transformed into adult recipes by adding a couple more ingredients. You can therefore make sure that whatever you feed them can also be delicious for you, which should spell the end of having to throw leftovers from their meal away.

Sam Walsh

Messy eating can be fun!

My child won't sit at the table to eat but is happy to snack and play. What can I do?

If your child won't sit at the table, then it's a sign for you to think about whether you've put a firm and familiar enough framework in place to show them how things work. Do you always eat meals together at the table? Is eating a family activity where your child knows exactly what happens or do you let them eat and play sometimes? Are you letting your child snack ad hoc? How much are they having at snack-time? How close is snack-time to mealtimes (i.e. do they have enough time to get hungry?)

It needs to be very clear to your child how eating works in your family, and that clarity is created by a familiar framework that doesn't change. We talk about this in depth on p.85 but here are a few quick troubleshooting ideas to bear in mind:

- If your child gets upset and refuses to eat at the table, comfort, empathize and explain, but don't move the boundaries (see p.91 for a case study)
- Watch portion sizes of snacks and construct a routine around eating
- Don't compound the problem by giving your child filling drinks (see p.150–51 for more)
- If your child refuses to eat a meal, don't give them extra snacks while they play because you're scared they won't get enough food. Don't be tempted to give them their meal while they're playing, either. Both of these coping strategies undermine the structure you're trying to put in place – that food is eaten at the table and that, if you're hungry, that is where you need to sit
- Put in place a routine that everyone has

Shutterstock

I don't want to sit at the table!

to say when they're finished and everyone gets down from the table at the same time (see p.34). Ask younger children who cannot yet verbalize their thoughts whether they're finished and answer for them – this way nobody is excluded

My 10-month-old isn't interested in solids. Is this okay?

Children develop at very different rates, and we often work with parents whose children don't seem interested in solids until much later than their peers. For most of these parents, our advice would be to relax and wait, while exposing your child to the opportunity to become interested in solids at their own pace.

There are, however, a small number of physical conditions that might lead to swallowing difficulties or muscle weakness, which make self-feeding and eating solid food challenging. If you have any concerns regarding your child's development – for example, if they have difficulty picking up and mouthing toys – then contact your GP or paediatrician as this apparent lack of interest could mean an underlying problem.

Final words

This is not a weaning-by-numbers book. In our practice, all the advice we give is based on the needs and circumstances of the individual family we are working with; therefore, the advice we have offered to parents, as described in the case studies, may or may not suit your needs. We have included them here as they are typical of what we have witnessed working time and time again with the families who have attended our workshops and our one-to-one consultations.

To recap, here are some of the more common elements of advice we have offered. We haven't included the justification and rationale behind each point here as these have all been covered previously in the book:

- Always sit down with your child at the table to eat main meals – snacks can be eaten in other locations (see p.108)
- Always eat the same foods as your child (see p.68)
- Even if your child refuses the food, everyone stays at the table until everyone has finished (see p.34)
- Avoid having toys, television or books at the table (see p.61)
- If your child is over twelve months, a milk feed is considered a meal so adjust your expectations of their solid food intake to reflect this (see p.24)
- Monitor the size of snacks: two small snacks a day are often suitable (see p.162)
- Play fair: serve foods you know your child 'likes' alongside unfamiliar foods (see p.184)

Conclusion

'What a child can do with assistance today she will be able to do by herself tomorrow.'
Lev Vygotsky

We hope that you have enjoyed reading this book and that you and your family now have a renewed enthusiasm for mealtimes. We have no wish to tell you what to do; rather, we hope that you can use this book and the information herein to make your own informed decisions as a parent when it comes to mealtimes. Just because your parenting style is different to someone else's, that doesn't make it wrong. Your baby and family situations are unique and there is no 'parenting-by-numbers'.

Having the confidence to make parenting decisions based on your instincts and a knowledge of current thinking on various issues rather than on the approval of outsiders will, we hope, enable you to raise your children in the way that best suits *your* family. Ignoring the one-size-fits-all calendar and using your child's unique developmental signs as a guide will encourage you to connect with your instincts instead of worrying so that you can relax and enjoy parenthood.

Research and guidelines are changing continuously. You can stay up-to-date with the latest approaches by visiting our website and signing up to our news bulletins at **www.yummydiscoveries.com**, which will also keep you updated with news of forthcoming Yummy Discoveries books.

To all the parents who have generously shared and contributed their own experiences to help us write this book, we thank you.

References

1   Rigal, N., Frelut, M.L., Monneuse, M.O. et al., 'Food neophobia in the context of a varied diet induced by a weight reduction program in massively obese adolescents', *Appetite*, 2006, Volume 46, Issue 2, pp.207–14.

2   Kaufman, F.R., 'Type 2 diabetes mellitus in children and youth: A new epidemic', *Journal of Pediatric Endocrinology and Metabolism*, 2002, Volume 15, Issue supplement 2, pp.737–44.

3   Garcia, A.L., Raza, S., Parrett, A. et al., 'Nutritional content of infant commercial weaning foods in the UK', *Archives of Disease in Childhood*, 2013, Volume 98, pp.793–7.

4   Ibid.

5   World Health Organization, http://www.who.int/nutrition/topics/exclusive_breastfeeding/en, accessed 20 March 2014.

6   The Department of Health Diet and Nutrition Survey of Infants and Young Children, 2011 Survey. http://webarchive.nationalarchives.gov.uk/20130402145952/http://transparency.dh.gov.uk/category/statistics/ndns, accessed 9 June 2014.

7   http://www.health.govt.nz/your-health/healthy-living/food-and-physical-activity/nutrition/baby-led-weaning, accessed 20 November 2013.

8   Puisais, J. and Pierre, C., *Le Goût de l' Enfant*, in Preedy, V.R., Watson, R.R. and Martin, C.R., *Handbook of Behavior, Food and Nutrition*, New York: Springer, 2011, pp.143–57.

9   National Guidelines on Infant and Young Child Feeding, Ministry of Human Resource Development, Department of Women and Child Development (food and nutrition board), Government of India, 2004.

10 Hambidge, K.M., Sheng, X., Habicht, J.P. et al., 'Evaluation of meat as a first complementary food for breastfed infants: impact on iron intake', *Nutrition Reviews*, 2011, Volume 69, Issue Supplement 1, pp.57–63.

11 Pelto, G.H., Zhang, Y. and Habicht, J.P., 'Premastication: the second arm of infant and young child feeding for health and survival?', *Maternal & Child Nutrition*, 2010, Volume 6, Issue 1, pp.4–18.

12 Ibid.

13 Ibid.

14 Ibid.

15 Ibid.

16 Lebanthal, E. and Lee, P.C., 'Development of functional responses in human exocrine pancreas', *Pediatrics*, 1980, Volume 66, pp.556-60.

17 Sevenhuysen, G.P., Holodinsky, C. and Dawes, C., 'Development of salivary alpha-amylase in infants from birth to 5 months', *American Journal of Clinical Nutrition*, 1984, Volume 39, Issue 4, pp.584–8.

18 Imong, S.M., Jackson, D.A., Rungruengthanakit, K. et al., 'Maternal behaviour and socio-economic influences on the bacterial content of infant weaning foods in rural northern Thailand', *Journal of Tropical Pediatrics*, 1995, Volume 41, Issue 4, pp.234–40.

19 Berkowitz, R.J., Turner, J. and Green, P., 'Maternal salivary levels of *Streptococcus mutans* and primary oral infection of infants', *Archives of Oral Biology*, 1981, Volume 26, Issue 2, pp.147–9.

20 http://www.thetimes.co.uk/tto/health/news/article3901745.ece, accessed 19 November 2013.

21 Fildes, V., 'Infant feeding practices and mortality in England 1900–1919', *Continuity and Change*, 1998, Volume 13, Issue 2, pp.251–80.

22 NHS infant feeding survey, http://www.unicef.org.uk/BabyFriendly/About-Baby-Friendly/Breastfeeding-in-the-UK/UK-Breast feeding-rates, accessed 12 September 2013.

23 American Academy of Pediatrics Committee on Nutrition, 'On the feeding of solid foods to infants', *Pediatrics*, 1958, Volume 21, pp.685–92.

24 Sackett, W.M., 'Results of three years experiences with a new concept of baby feeding', *Southern Medical Journal*, 1953, Volume 46, Issue 4, pp.358–63.

25 Ibid.

26 Oates, R.K., 'Infant feeding practices', *British Medical Journal*, 1973, Volume 2, Issue 5869, pp.762–4.

27 Wilkinson, P.W. and Davies, D.P., 'When and why are babies weaned?', *British Medical Journal*, 1978, Volume 1, Issue 6128, pp.1682–3.

28 Forsyth, J.S., Ogston, A.S., Clark, A. et al., 'Relation between early introduction of solid food to infants and their weight and illnesses during the first two years of life', *British Medical Journal*, 1993, Volume 306, Issue 6892, pp.1572–6.

29 Fewtrell, M.S., Morgan, J.B., Duggan, C. et al., 'Optimal duration of exclusive breast-feeding: what is the evidence to support current recommendations?' *American Journal of Clinical Nutrition*, February 2007, Volume 85, Issue 2, pp.635S–8S.

30 American Academy of Pediatrics Committee on Nutrition, *Pediatric Nutrition Handbook*, 5th edn, 2004.

31 World Health Organization, Prevention of allergy and allergic asthma paper presented at: WHO/WAO Meeting on the Prevention of Allergy and Allergic Asthma, 8–9 January 2002, Geneva, Switzerland.

32 Muraro, A., Dreborg, S., Halken, S. et al., 'Dietary prevention of allergic diseases in infants and small children, part III: critical review of published peer-reviewed observational and interventional studies and final recommendations', *Pediatric Allergy and Immunology*, 2004, Volume 15, pp.291–307.

33 Tarini, B.A., Carroll, A.E., Sox, C.M. et al., 'Systematic review of the relationship between early introduction of solid foods to infants and the development of allergic disease', *Archives of Pediatric and Adolescent Medicine*, 2006, 160(5), pp.502–7.

34 Fewtrell, M.S., Morgan, J.B., Duggan, C. et al., 'Optimal duration of exclusive breast-feeding: what is the evidence to support current recommendations?' *American Journal of Clinical Nutrition*, February 2007, Volume 85, Issue 2, pp.635S–8S.

35 Foote, K. and Marriott, L., 'Weaning of infants', *Archives of Diseases in Childhood*, 2003, Volume 88, Issue 6, pp.488–92.

36 Lanigan, J.A., Bishop, J.A., Kimber, A.C. et al., 'Systematic review concerning the age of introduction of complementary foods to the healthy full-term infant', *European Journal of Clinical Nutrition*, 2001, Volume 55, Issue 5, pp.309–20.

37 Quigley, M.A., Kelly, Y.J. and Sacker, A., 'Breastfeeding and hospitalization for diarrheal and respiratory infection in the United Kingdom: Millennium Cohort Study', *Pediatrics*, 2007, Volume 119, pp.E837–42.

38 British Dietetic Association, Complementary feeding: introduction of solid food to an infant's diet, April 2013. http://www.bda.uk.com/policies/WeaningPolicyStatement.pdf, accessed 5 March 2014.

39 Richter J., 'Public-private Partnerships and International Health Policy-making: How Can Public Interests be Safeguarded?',

Ministry of Foreign Affairs of Finland, Development Policy Information Unit, 2004.

40 World Health Organization, Guiding principles for complementary feeding of the breastfed child, 2004. http://whqlibdoc.who.int/paho/2003/a85622.pdf, accessed 28 February 2014.

41 Henderson, G., Anthony, M.Y., McGuire, W. et al., 'Formula milk versus maternal breast milk for feeding preterm or low birth weight infants', Cochrane Neonatal Reviews, 2007, http://www.nichd.nih.gov/cochrane_data/hendersong_01/hendersong_01.html, accessed 28 February 2014.

42 WHO/UNICEF (1998), quoted in World Health Organization, Guiding principles for complementary feeding of the breastfed child, 2004. http://whqlibdoc.who.int/paho/2003/a85622.pdf, accessed 28 February 2014.

43 Sproston, K. and Mindell, J. (eds), *Health Survey for England 2004*, London: The Information Centre, 2006.

44 Gisel, E.G., 'Effect of food texture on the development of chewing of children between six months and two years of age', *Developmental Medicine and Child Neurology*, January 1991, pp.69–79.

45 http://www.rapleyweaning.com/assets/blwleaflet.pdf, accessed 6 June 2013.

46 Bowlby, J., *A Secure Base: Parent-child Attachment and Healthy Human Development*, New York: Basic Books, 1988.

47 The phrase was coined by the paediatrician William Sears: http://www.askdrsears.com/topics/attachment-parenting/what-ap-7-baby-bs, accessed 5 March 2014.

48 Drotar, D. and Eckerle, D., 'The family environment in non-organic failure to thrive: a controlled study', *Journal of Pediatric Psychology*, 1989, Volume 14, Issue 2, pp.245–57.

49 Rabinowitz, S.S. and Alvarez, R., 'Nutritional Considerations in failure to thrive', *Medscape*, July 2012, http://emedicine.medscape.com/article/985007-overview, accessed 18 March 2014.

50 Weston, J.A., Colloton, M., Halsey, S. et al., 'A legacy of violence in nonorganic failure to thrive', *Child Abuse and Neglect*, 1993, Volume 17, Issue 6, pp.709–14.

51 Oates, R.K. and Kempe, R.S., 'Growth failure in infants', in Helfer, M.A., Kempe, R.S. and Krugman, R.D. (eds), *The Battered Child*, 5th edn, Chicago: University of Chicago Press, 1997, pp.374–91.

52 World Health Organization, Global strategy for infant and young child feeding, Geneva: World Health Organization, 2003, http://www.who.int/nutrition/publications/infantfeeding/9241562218/en, accessed 11 March 2014.

53 Issanchou, S., 'Food habit formation and breaking in early childhood', *Habeat EU*, 2010, p.5.

54 http://www.rapleyweaning.com/assets/blwleaflet.pdf, accessed 20 March 2014.

55 Rapley, G. and Murkett, T., *Baby-Led Weaning: Helping Your Baby Love Good Food*, London: Vermilion, 2008.

56 Ibid.

57 Ibid.

58 Ibid.

59 Wilson, B., *Swindled: The Dark History of Food Cheats*, London: John Murray, 2008.

60 http://www.dailymail.co.uk/health/article-462599/Does-feeding-babies-pureed-food-harm-health.html, accessed 10 October 2013.

61 Garcia, A.L., Raza, S., Parrett, A. et al. 'Nutritional content of infant commercial weaning foods in the UK', *Archives of*

Disease in Childhood, 2013, DOI: 10.1136/archdischild-2012-303386.

62   McCraty, R., Atkinson, M., Tomasino, D. et al., 'The electricity of touch: detection and measurement of cardiac energy exchange between people' in Pribram, Karl H. (ed.), *Brain and Values: Is a Biological Science of Values Possible?*, New Jersey: Lawrence Erlbaum Associates, 1998, pp.359–79.

63   British Dietetic Association, Weaning policy statement, April 2013. www.bda.uk.com/policies/WeaningPolicyStatement.pdf, accessed 5 March 2014.

64   Naylor, A. and Morrow, A. (eds), 'Developmental Readiness of Normal Full Term Infants to Progress from Exclusive Breastfeeding to the Introduction of Complementary Foods: Reviews of the Relevant Literature Concerning Infant Immunologic, Gastrointestinal, Oral Motor and Maternal Reproductive and Lactational Development', Wellstart International and the LINKAGES Project Academy for Educational Development, Washington, DC, USA, 2001.

65   Kuhn, C.M., Schanberg, S.M., Field, T. et al., 'Tactile-kinesthetic stimulation effects on sympathetic and adrenocortical function in preterm infants', *Journal of Pediatrics*, September 1991, Volume 119, Issue 3, pp.434–40.

66   Mennella, J.A., Jagnow, C.P. and Beauchamp, G.K., 'Prenatal and postnatal flavor learning by human infants', *Pediatrics*, June 2001, Volume 107, Issue 6, p.E88.

67   Mennella, J.A., Johnson, A. and Beauchamp, G.K., 'Garlic ingestion by pregnant women alters the odor of amniotic fluid', *Chemical Senses*, April 1995, Volume 20, Issue 2, pp.207–9.

68   Schaal, B., Marlier, L. and Soussignan, R., 'Human foetuses learn odours from their pregnant mother's diet'. *Chemical Senses*, December 2000, Volume 25, Issue 6, pp.729–37.

69   Mennella, J.A., Jagnow, C.P. and Beauchamp, G.K, 'Prenatal and postnatal flavor learning by human infants', *Pediatrics*, June 2001, Volume 107, Issue 6, p.E88.

70   Ibid.

71   Hausner, H., Nicklaus, S., Issanchou, S. et al., 'Breastfeeding facilitates acceptance of a novel dietary flavour compound', *Clinical Nutrition*, February 2010, Volume 29, Issue 1, pp.141–8.

72   Hausner, H., Bredie, W.L., Mølgaard, C. et al., 'Differential transfer of dietary flavour compounds into human breast milk', *Physiology & Behavior*, September 2008, Volume 95, Issues 1–2, 3, pp.118–24.

73   Mennella, J.A., Kennedy, J. and Beauchamp, G.K., 'The type of formula fed to infants modifies vegetable acceptance', *Early Human Development*, 2006, Volume 82, pp.263–8.

74   Bolhuis, D.P., Lakemond, C.M., de Wijk, R.A. et al., 'Consumption with large sip sizes increases food intake and leads to underestimation of the amount consumed', *PLoS One*, 2013, Volume 8, Issue 1, p.E53288.

75   Dwyer, T., 'Shaping habits that shape obesity' presentation, The Feeding Infants And Toddlers Study (FITS), 2004.

76   Elder, S.H., Perry, C.L., Klepp, K.I. et al., 'Longitudinal tracking of adolescent smoking, physical activity and food choice behaviors', *American Journal of Public Health*, 1994, Volume 84, Issue 7, pp.1121–6.

77   Shim, J.E., Kim, J., Mathai, R.A. et al., 'Associations of infant feeding practices and picky eating behaviors of preschool children', *Journal of the American Dietetic Association*, 2011, Volume 111, Issue 9, pp.1363–8.

78   Mahmoudzadeh, M., Dehaene-Lambertz, G., Fournier M. et al., 'Syllabic discrimination in premature human infants prior to complete formation of cortical layers', *Proceedings of The National Academy of Sciences of the*

United States of America, 2012, Volume 110, Issue 12, pp.4846–51.

79 Querleu, D., Renard, X., Versyp, F. et al., 'Fetal hearing', *European Journal of Obstetrics and Gynecology and Reproductive Biology*, 1988, Volume 29, pp.191–212.

80 Moon, C., Cooper, R.P. and Fifer, W.P., 'Two-day-olds prefer their native language', *Infant Behavior and Development*, 1991, Volume 16, Issue 4, pp.495–500.

81 Goren, C.C., Sarty, M. and Wu, P.Y.K., 'Visual following and pattern discrimination of face-like stimuli by newborn infants', *Pediatrics*, 1975, Volume 56, Issue 4, pp.544–9.

82 Bushnell, I.W.R., Sai, F. and Mullin, J.T., 'Neonatal recognition of the mother's face', *British Journal of Developmental Psychology*, Volume 7, Issue 1, pp.3–15.

83 Mennella, J.A., Pepino, M.Y. and Reed, D.R., 'Genetic and environmental determinants of bitter perception and sweet preferences', *Pediatrics*, 2005, Volume 115, Issue 2, pp.E216–22.

84 Liem, D.G., Zandstra, L. and Thomas, A., 'Prediction of children's flavour preferences. Effect of age and stability in reported preferences', *Appetite*, 2010, Volume 55, Issue 1, pp.69–75.

85 Bradfield, J.P., Taal, H.R., Timpson, N.J. et al., 'A genome-wide association meta-analysis identifies new childhood obesity loci', *Nature Genetics*, 2012, Volume 44, Issue 5, pp.526–31.

86 Liem, D.G., Zandstra, L. and Thomas, A., 'Prediction of children's flavour preferences. Effect of age and stability in reported preferences', *Appetite*, 2010, Volume 55, Issue 1, pp.69–75.

87 Lado, R., *Language Teaching: A Scientific Approach*, New York: McGraw-Hill, 1964, p.53.

88 Martins, Y., Pelchat, P.L. and Pliner, P., '"Try it; it's good and it's good for you": Effects of taste and nutrition information on willingness to try novel foods', *Appetite*, 1997, Volume 28, Issue 2, pp.89–102.

89 McFarlane, T. and Pliner, P., 'Increased willingness to taste novel foods: Effects of nutrition and taste information', *Appetite*, 1997, Volume 28, Issue 3, pp.227–38.

90 Pelchat, M.L. and Pliner, P., 'Try it. You'll like it. Effects of information on willingness to try novel foods' *Appetite*, 1995, Volume 24, Issue 2, pp.153–66.

91 Fisher, J.O., Mitchell, D.C., Smiciklas-Wright, H. et al., 'Parental influences on young girls' fruit and vegetable, micronutrient, and fat intakes', *Journal of the American Dietetic Association*, 2002, Volume 102, Issue 1, pp.58–64.

92 Galloway, A.T., Fiorito, L.M., Francis, L.A. et al., '"Finish your soup": Counterproductive effects of pressuring children to eat on intake and affect', *Appetite*, 2006, Volume 46, Issue 3, pp.318–23.

93 Anderson, J.W., Johnstone, B.M. and Remley, D.T., 'Breast-feeding and cognitive development: a meta-analysis', *American Journal of Clinical Nutrition*, 1999, Volume 70, Issue 4, pp.525–35.

94 Ramsden, S.R. and Hubbard, J.A., 'Family expressiveness and parental emotion coaching: Their role in children's emotion regulation and aggression', *Journal of Abnormal Child Psychology*, 2002, Volume 30, Issue 6, pp.657–67.

95 Zeman, J., Cassano, M., Perry-Parrish, C. et al., 'Emotion regulation in children and adolescents', *Journal of Developmental & Behavioral Pediatrics*, 2006, Volume 27, Issue 2, pp.155–68.

96 Morris, A.S., Silk, J.S., Steinberg, L. et al., 'The role of the family context in the development

of emotion regulation', *Social Development*, 2007, Volume 16, Issue 2, pp.361–88.

97   Bowlby, J., *A Secure Base: Parent-child Attachment and Healthy Human Development*, New York: Basic Books, 2008.

98   Sarason, I.G., 'Stress, anxiety, and cognitive interference: reactions to tests', *Journal of Personality and Social Psychology*, 1984, Volume 46, Issue 4, p.929.

99   Watson, J.B., *Psychological Care of Infant and Child*, New York:W.W. Norton, 1928.

100 Esposito, G., Yoshida, S., Ohnishi, R. et al., 'Infant calming responses during maternal carrying in humans and mice', *Current Biology*, 2013, Volume 23, Issue 9, pp.739–45.

101 Center on the Developing Child at Harvard University, 'The foundations of lifelong health are built in early childhood', 2010, available at: http://www.developingchild.harvard.edu, accessed 18 March 2014.

102 Middlemiss, W., Granger, D.A., Goldberg, W.A. and Nathans, L., 'Asynchrony of mother–infant hypothalamic–pituitary–adrenal axis activity following extinction of infant crying responses induced during the transition to sleep', *Early Human Development*, 2012, Volume 88, Issue 4, pp.227–32.

103 Henry, J.P. and Wang, S., 'Effects of early stress on adult affiliative behavior', *Psychoneuroendocrinology*, 1998, Volume 23, Issue 8, pp.863–75.

104 Blunden, S.L., Thompson, K.R. and Dawson, D., 'Behavioural sleep treatments and night time crying in infants: challenging the status quo', *Sleep Medicine Review*, 2011, Volume 15, Issue 5, pp.327–34.

105 Price, A., Wake, M., Ukoumunne, O. et al., 'Five-year follow-up of harms and benefits of behavioral infant sleep intervention: randomized trial', *Pediatrics*, 2012, Volume 130, Issue 4, pp.643–51.

106 Naylor, A. and Morrow, A. (eds), 'Developmental Readiness of Normal Full Term Infants to Progress from Exclusive Breastfeeding to the Introduction of Complementary Foods: Reviews of the Relevant Literature Concerning Infant Immunologic, Gastrointestinal, Oral Motor and Maternal Reproductive and Lactational Development', Wellstart International and the LINKAGES Project Academy for Educational Development, Washington, DC, USA, 2001.

107 Wright, C.M., Parkinson, K.N. and Drewett, R.F., 'Why are babies weaned early? Data from a prospective population cohort study', *Archives of Diseases in Childhood*, 2003, Volume 89, Issue 9, pp.813–16.

108 British Dietetic Association, Complementary feeding: introduction of solid food to an infant's diet, April 2013. http://www.bda.uk.com/policies/WeaningPolicyStatement.pdf, accessed 5 March 2014.

109 Northstone, K., Emmett, P., Nethersole, F. et al., 'The effect of age of introduction to lumpy solids on foods eaten and reported feeding difficulties at 6 and 15 months', *Journal of Human Nutrition and Dietetics*, 2001, pp.43–54.

110 Mason, S., Harris, G. and Blissett, J., 'Tube feeding in infancy: implications for the development of normal eating and drinking skills', *Dysphagia*, 2005, Volume 20, Issue 1, p.1.

111 Suskind, D. and Lenssen, P. (eds), *Pediatric Nutrition Handbook*, Seattle: Wiley-Blackwell, 2011.

112 Naylor, A. and Morrow, A. (eds), 'Developmental Readiness of Normal Full Term Infants to Progress from Exclusive Breastfeeding to the Introduction of Complementary Foods: Reviews of the Relevant Literature Concerning Infant Immunologic, Gastrointestinal, Oral Motor and Maternal Reproductive and Lactational Development', Wellstart International and the LINKAGES Project Academy for Educational Development, Washington, DC, USA, 2001.

113 Wright, C. and Birks, E., 'Risk factors for failure to thrive: A population-based survey', *Child Care Health and Development*, 2000, Volume 26, Issue 1, pp.5–16.

114 Gesell, A., 'The ontogenesis of infant behavior' in Carmichael, L. (ed.), *Manual of Child Psychology*, New York: Wiley, 1946, p.295.

115 Bayley, N., *The California Infant Scale of Motor Development*, Berkeley: University of California Press, 1936.

116 Carruth, B.R. and Skinner, J.D., 'Feeding behaviors and other motor development in healthy children (2–24 months)', *Journal of the American College of Nutrition*, 2002, Volume 21, Issue 2, pp.88–96.

117 Gesell, A., 'The ontogenesis of infant behavior' in Carmichael, L. (ed.), *Manual of Child Psychology*, New York: Wiley, 1946, p.295.

118 Bayley, N., *The California Infant Scale of Motor Development*; Berkeley: University of California Press, 1936.

119 Bruner, J.S. and Koslowski, B., 'Visually preadapted constituents of manipulatory action', *Perception*, 1972, Volume 1, Issue 1, pp.3–14.

120 Rochat, P., 'Self-sitting and reaching in 5- to 8-month-old infants: The impact of posture and its development on early eye-hand coordination', *Journal of Motor Behavior*, 1992, Volume 24, Issue 2, pp.210–20.

121 Ibid.

122 Von Hofsten, C. and Ronnqvist, L., 'Preparation for grasping an object: A developmental study', *Journal of Experimental Psychology*, 1988, Volume 14, Issue 4, pp.610–21.

123 Margulies, Sheldon, MD, *The Fascinating Body: How It Works*, Washington, DC: ScarecrowEducation, 2004, p.148.

124 Brown, A. and Lee, M., 'An exploration of experiences of mothers following a baby-led weaning style: Developmental readiness for complementary foods', *Maternal and Child Nutrition*, 2013, Volume 9, Issue 2, pp.233–43.

125 Morgan, J., Taylor, A. and Fewtrell, M., 'Meat consumption is positively associated with psychomotor outcome in children up to 24 months of age', *Journal of Pediatric Gastroenterology and Nutrition*, 2004, Volume 39, Issue 5, pp.493–8.

126 Jalla, S., Westcott, J., Steirn, M. et al., 'Zinc absorption and exchangeable zinc pool sizes in breast-fed infants fed meat or cereal as first complementary food', *Journal of Pediatric Gastroenterology and Nutrition*, 2002, Volume 34, Issue 1, pp.35–41.

127 Fox, M.K., Devaney, B., Reidy, K. et al., 'Relationship between portion size and energy intake among infants and toddlers: Evidence of self-regulation', *Journal of the American Dietetic Association*, 2006, Volume 106, Supplement 1, pp.S77–83.

128 World Health Organization, 'Physiological development of the infant and its implications for complementary feeding', *Bulletin of the World Health Organization*, 1989, Volume 67, pp.55–67.

129 Townsend, E. and Pitchford, N., 'Baby knows best? The impact of weaning style on food preferences and body mass index in early childhood in a case-controlled sample', *BMJ Open*, 2012, Volume 2, Issue 1, p.E000298.

130 Uvnas-Moberg, K. and Francis, B., *The Oxytocin Factor: Tapping the Hormone of Calm, Love and Healing*, Cambridge, MA: Da Capo Press, 2003.

131 Neumark-Sztainer, D., Larson, N.I., Fulkerson, J.A. et al., 'Family meals and adolescents: What have we learned from project eat (eating among teens)?', *Public Health Nutrition*, 2010, Volume 13, Issue 7, pp.1113–21.

132 Eisenberg, M.E., Olson, R.E., Neumark-Sztainer, D. et al., 'Correlations between

family meals and psychosocial well-being among adolescents', *Archives of Pediatrics and Adolescent Medicine*, 2004, Volume 158, Issue 8, pp.792–6.

133 Dovey, Terence M., 'Food neophobia and "picky/fussy" eating in children: a review', *Appetite*, 2008, Volume 50, Issues 2–3, pp.181–93.

134 Birch, L.L., 'Effects of peer model's food choices and eating behaviours on preschooler's food preferences', *Child Development*, 1980, Volume 51, pp.489–96.

135 Ibid.

136 Shepard, R. and Dennison, C.M., 'Influences on adolescent food choice', *Proceedings of the Nutritional Society*, 1996, Volume 55, Issue 1B, pp.345–57.

137 Reddy, S., 'Food allergy advice for kids: don't delay peanuts, eggs', *Wall Street Journal*, http://online.wsj.com/news/articles/SB1000142412788732466240457833442 3524696016, accessed 29 November 2013.

138 Department of Health, 'Introducing Solid Foods: Giving Your Baby a Better Start in Life', in *Policy: Giving all children a healthy start in life*, 2011, https://www.gov.uk/government/publications/introducing-solid-foods-giving-your-baby-a-better-start-in-life, accessed 25 October 2013.

139 Sampson, H.A., 'Food allergy. Part 1: Immunopathogenesis and clinical disorders', *Journal of Allergy and Clinical Immunology*, 1999, Volume 103, Issue 5, Part 1, pp.717–28.

140 Poole, J.A., Barriga, K., Leung, D.Y. et al., 'Timing of initial exposure to cereal grains and the risk of wheat allergy', *Pediatrics*, 2006, Volume 117, Issue 6, pp.2175–82.

141 Zutavern, A., von Mutius, E., Harris, J. et al., 'The introduction of solids in relation to asthma and eczema', *Archives of Disease in Childhood*, 2004, Volume 89, Issue 4, pp.303–8.

142 Zutavern, A., Brockow, I., Schaaf, B. et al., 'Timing of solid food introduction in relation to eczema, asthma, allergic rhinitis, and food and inhalant sensitization at the age of 6 years: Results from the prospective birth cohort study LISA', *Pediatrics*, 2008, Volume 121, Issue 1, pp.E44–52.

143 Snijders, B.E., Thijs, C., van Ree, R. et al., 'Age at first introduction of cow milk products and other food products in relation to infant atopic manifestations in the first 2 years of life: The KOALA birth cohort study', *Pediatrics*, 2008, Volume 121, Issue 1, pp.E115–22.

144 Roduit, C., Frei, R., Depner, M. et al., 'Increased food diversity in the first year of life is inversely associated with allergic diseases', *Journal of Allergy and Clinical Immunology*, 2014, Volume 4, pp.1056–64.

145 NIAID-Sponsored Expert Panel, 'Guidelines for the Diagnosis and Management of Food Allergy in the United States: Report of the NIAID-Sponsored Expert Panel', *Journal of Allergy and Clinical Immunology*, 2010, Volume 126, Issue 6, Supplement, pp.S1-S58.

146 www.eatstudy.co.uk, accessed 25 March 2014.

147 Ministry of Health, *Food and Nutrition Guidelines for Healthy Infants and Toddlers (Aged 0–2): A Background Paper*, 4th edn, Wellington: Ministry of Health, 2008.

148 Health Canada, *Nutrition for Healthy Term Infants: Statement of the Joint Working Group: Canadian Paediatric Society, Dietitians of Canada and Health Canada*, Ottawa: Canadian Government Publishing, 2005.

149 Carruth, B.R. and Skinner, J.D., 'Feeding behaviors and other motor development in healthy children (2–24 months)', *Journal of the American College of Nutrition*, 2002, Volume 21, Issue 2, pp.88–96.

150 Cameron, S.L., Heath, A.L. and Taylor, R.W., 'Healthcare professionals' and mothers'

knowledge of, attitudes to, and experiences with, baby-led weaning: A content analysis study', *BMJ Open*, 2012, Volume 2, Issue 6, p.E001542.

151 Byard, R.W., Gallard, V., Johnson, A. et al., 'Safe feeding practices for infants and young children', *Journal of Paediatric Child Health*, 1996, Volume 32, Issue 4, pp.327–29.

152 Glander, K., 'The impact of plant secondary compounds on primate feeding behavior', *American Journal of Physical Anthropology*, 1982, pp.1–18.

153 Cooke, L., 'The development and modification of children's eating habits', *Nutrition Bulletin*, 2004, Volume 29, Issue 1, pp.31–5.

154 Cooke, L., Wardle, J. and Gibson, E.L., 'The relationship between child food neophobia and everyday food consumption', *Appetite*, 2003, Volume 41, Issue 2, pp.205–6.

155 Bell, K.I. and Tepper, B.J., 'Short-term vegetable intake by young children classified by 6-n-propylthoiuracil bitter-taste phenotype', *Americal Journal of Clinical Nutrition*, 2006, Volume 84, Issue 1, pp.245–51.

156 Popper, R. and Kroll, J.J., 'Conducting sensory research with children', *Journal of Sensory Studies*, 2005, Volume 20, Issue 1, pp.75–87.

Pliner, P., Pelchat, M. and Grabski, M., 'Reduction of neophobia in humans by exposure to novel foods', *Appetite*, 1993, Volume 20, Issue 2, pp.111–23.

157 Addessi, E., Galloway, A.T., Visalberghi, E. et al., 'Specific social influences on the acceptance of novel foods in 2–5-year-old children', *Appetite*, 2005, Volume 45, Issue 3, pp.264–71.

Cooke, L.J., Wardle, J. and Gibson, E.L., 'Relationship between parental report of food neophobia and everyday food consumption in 2–6-year-old children', *Appetite*, 2003, Volume 41, Issue 2, pp.205–6.

158 Cashdan, E., 'A sensitive period for learning about food', *Human Nature*, 1994, Volume 5, Issue 3, pp.279–91.

159 McFarlane, T. and Pliner, P., 'Increased willingness to taste novel foods: Effects of nutrition and taste information', *Appetite*, 1997, Volume 28, Issue 3, pp.227–38.

160 Raynor, H.A. and Epstein, L.H., 'Dietary variety, energy regulation and obesity', *Psychological Bulletin*, 2001, Volume 127, Issue 3, pp.325–41.

161 Otis, L.P., 'Factors influencing willingness to taste unusual foods', *Psychological Reports*, 1984, Volume 54, Issue 3, pp.739–45.

162 Birch, L.L., Gunder, L., Grimm-Thomas, K. et al., 'Infants' consumption of a new food enhances acceptance of similar foods', *Appetite*, 1998, Volume 30, Issue 3, pp.283–95.

163 Birch, L.L., McPhee, L., Shoba, B.C. et al., 'What kind of exposure reduces children's food neophobia? Looking vs tasting', *Appetite*, 1987, Volume 9, Issue 3, pp.171–8.

Wardle, J., Cooke, L.J. and Gibson, E.L., 'Increasing children's acceptance of vegetables: A randomised trial of parent-led exposure', *Appetite*, 2003, Volume 40, Issue 2, pp.155–62.

164 Wardle, J., Carnell, S. and Cooke, L., 'Parental control over feeding and children's fruit and vegetable intake: How are they related?', *Journal of the American Dietetic Association*, 2005, Volume 105, Issue 2, pp.227–32.

165 Rigal, N., Frelut, M.L. and Monneuse, M.O., 'Food neophobia in the context of a varied diet induced by a weight reduction program in massively obese adolescents', *Appetite*, 2006, Volume 46, Issue 2, pp.207–14.

166 Harris, G., 'Introducing the infant's first solid food', *British Food Journal*, 1993, Volume 95, Issue 9, pp.7–10.

167 Blossfield, I., Collins, A., Kiely, M. et al.,

'Texture preferences of 12-month-old infants and the role of early experiences', *Food Quality and Preference*, 2007, Volume 18, Issue 2, pp.396–404.

168 Northstone, K., Emmett, P., Nethersole, F. et al., 'The effect of age of introduction to lumpy solids on foods eaten and reported feeding difficulties at 6 and 15 months', *Journal of Human Nutrition and Dietetics*, 2001, Volume 14, Issue 1, pp.43–54.

169 Brown, S.D., Harris, G., Bell, L. et al., 'Disliked food acting as a contaminant in a sample of young children', *Appetite*, 2012, Volume 58, Issue 3, pp.991–6.

170 Birch, L., 'Development of food preferences', *Annual Review of Nutrition*, 1999, Volume 19, pp.41–62.

171 Maier, A., Chabanet, C., Schaal, B. et al., 'Effects of repeated exposure on acceptance of initially disliked vegetables in 7-month-old infants', *Food Quality and Preference*, 2007, Volume 18, Issue 8, pp.1023–32.

172 Carruth, B., Ziegler, P., Gordon, A. et al., 'Prevalence of picky eaters among infants and toddlers and their caregivers' decisions about offering a new food', *Journal of the American Dietetic Association*, 2004, Volume 104, Issue Supplement 1, pp.S57–64.

173 University of Greenwich, 'Jars of baby food very low in micro-nutrients, UK study suggests', *ScienceDaily*, 2012, available at: http://www.sciencedaily.com/releases/2012/0 4/120413101119.htm, accessed 22 November 2013.

174 Kramer, M.S., Guo, T., Platt, R.W. et al., 'Feeding effects on growth during infancy', *Journal of Pediatrics*, 2004, Volume 145, Issue 5, pp.600–605.

175 Ibid.

176 Li, R., Fein, S.B. and Grummer-Strawn, L.M., 'Association of breastfeeding intensity and bottle-emptying behaviors at early infancy with infants' risk for excess weight at late infancy', *Pediatrics*, 2008, Volume 122, Supplement 2, pp.S77–84.

177 Farrow, C. and Blissett, J., 'Breast-feeding, maternal feeding practices and mealtime negativity at one year', *Appetite*, 2006, Volume 46, Issue 1, pp.49–56.

178 Black, M.M. and Aboud, F.E., 'Responsive feeding is embedded in a theoretical framework of responsive parenting', *Journal of Nutrition*, 2011, Volume 141, Issue 3, pp.490–94.

179 Schwartz, C., Scholtens, P.A., Lalanne, A. et al., 'Development of healthy eating habits early in life. Review of recent evidence and selected guidelines', *Appetite*, 2011, Volume 57, Issue 3, pp.796–807.

180 Iacovou, M. and Sevilla, A., 'Infant feeding: the effects of scheduled vs. on-demand feeding on mothers' wellbeing and children's cognitive development', *European Journal of Public Health*, 2012, Volume 23, Issue 1, pp.13–19.

181 Disantis, K.I., Collins, B.N., Fisher, J.O. et al., 'Do infants fed directly from the breast have improved appetite regulation and slower growth during early childhood compared with infants fed from a bottle?', *International Journal of Behavioral Nutrition and Physical Activity*, 2011, Volume 8, Issue 89, available at: http://www.biomed-central.com/content/pdf/1479-5868-8-89.pdf , accessed 19 March 2014.

182 Li, R., Fein, S.B. and Grummer-Strawn, L.M., 'Do infants fed from bottles lack self-regulation of milk intake compared with directly breastfed infants?', *Pediatrics*, 2010, Volume 125, Issue 6, pp.E1386–93.

183 Huh, S.Y., Rifas-Shiman, S.L., Taveras, E.M. et al., 'Timing of solid food introduction and risk of obesity in preschool-aged children', *Pediatrics*, 2011, Volume 127, pp.E544 –1.

184 Li, R., Fein, S.B. and Grummer-Strawn, L.M., 'Do infants fed from bottles lack self-regulation of milk intake compared with

directly breastfed infants?', *Pediatrics*, 2010, Volume 125, Issue 6, pp.E1386–93.

185 Li, R., Fein, S.B. and Grummer-Strawn, L.M., 'Association of breastfeeding intensity and bottle-emptying behaviors at early infancy with infants' risk for excess weight at late infancy', *Pediatrics*, 2008, Volume 122, Supplement 2, pp.S77–84.

186 Brown, A. and Lee, M., 'Breastfeeding during the first year promotes satiety responsiveness in children aged 18–24 months', *Pediatric Obesity*, 2012, Volume 7, Issue 5, pp.382–90.

187 Companies Act 2006, http://www.legislation.gov.uk/ukpga/2006/46/contents, accessed 6 March 2014.

188 Macknin, M.L., Medendorp, S.V. and Maier, M.C., 'Infant sleep and bedtime cereal', *American Journal of Diseases of Children*, 1989, Volume 143, Issue 9, pp.1066–8.

189 Keane, V., Charney, E., Strauss, J. et al., 'Do solids help baby sleep through the night?', *American Journal of Diseases of Children*, 1988, Volume 142, pp.404–5.

190 Daly, S.E., Kent, J.C., Owens, R.A. et al., 'Frequency and degree of milk removal and the short-term control of human milk synthesis', *Experimental Physiology*, 1996, Volume 81, Issue 5, pp.861–75.

191 Kent, J.C., Mitoulas, L.R., Cregan, M.D. et al., 'Volume and frequency of breastfeedings and fat content of breast milk throughout the day', *Pediatrics*, 2006, Volume 117, Issue 3, pp.E387–95.

192 Shea, S., Stein, A.D., Basch, C.E. et al., 'Variability and self-regulation of energy intake in young children in their everyday environment', *Pediatrics*, 1992, Volume 90, Issue 4, pp.542–6.

193 Scaglioni, S., Salvioni, M. and Galimberti, C., 'Influence of parental attitudes in the development of children's eating behaviour',

British Journal of Nutrition, 2008, Issue 99, Supplement 1, pp.S22–5.

194 Bonyata, K., 'Spitting up & reflux in the breastfed baby', 2011, http://kellymom.com/health/baby-health/reflux, accessed 26 October 2013.

195 Eidelman, A.I., Schanler, R.J., Johnston, M. et al., 'Breastfeeding and the use of human milk', *Pediatrics*, 2012, Volume 129, Issue 3, pp.E827–41.

196 Scaglioni, S., Salvioni, M. and Galimberti, C., 'Influence of parental attitudes in the development of children's eating behaviour', *British Journal of Nutrition*, 2008, Issue 99, Supplement 1, pp.S22–5.

197 Barmby, L., 'Breastfeeding the baby with gastroesophageal reflux' (updated 2004), *New Beginnings*, 1998, Volume 15, Issue 6, pp.175–6. Available at www.lalecheleague.org/nb/nbnovdec98p175.html, accessed 26 October 2013.

198 The British Dietetic Association, 'Complementary feeding: introduction of solid foods to an infant's diet', www.bda.uk.com/policies/WeaningPolicyStatement.pdf, accessed 29 November 2013.

199 Bliss, 'Weaning your premature baby', 7th edn, 2011, available at: http://www.bliss.org.uk/wp content/uploads/2012/02/Weaning.pdf, accessed 29 November 2013.

200 The British Dietetic Association, 'Complementary feeding: introduction of solid foods to an infant's diet', www.bda.uk.com/policies/WeaningPolicyStatement.pdf , accessed 29 November 2013.

201 BBC News, 'Increase in rickets in Southampton astonishes doctors', 2010, http://www.bbc.co.uk/news/uk-england-hampshire-11741262, accessed 20 November 2013.

202 Department of Health, 'Vitamin D – advice on supplements for at risk groups', 2012,

https://www.gov.uk/government/uploads/syst
em/uploads/attachment_data/file/213703/dh_
132508.pdf, accessed 9 March 2014.

203 Bonyata, K., 'Is iron-supplementation necessary?', http://kellymom.com/nutrition/
vitamins/iron, accessed 21 March 2014.

204 Voigt, C.C., Capps, K.A., Dechmann, D.K. et
al., 'Nutrition or detoxification: why bats visit
mineral licks of the Amazonian rainforest',
PLoS One, 2008, Volume 3, Issue 4, p.E2011.

205 World Health Organization, 'Cord clamping
for the prevention of iron deficiency anaemia
in infants: optimal timing',
http://www.who.int/elena/titles/cord_clamping
/en, accessed 23 October 2013.

206 American College of Obstetricians and Gyne-
cologists, 'Time to clamp the cord? Cord
clamping for the prevention of iron deficiency anaemia in infants: optimal timing',
www.acog.org/About_ACOG/News_Room/
News_Releases/2012/Time_to_Clamp_the_
Cord, accessed 23 October 2013.

207 Uauy, R., Hertrampf, E. and Reddy, M., 'Iron
fortification of foods: overcoming technical
and practical barriers', *Journal of Nutrition*,
Volume 132, Issue Supplement 4, 2002,
pp.849S–52S.

208 Ibid.

209 James Randerson, 'Arsenic in baby rice is a
cancer risk, say scientists',
http://www.theguardian.com/science/2008/ap
r/30/medicalresearch.cancer, accessed 26
March 2014.

210 NHS, 'Arsenic in baby rice', 2008,
http://www.nhs.uk/news/2008/04April/Pages/
Arsenicinbabyrice.aspx, accessed 10 October
2013.

211 Ibid.

212 Barrett, J.R., 'The science of soy: what do we
really know?', *Environmental Health
Perspectives*, 2006, Volume 114, Issue 6,
pp.A352–8.

213 Moynihan P., *Dental Disease: In Human
Nutrition*, 11th edn, ed. by Geissler, C. and
Powers, H., London: Elsevier/Churchill
Livingstone, 2005, pp.461–78.

214 Bray, G.A., Nielsen, S.J. and Popkin, B.M.,
'Consumption of high-fructose corn syrup in
beverages may play a role in the epidemic of
obesity', *American Journal of Clinical Nutrition*, April 2004, Volume 79, Issue 4,
pp.537–43.

215 Menella, J.A. and Pepino, M.Y., 'Sucrose-
induced analgesia is related to sweet
preferences in children but not adults', *Pain*,
2005, Volume 15, Issue 119, Supplement 1–3,
pp.210–18.

216 Lustig, R.H., Schmidt, L.A. and Brindis,
C.D., 'Public health: The toxic truth about
sugar', *Nature*, 2012, Volume 482, Issue
7383, pp.27–9.

217 Reilly, J.J., Armstrong J., Dorosty, A.R. et al.,
'Early life risk factors for obesity in childhood: cohort study', *British Medical Journal*,
2005, Volume 330, p.1357.

218 Taheri, S., Lin, L., Austin, D. et al., 'Short
sleep duration is associated with reduced
leptin, elevated ghrelin, and increased body
Mass Index', *PLoS Medicine*, 2004, Volume
1, Issue 3, p.E62.

219 Ibid.

220 Spiegel, K., Leproult, R., Tasali, E. et al.,
'Sleep curtailment results in decreased leptin
levels and increased hunger and appetite',
Sleep, 2003, Volume 26, p.A174.

221 Taheri, S., Lin, L., Austin, D. et al., 'Short
sleep duration is associated with reduced
leptin, elevated ghrelin, and increased body
mass index', *PLoS Medicine*, 2004, Volume
1, Issue 3, p.E62.

222 Hart, C.N., Carskadon, M.A., Considine, R.V.
et al., 'Changes in children's sleep duration
on food intake, weight, and leptin', *Pediatrics*, 2013, Volume 132, Issue 6,
pp.1473–80.

223 Keskitalo, K., Knaapila, A., Kallela, M. et al., 'Sweet taste preferences are partly genetically determined: identification of a trait locus on chromosome 161,2,3', *American Journal of Clinical Nutrition*, July 2007, Volume 86, Issue 1, pp.55–63.

224 Flood-Obbagy, J.E. and Rolls, B.J., 'The effect of fruit in different forms on energy intake and satiety at a meal', *Appetite*, 2009, Volume 52, Issue 2, pp.416–22.

225 Ritchel, M., 'Putting the squeeze on a family ritual', http://www.nytimes.com/2012/06/21/garden/food-pouches-let-little-ones-serve-themselves.html?pagewanted=all&_r=1&, accessed 27 March 2014.

226 The UK Food Guide, 'Broccoli', http://ukfoodguide.net/broccoli.htm, accessed 6 March 2014.

227 Jahns, L., Siega-Riz, A.M. and Popkin, B.M., 'The increasing prevalence of snacking among US children from 1977 to 1996', *Journal of Pediatrics*, 2001, Volume 138, Issue 4, pp.493–8.

228 Which?, 'Healthy snacks?', 2012, http://www.which.co.uk/documents/pdf/cereal-bars-full-report-293495.pdf, accessed 6 March 2014.

229 Fomon, S.J., 'Assessment of growth of formula-fed infants: evolutionary considerations', *Pediatrics*, 2004, Volume 113, Issue 2, pp.389–93.

230 Johnson, S.L., 'Improving preschoolers' self-regulation of energy intake', *Pediatrics*, 2000, Volume 106, Issue 6, pp.1429–35.

231 Fox, M.K., Devaney, B., Reidy, K. et al., 'Relationship between portion size and energy intake among infants and toddlers: evidence of self-regulation', *Journal of the American Dietetic Association*, Volume 106, Issue 1, Supplement 1, pp.S77–83.

232 Townsend, E. and Pitchford, N.J., 'Baby knows best? The impact of weaning style on food preferences and body mass index in early childhood in a case–controlled sample', *BMJ Open*, 2012, Volume 2, Issue 1, p.2.

233 Fomon, S.J., *Nutritional Disorders of Children: Prevention, Screening, and Follow-up*, Washington, DC: Department of Health, Education, and Welfare, 1976.

234 Kochanska, G., Murray, K.T. and Harlan, E.T., 'Effortful control in early childhood: continuity and change, antecedents, and implications for social development', *Developmental Psychology*, 2000, Issue 36, Volume 2, p.220.

235 Halberstadt, J., Makkes, S., De Vet, E. et al., 'The role of self-regulating abilities in long-term weight loss in severely obese children and adolescents undergoing intensive combined lifestyle interventions (HELIOS); rationale, design and methods', *BMC Pediatrics*, 2013, Volume 13, p.41.

236 Appelhans, B.M., Woolf, K., Pagoto, S.L. et al., 'Inhibiting food reward: delay discounting, food reward sensitivity, and palatable food intake in overweight and obese women', *Obesity*, 2011, Volume 19, Issue 11, pp.2175–82.

237 Epstein, L.H., Dearing, K.K., Temple, J.L. et al., 'Food reinforcement and impulsivity in overweight children and their parents', *Eating Behaviors*, 2008, Volume 9, Issue 3, pp.319–27.

238 Nederkoorn, C., Braet, C., Van Eijs, Y. et al., 'Why obese children cannot resist food: the role of impulsivity', *Eating Behaviors*, 2006, Volume 7, Issue 4, pp.315–22.

239 Manian, N., Papadakis, A.A., Strauman, T.J. et al., 'The development of children's ideal and ought self-guides: parenting, temperament, and individual differences in guide strength', *Journal of Personality*, 2006, Volume 74, Issue 6, pp.1619–46.

240 Birch, L.L. and Fisher, J.O., 'Development of eating behaviors among children and adolescents', *Pediatrics*, 1998, Volume 101, Supplement 2, pp.539–49.

241 Piaget, J., *Origins of Intelligence in the Child*,
     London: Routledge & Kegan Paul, 1936.

242 Sheridan, Mary, *Children's Developmental
     Progress from Birth to Five Years: Stycar
     Sequences*, Slough: NFER Publishing, 1975,
     p.30.

243 Butte, N.F., Wong, W.W., Hopkinson, J.M. et
     al., 'Energy requirements derived from total
     energy expenditure and energy deposition
     during the first 2 y of life', *American Journal
     of Clinical Nutrition*, 2000, Volume 72, Issue
     6, pp.1558–9.

244 Perry, L.K., Samuelson, L.K. and Burdinie,
     J.B., 'Highchair philosophers: the impact of
     seating context-dependent exploration on
     children's naming biases', *Developmental
     Science*, December 2013, DOI:
     10.1111/desc.12147.

Index